Living with A Creative Mind

JEFF CRABTREE
JULIE CRABTREE

Zebra Collective

©2011 Jeff Crabtree and Julie Crabtree

Published by Zebra Collective
P.O. Box 1448, Manly NSW 1655
For further information about orders:
www.livingwithacreativemind.com
Phone: +61 2 99751136
Email: marnico@me.com

National Library of Australia Cataloging-in-Publication Data:
Crabtree, Jeffrey Robert and Crabtree, Julie Margaret
Living with a creative mind / by Jeff Crabtree and Julie Crabtree.
2nd ed. 2nd imprint 2013
ISBN: 9780987104601 (paperback)
Includes bibliographical references.

Crabtree, Jeffrey Robert and Crabtree, Julie Margaret. 1. Creative ability. 2. Creative thinking.
I. Title.
Dewey Number: 153.35

Design by Imperical Metric, Manly NSW
Cover Art and illustrations by Simon Ray and Nicholas Goodger, Imperial Metric.
www.imperialmetric.tv
Back Cover Photograph by Melinda DiMauro, New York, NY.
www.melindadimauro.com
Edited by Russell Thomson and Peter Gray, Clear Communications, Dulwich Hill. NSW.
www.clearcommunications.net.au
2nd edition revision by Cyberbia Interactive, Crows Nest, NSW, www.cyberbia.com.au
Proofreading by Blake Antrobus

To our very own home grown creative minds,
Jessica and Madeline and to our son-in-law Jason.
May your journey be as beautiful and as full of the love,
the wonder and the laughter that you have brought to us.

And with grateful thanks to all of our past students,
staff and teaching faculty over nineteen years.
Much of what we learnt on our journey
we learnt from working next to you.

ABOUT THE AUTHORS

JEFF CRABTREE holds a Bachelor of Arts in English Literature and a Master of Arts with Honours in Music and Cultural Studies. He is an award winning professional composer and musician specializing in the diametrically opposite genres of acid gospel blues and film scoring. Following a career as a performance blues artist he was the Principal of the School of Creative Arts for 16 years. He is a speaker and consultant, particularly in the area of creative arts practice.

JULIE CRABTREE has been a registered Psychologist for over 28 years and is currently in private practice, primarily seeing clients across the whole spectrum of the creative industries. She is engaged in doctoral research at UNSW in the School of Psychiatry. Her area of research is creativity and mental health, specifically how the potential of creative people can be harnessed.

CONTENTS

INTRO-
DUCTION

WHY THIS BOOK?

JEFF: In 1993 I found myself in a career change. Suddenly from being a professional musician, I was running an arts college. People from all over the world came to study at this place and even though I was experienced as a performer and as an educator, I wasn't quite prepared for what it meant when you put all those different types of creative people together. We had musicians, singers, actors and artists at first. Later we were attracting songwriters, dancers and filmmakers. Even though what we were teaching these students was quite different from day to day, I began to notice that a lot of the ways that they lived and worked – and even their personal issues, had some similarities.

JULIE: Part of my work when Jeff was the principal of the college was managing a community support and counselling service. As a psychologist I was intrigued to see themes emerging in the people that Jeff was training, and in particular those who came into my care. We compared notes about the recurring patterns, and from those early days we began to form some ideas about how creative people seem to be wired differently.

In so many different places we have had to fight to overcome a prevailing view that creative people were in some way second-class citizens in the workplace. All too often this came in the form of a put down disguised as a joke. We have found this idea has always surfaced whenever we are invited to talk about creativity. There is a dividing line in organizations that looks something like: "Here are the 'creatives' –the weirdos – and here are the rest of us who do the 'real' work."

Thus we began the journey that has culminated in the principles we have documented in this book. It is through our students sharing their lives, their pain and triumphs with us that we began to answer the question – what makes creative people tick? By understanding how the creative mind works we discovered what enables creatives to realize their full potential and, conversely, what disempowers and frustrates them. We found keys that make creative people easier to understand, and easier to work and live with. These keys and principles began to be applied to a large sample of over one thousand creative graduates the vast majority of whom have gone on to continue creating and enjoy success all over the world.

A MAP

This book is about:

- A model of creativity – it has three parts.
- A model of the creative mind – it has nine parts.
- One principle for long-term success.
- Four reasons why creative people have such problems.
- Three strategies to make the one principle happen.

To make it easy to understand the terms we use on this journey we have included a glossary at the end of the book.

As part of our preparation we conducted a number of surveys and interviews with creative people. Their thoughts are quoted throughout the book. Many of them wished to remain anonymous. (These survey respondents are identified only by their initials.)

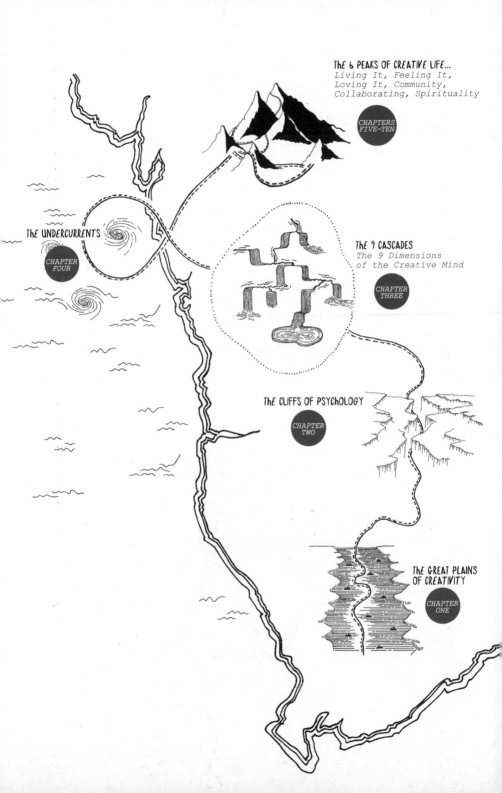

THE 6 PEAKS OF CREATIVE LIFE...
*Living It, Feeling It,
Loving It, Community,
Collaborating, Spirituality*

CHAPTERS
FIVE-TEN

THE UNDERCURRENTS

CHAPTER
FOUR

THE 9 CASCADES
*The 9 Dimensions
of the Creative Mind*

CHAPTER
THREE

THE CLIFFS OF PSYCHOLOGY

CHAPTER
TWO

THE GREAT PLAINS
OF CREATIVITY

CHAPTER
ONE

ONE BIG THING

Here it is: you get the best out of something by using it for what it was intended for. In human terms, our best life is found by positioning ourselves to live in the way that best suits our talents.

Fulfilment lies in being true to who we really are. Those who were made for a creative life are drawn to situations where their unusual inner wiring will be harnessed helpfully and productively over the longest period of time.

Creative people want to be productive and to have a long creative life. This book will help them. It will also help those who live and work with creatives to have a better life by making the chaos creatives seem to inflict on them more comprehensible and therefore more manageable.

WHAT'S WITH THE ZEBRA?

The zebra is a symbol of the creative mind because it is a creature of contradictions.

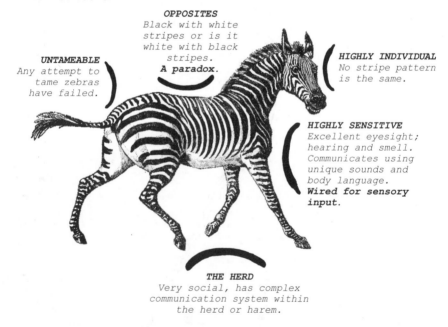

OPPOSITES
Black with white stripes or is it white with black stripes.
A paradox.

UNTAMEABLE
Any attempt to tame zebras have failed.

HIGHLY INDIVIDUAL
No stripe pattern is the same.

HIGHLY SENSITIVE
Excellent eyesight; hearing and smell. Communicates using unique sounds and body language.
Wired for sensory input.

THE HERD
Very social, has complex communication system within the herd or harem.

A WORD OF CAUTION

In this book we propose a model of the creative process, a model of the creative mind and a fundamental strategy to make them work well together.

However, people are people; not models, processes, strategies, formulas and methods. It would be tempting to just take the material in this book and make a set of rules and principles and try to apply them rigidly to our colleagues.

To use this book in such a fashion would be to completely miss the point.

In practice, you will find that the principles interact together in an endlessly varying, infinitely complex way. You will have to adapt to individual differences and make allowance for things not always working out according to plan. In short, while all creative minds work in similar ways, no two creative minds work in exactly the same way. They are the same - but different.

CHAPTER ONE

CREATIVITY

CREATIVITY

*YOU COULD KNOW EVERY BIT OF NEUROCIRCUITRY IN
SOMEBODY'S HEAD, AND YOU STILL WOULD NOT KNOW
WHETHER OR NOT THAT PERSON WAS CREATIVE.[1]*
- HOWARD GARDNER

Over years of working with creative people, we discovered that artists and performers with long productive careers had at least one thing in common; they had figured out how to work their creativity.

For young or less experienced artists, creativity seems more magical and mysterious, and is something that they feel at the mercy of. We found that the seasoned veteran is able to access their creativity more readily. It seemed to us that if you can weather the storms of your early career – working out how you ticked made it easier to manage living with a creative mind. So we began to realise there was hope for the so-called 'tortured artist' – that they might not need to be quite so tortured after all.

Even though young artists can't really pinpoint what's happening to them when they are being creative, they are subject to it anyway. Rather than managing it, it has control of them. Ninety percent of the younger creative people in our research commented on the negative effect their creativity had on their relationships and on aspects of their general wellbeing. However being creative does not mean that you are sentenced to an unhappy life!

So, why do creatives have such a tough time? We discovered it is because their minds are not wired the way we conventionally expect. Rather they are particularly wired to be creative. This is because the different ways in which they feel and think are uniquely suited to locking in to the creative process.

If you are creative – the creative process is how you paint, write, sing, dance or whatever. It is how you get from nothing to something.

So in order to understand the creative mind we have to understand the creative process. So let's begin the journey! What is it all about and what is going on in there?

DEFINING CREATIVITY

So – what is creativity? Is it a matter of genius? Is it magic, mystery or madness? Is it a gift or a curse? It is none of these. Rather, as Ken Robinson says, "Creativity is the process of having original ideas that have value."[2] Easy.

This is a pretty broad definition, and it means that everybody is creative because everyone has the ability to have new ideas or solve problems. That doesn't mean everyone can write a bestselling novel though. There are different types of creativity. The real differences boil down to the skills involved and what kind of creative outcome emerges from an individual. A lot of people are good at everyday creativity such as an ingenious idea to solve a problem. Then there is the making of art, music, film and literature; a lot of people are also good at these, whether they make a living from them or whether they are a hobby. There is even the kind of creativity that is found in people who possess skill in technical creative fields – like cinematography, video editing or software programming. It's a big enough topic that entire books have been written just discussing and refining the definition of creativity, so we are not going to do that here. We will just stick to what is important for understanding the creative mind.

We all possess different potential in each type of creativity. Just because you may be good at one, doesn't necessarily mean you'll be good at the others. Some creative ideas require the use of high-level artistic skills (such as in dance or music), and some don't. A part of the secret to being creative is the secret of learning the skills – whether they are to do with harmony, melody and rhythm or light, colour, space or movement. While all creativity is important, we are going to confine ourselves to the issues of those involved in the arts, entertainment and design.

So if creativity is the process of having original ideas that have value, then this lets us into another secret. Creativity is a process. It is not a thing; nor is it magic or a mystery. It is a process that is dynamic and fluid and never occurs in isolation. Because it is a process, we can work out what parts there are to it - and we can work out what kind of things either fuel or frustrate it.

In the past people have focused on single aspects of creativity: the mental process, the type of person you need to be or the kind of environment you need to be in. In practice these three things are in a state of constant interaction – you can't separate the process from the person, and you can't separate the person from their environment.

However, the main thing to remember is that whether you are involved in music, film, writing, painting, sculpting, dance, acting, designing, writing software, editing, composing or performing – the creative process is the same. The process is the same no matter what you do, even if the expression of it is different from everyone else.

Understanding the creative process means we can begin to understand the creative mind.

THE CREATIVE PROCESS

I see, I think, I make.

The creative process has three phases:

- Perception – where something is seen, revealed, felt or recognized.
- Discovery – where something is interpreted, known or found out.
- Production – where something is made, performed or realized.

From here on we are going to refer to perception, discovery and production quite specifically in these terms. They are crucial to what follows in the rest of this book. Understanding each of the three phases means that we catch a glimpse of what the creative mind is trying to do at each part of the process.

A Process

- Takes time
- Has a beginning and an ending
- Has specific phases
- Can be initiated or blocked
- Can be set in motion again after it gets stalled

HOW DOES IT WORK?

A creative work begins with a perception i.e. a way of seeing something that is different from everyone else, or something that you have not seen before. What happens next is that perception evolves into discovery, an internalisation of the new seeing, where the filters of your life experience, knowledge, emotions and beliefs interact with the new thing. Finally something about this interpretation of the perception goes into production. That is when it is formed into something others can experience.

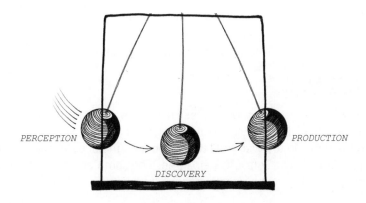

Perception happens when something comes within the focus of the creative person – so this phase is all about the senses. Discovery happens when all of their experiences and beliefs impact on what the new perception means – so it's all about the internal world of the artist. This phase is a lot like a gigantic melting pot. Then there is production, which is all about doing the work. It happens when an artist or performer goes about producing something that is a result of perception and discovery.

Each kind of art form and genre (or style) is influenced by a different set of skills, techniques and disciplines that change how the perception and discovery are going to be turned into something real.

> *It's still the same process. I see something, I react, I internalize it, and I externalize it as music. I have probably saved myself several million dollars in psychiatry bills because I talk to myself a lot. I think most songwriters do. I think most people do, have internal dialogues. I just happen to have trained the internal muscles and the internal spirit to create music.[3] - **Graham Nash***

Even though the skills and the forms are different from art-form to art-form the process is always the same. For example, the form and culture of ballet is really different to that of hip-hop, but the choreographer's journey always involves perception, discovery and production.

The development of a creative or performing artist involves a lengthy and highly focused gathering of artistic skills and techniques, the storing of creative experiences and the referencing of artistic knowledge as well as interactions with other artists. These things lead to the formation of an internal set of rules or disciplines concerning the way these techniques are best used, i.e. a developed sense of harmony or order in a creative discipline.[4]

IT'S ORGANIC

Now we know that the creative process has these three phases, it's tempting to think that creativity is as simple and straightforward as we have just drawn it – like the desktop toy with the little suspended metal balls: step one leads to step two and that sets off step three. For some artists, and for some projects, that is exactly how they describe it.

My projects are generally paintings. When I get the original idea, I make a quick sketch and write around it my initial impression, including colours and shapes. I know it is nowhere near ready, it is just an idea and so I let it sit and grow inside. Some paintings can take months of mulling around on the inside before they are ready to paint. **- AK**

However, it is rare that the creative process works so neatly. It is far more common for creativity to lack this kind of linear progression. Perception, discovery and production more frequently happen intuitively, non-sequentially, unconsciously and sometimes in a circular fashion, with one part of the process stimulating and affecting another in a feedback loop. Sometimes the phases occur almost simultaneously – intermingled with each other. This is because the creative process does not involve conventional ways of thinking. Artists are often 'thinking' physically, aurally or visually – things that we don't think of as thinking in the traditional sense.

We think about the world in all the ways that we experience it. We think visually, we think in sound, we think kinaesthetically. We think in abstract terms, we think in movement...[5] **- Ken Robinson**

The 'thinking' that goes on in a creative person may not look like the kind of thinking that the rest of us call rational. Singers think in melody – they think with their voice, and dancers think with their body – they think in movement.

I find it easier to express my emotions through my art, especially when I can't articulate how I feel – so basically I dance it out. **- AW**

The creative process is not linear – it's organic. It's more like a lava lamp, in which everything is bubbling up and down, and where a hot lamp drives globules of wax through coloured oil in endlessly changing patterns that change as the wax heats up, cools down and repeats over and over.

The progression of the phases is not always orderly and linear, so it can be difficult to figure out from an observer's point of view, not to mention for someone who is actually involved in it.

*Frequently I have written music and lyrics without any clue as to what I am writing about. In fact many times almost complete songs have emerged in what I can only describe as a discovery kind of experience – with the realization of meaning coming right at the end. Sometimes a melodic phrase was the starting point, because it sounded great – and then got attached something I saw much later. In the case of one song, the main melodic hook was in existence for about three years before the rest of the song was written. It was as if that phrase was the first piece of the puzzle. The rest of the pieces had to be discovered and then put in their places later on. - **JV.***

The creative process is alive and dynamic, with parts of the creative process referencing and affecting other parts, and all emerging through the filter of techniques and experiences that have been acquired over a lifetime.

*I follow it where it goes. Often I don't know what it means until the song is finished. Sometimes months later. I don't think that's bad. It implies that I don't know what I'm doing but I don't think that's the case. I think that if you're able to follow your instincts, then that is knowing what you're doing.[6] - **David Byrne***

So the intricate workings of the creative process are often beyond the conscious articulation of those doing it. How frustrating is that? Even the experts can't explain to you exactly what is happening as they do their job. Most people find that difficult to comprehend. How can you not know what you are doing when you are doing it? Creative people have a high tolerance for ambiguity, they don't mind things not falling into line, they are curious about everything around them, and don't need to know all the answers. To the creative mind, having all the answers is often boring whereas having a whole lot of questions is fun.

Interesting? Scary? Let's look at each of the phases in a little more detail in order to have a good grasp of what is going on for the creative mind when they are working.

PERCEPTION - SEEING

If I'm moved by a scene – a situation – a character; if I portray that, just the way I see it - in both places, heart and head, I have to assume that that's going to work for an audience.[7] *- Sidney Lumet*

Perception is the act of seeing or the moment when something is revealed in a unique perspective. It's when external circumstances come within the field of awareness of a creative person. Perception requires a willingness to be open to new experiences. It requires the willingness to be alive to our senses and the ability to focus.

Focus

Focus is the capacity to concentrate on something to the exclusion of everything else. It is an active process; like shining a torch around a dark room. Whatever we are paying attention to is what we perceive. However, there are two levels to this.

> **Jeff:** I can be so focused on something that it is possible for things to go on around me without my having any awareness of them. I am famous in my family for not finishing sentences. It seems like I suddenly drift off in the middle of a conversation. What has happened is that my awareness has suddenly been captured by something else – a memory or a brilliant new idea, and I have forgotten to speak while in my mind I have gone off chasing imaginary butterflies.

Therefore it is important to think of perception as a kind of constant filtering of sensory input, a constant shifting of focus. We actively filter our senses all the time, consciously and unconsciously, as if our mind is not just like the beam of a torch, but it is also simultaneously like a little radar scanner looking for other interesting things while we are fully focused on what is in front of us. Incidentally, our unconscious filtering is really a good indication of our deepest intentions and values.

Generally we can only pay close attention to one thing at a time – but we can pay less detailed attention to a few things in a way that seems simultaneous. Visual artist and music producer Brian Eno describes the relationship between himself and his wife, Andrea, in terms of the kind of attention focus they generally hold. He says that she refers to him as 'zoom' and he refers to her as 'wide angle'. These terms relate to the field of view you get from different types of camera lens. He sees a narrow range of things close up and in detail. She sees lots of things and their connections but in a lot less detail. These differences complement each other in the way they work and in their relationship.[8] One kind of attention is best for working on creative projects, and the other is best for managing the finances.

Even though we talk about perception as seeing, it's actually much bigger than this. When we say 'seeing' we talking about the means by which our attention is focused, as well as everything that we take in about our inner world and the world around us.

> *Seeing comes before words. The child looks and recognizes before it can speak.[9]*
> *- John Berger*

The Senses

Perception includes all of the five senses: seeing, touching, hearing, tasting, and smelling. It also incorporates the emotional: all of our inmost feelings. Perception can also be about ideas, which come unbidden to our awareness like a sudden moment of recognition or a flash of insight, and also includes memories that suddenly come to the forefront of our mind. These may come from our unconscious, or they may be the product of transcendence, i.e. something that has come from outside our physical frame of reference.

Perception is not neutral, nor is it a mirror of reality; rather it is a view of reality that we make for ourselves.

> *...what a piece of bread looks like depends on whether you're hungry or not. Our notion of reality is moulded by our parents, schooling and culture. Since we all come from differing backgrounds so do our perceptions of things. That is not to say we experience totally different things but different aspects of those things. The Hindu's view of a cow in no way corresponds to that of a canning factory meatpacker ... to alter our particular personal construct requires a substantial leap of imagination as we need to see things from a new angle. And only when this is expressed through a creative action, can it be experienced by others.[10]*
> *- Alan Fletcher*

So the moment of perception is always a subjective moment. For the creative artist this is something to be embraced, because the secret of originality is that no one is like you, so no one sees, perceives or puts value on things in quite the way you do. We are all subject to the filters of culture, experience and the rest, so your filters are not our filters. This means the things you do or make will be different from the things we do or make, even if we are all provided with an identical starting point.

> *We are never looking at just one thing; we are always looking at the relation between things and ourselves. Our vision is continually active, continually moving, continually holding things in a circle around itself, constituting what is present to us as we are.*[11] *- John Berger*

Our emotional state affects our perception at any given moment. If we are angry then something inoffensive becomes offensive - if we are depressed, then something innocent becomes an accusation.

Where does perception end and discovery begin? Creative people commonly describe perception as the flash of insight, inspiration or revelation. But when we experience a perception there is an instant mixing of what we are seeing with what we already know – so really there is a morphing together of what is inside of us with what we are seeing afresh. Think back to the lava lamp. It's organic.

It is helpful to think of the discovery phase as distinct from perception because an interpretation of a new thing can sometimes take a long time to come to the surface.

What Makes Us Get A New Perception?

Truly it can be anything either outside of us, or from within. It might be a casual remark by someone at a party; it might be a particularly beautiful sunset; or the sudden emergence of a memory. It can be:

a pain, a problem, a question, a bout of depression, a burst of elation, a frustration, a deadline, a conviction, a provocation, a commission, a creative brief, a piece of music, a film, a book, a poem, a caress, food, a colour, the feel of something on your skin, a feeling, a spiritual experience, sadness, a loss, grief, joy, a betrayal, regret, guilt, taking stock, a challenge, an expectation, a responsibility, a birth, a death, a trauma, a victory, a sound, a sight, a smell, a taste, touch, a recollection, an association, an injustice, a wrong, a right, a place, a new thing, a new place, a new day …

The list is endless. However it is things like them that provoke us, and sometimes force us to see things in a different way – if we are willing. Actually everyone has these kinds of moments, they don't belong solely to the creative mind. To perceive is to be human. The creative mind just deals with it differently. For most of us a moment of perception can present a challenge to our view of the world. When that happens it is common to dismiss the new idea because it doesn't fit our thinking.

> *We build up whole cultural patterns based on past 'facts' which are extremely selective. When a new fact comes in that does not fit the pattern we don't throw out the pattern. We throw out the fact.*[12] - **Robert Pirsig**

However, the creative mind thrives on ambiguity and stuff that challenges preconceptions.[13] The other factor is that an artist feels compelled to articulate what they have seen. Then to add to that; they have developed the skills to do it in music or film or whatever. To take advantage of perception, you have to be brave enough to deal with things that don't fit, sometimes in the face of opposing opinion.

The ability of the creative mind to function like this is a product of the unique wiring of their mind. Needless to say this kind of openness places unusual demands on them. Most of us prefer to block out dissonance. Understanding these demands is a significant key to living with a creative person, but more on that later.

Perception Gets Blocked When:

- Feelings are shut down, senses are dulled or heart is hardened.
- We are frightened.
- We are forced to conform.
- We are exhausted or time poor.
- We are bored.

Perception Gets Activated When:

- Feelings are alive, senses are awake or heart is soft.
- We are encouraged.
- We have permission to be different.
- We are in good physical condition, and there is time and space.
- There are new experiences.

DISCOVERY - INTERPRETING

It's not here yet but I'm watching it and it's like an egg incubating. You got a little bit of heat, and some chicken's hatched. It's no good cracking open the shell before the chicken's ready to hatch - otherwise you kill the chicken.[14] - Ken Duncan

Discovery is the phase where a perception interacts with our inner world. The internal filters of experience, knowledge, emotions and beliefs shape the final product or performance. Discovery is about internal reconciliation, reorganization, reinforcement or rejection of beliefs, ideas and understandings.

Between the moment of perception and the beginning of production the discovery phase works and reworks on an idea - building and deconstructing, looking from different angles and finding out whether there is something new in the perception or something new about what is already believed. The discovery phase is often described using phrases like 'mulling around' or 'chewing it over'.

Developing the idea will sometimes happen in my subconscious...I will have several paintings or themes developing at any given time. - MD

I'm never not working. Even as I sit here chatting ... my mind is simultaneously glued to the piece I am currently creating; the physical act ... is merely a necessary afterthought.[15] - Ned Rorem

Sometimes the boundary between perception and discovery phases is well delineated and sometimes it is really unclear. Sometimes the discovery seems to happen in the blink of an eye, and sometimes it is laborious.

The human mind seems designed to do two things really well:

- To try and make sense out of what looks like chaos.
- To try and imagine the possibilities – to dream.

These are what drives the creative mind when it is engaged in discovery. Making sense and dreaming seem to be complete opposites. In fact they are totally different ways of thinking, and on the face of it – one has almost nothing to do with the other. Daydreaming is such a frowned on activity. It's considered frivolous and a time waster – but we need both kinds of thinking to be truly in discovery. It's a paradox. We need to imagine and we also need to create a sense of meaning in things. This side of discovery is most deeply affected by our life history. No two individuals on earth are the same in terms of experience, imagination and belief.[16]

Everything about our past is unalterable except for what we believe about it. Beliefs get changed in the present as our experiences alter our view of the world. Everything about our future is open to change but we have to be willing to imagine and dream.

Discovery can occur in the forefront of consciousness, but is almost always occurring below the immediate level of our awareness. The creative mind is never really switched off.

ASPECTS OF DISCOVERY

Dreaming: The Imagination

Then they said to one another, "Look, this dreamer is coming! Come therefore, let us now kill him and cast him into some pit... We shall see what will become of his dreams!" - Genesis 37:19–20

Dreamers are often dismissed, yet is there a person who lives without dreaming or daydreaming? People are imagining all the time, and it is rare for people not to wonder about the future, or not to try and weigh up the consequences when it comes to making an important decision. The imagination is essential to such basic things as planning and preparing. It's what lies behind the experience of getting excited, or apprehensive about upcoming events. Anticipation is evidence of an imagination at work, as is the ability to put off an immediate short-term pleasure (e.g. eating that extra slice of chocolate cake) for a long-term benefit (e.g. a trimmer waistline). Laughter is a pretty good clue that the imagination is at work. Most jokes work because we can imagine an unfolding scene, as someone tells us a funny story. Our mind fills in the blanks, or creates the visuals that are suggested by the words.

Most people impose internal limits on their imaginations – but the creative mind has to regularly go beyond what most of us think of as normal limits.

> *When I examine myself and my methods of thought, I come to the conclusion that the gift of fantasy has meant more to me than my talent for absorbing positive knowledge.*[17] *- Albert Einstein*

Freedom to imagine is extraordinarily valuable to the creative mind. A constrained imagination prevents us dreaming up new possibilities. Those internal limits also prevent us considering alternatives or asking questions. The imagination allows us to invent, because an unfettered imagination is the original blueprint for virtual reality. Where can we put aside the problems that we face in real life, and where can we have no boundaries? In our dream world it is possible to violate the laws of nature. We can travel through time, swim underwater without a breathing apparatus, meet our handsome prince (or princess), change the past and even try out what it's like to be someone else. Of course we must remember that dreams and the real world are different. People who genuinely get these two worlds confused have lots of problems.

During discovery, creative people are alternating between trying to make meaning out of a perception and then dreaming about what might be…'if only'. They are trying to bring something into focus from within their dream world so they can eventually turn it into something in the real world. Sometimes they are attempting to form an inner vision of how a song should be performed or what the film should look like – or what the story really is, and so on. Sometimes they don't know exactly what it is, only that there is something going on inside that they need to bring out into the real world.

> *I like to think of computer programming as art. In the industry we are known as software engineers, but in the geek community, I think we are more like abstract artists ... Programmers work in the abstract. They work in a space that can't be modelled in a way that traditional engineering can model a bridge, an airplane*

*or a building. So when a programmer builds software he has to somehow capture what is happening in an intangible space. We have to mentally visualize how the program will flow... - **DS***

For the discovery part of the creative process to really work, the imagination must be allowed to roam free: it must be unfettered. The creative mind must also be able to call upon the whole of their experience to work out what it all means to them. This kind of task can take a lot of time and space. A creative mind needs to be allowed the freedom to feed the imaginative world but also needs to be able to keep having experiences that provide the raw material for the 'making sense' side of discovery.

What Stops People Dreaming?

Some cultures or workplaces steer people towards logical/rational thinking by rewarding that ability. Some jobs demand an intensely objective or pragmatic approach to dealing with information. Training for this kind of work invariably discourages imaginative thinking and instead rewards you for thinking like everybody else.

Also, like any ability, imagination can be stunted by lack of attention or discouragement in the early years. A childhood where fantasy play was disapproved doesn't help things. Growing up surrounded by music, movies, books or comic books is like a caffeine shot to the imaginative world. Even TV is good when the programs involve storytelling.

One of the most significant killers of a young imagination is fear. At one level, the dream world offers almost unlimited possibilities for discovery, but people who have been terrorized at a young age often avoid inner reflection because they are afraid of reliving painful experiences. Some, however, use their dream world to escape from a fearful reality, and thus have a rich inner life.

Creative people who have suffered through prolonged abusive episodes often emerge with such a loss of self-worth, that their dream world has closed down.

Keeping the Well Full

Think of the inner world of experiences, memories and understandings as a huge well that the creative person draws from in order to make sense of what they see and feel. If the well is full, then there is plenty to draw from. If the well is empty, or all too familiar, then discovery is going to be difficult.

> *I read all the time, absolutely everything...So I file away interesting little snippets – not on paper, but in the back of my mind. Then they eventually float to the surface and get used.*[18] *- Lee Child*

Creative people need to keep their well full by seeking new experiences, and by dreaming a lot. If an artist doesn't treat this aspect of their creativity as a discipline they need to maintain, then they risk the well running dry. When this happens they become repetitive, unproductive or even unable to create at all. When a creative person is feeling bored, empty, restless, dissatisfied, frustrated, worthless, afraid, hopeless, or they feel like a fake, uninspired and incapable; one of the reasons might be that they have failed to keep their well full. While creative blockages are a normal part of the creative life, they are actually frightening and distressing episodes for a creative person. Just patting them on the back and saying they'll get through it is not really helpful. Some of these episodes can be so bad that they involve a kind of loss of faith. An artist can lose confidence in their skill and their experience. They can lose faith in their entire social network. They can begin to question their core beliefs and begin to doubt themselves and the very things that they treasure.

Most creative people instinctively know the importance of the well, although they may not be able to articulate it in this kind of detail. However, when the well starts to run dry, it is such a crisis that they can start behaving in ways that appear bizarre and unreasonable. Although they may not be able to talk about what is happening to them, they are in a kind of creative panic and will attempt to fill up the empty well in any number of ways, mostly by seeking out any kind of new experience regardless of its helpfulness or its safety.

Discovery Gets Blocked When:

- The well is empty.
- The imagination has been shut down.
- We are frightened.
- We are forced to conform.
- There is no time or space.

Discovery Gets Activated When:

- The well gets filled with new experiences.
- There is freedom to dream.
- The source of fear can be removed.
- We have permission to be different.
- We are in good physical condition.
- There is time and space.

PRODUCTION - MAKING

This is the part that most people think of as creativity, because something is made or performed. Also, during production the machinery of the art is most obvious. Production, however, is only the tip of the iceberg. It happens at the point where the first two phases have gone far enough for the artist to begin to come up with something material. This phase is also the most affected by the nature of the art form itself (musicians make different things than painters).

Remember the lava lamp! Frequently things emerge in production that reawaken discovery, or that start a new perception. Often the whole business of production is a kind of constant bubbling interaction between making, interpreting and seeing, and making again.

This phase is more about an intensity of focus on the work, where the making, reviewing and re-evaluating something demands a high level of concentration. It is here where it seems that the artist gets 'lost' inside what they are doing. Production also takes different kinds of focus – alternating between a concentration on the details and a stepping back to look at the big picture or the overall effect. For performers, you can see this at work more in the rehearsal process than in the actual performance. Rehearsal allows space to experiment with the techniques and find ways to bring the inner vision to life.

Practice, Practice, Practice.

Even though financial success can never be guaranteed in the arts, it is normal for an artist to spend years developing technical skill. This is because the production phase is all about how well someone can use their skills. Technique is so crucial to the artist or performer that they pay a high price in order to get it. Outside of their professional colleagues, most people never fully appreciate the personal cost involved. There is a story, possibly apocryphal, about pianist Richard Clayderman being visited backstage by a wealthy New York business identity after a recital at Carnegie Hall. The businessman brought his friends backstage and the conversation apparently went like this:

Businessman: *I would give my life to play piano like that.*

Clayderman: *I did!*[19]

Whether its true or not, we know musicians who tell this story from time to time – probably to encourage each other that all that time and energy hasn't been wasted! Creative people are really aware of the personal cost of developing skill and technique; and they recognise it in other artists. A by-product of this is the tendency to compare themselves with everyone else in their field – as measured by their technique.

If the artist's level of technique is a good match for the kind of work they have to do, then they can give intense concentration to the exclusion of everything else for long periods of time, without seeming to get tired. The focus of production is just like the focus of perception – but it works for a different purpose[20]. Although they appear to be ignoring the rest of the world, they are in fact engaged in a world of their own – which is more fun than the 'real world'. At times like this, it's a sign that the production phase is going really well. The artist will feel as if they are really achieving something. If you try to break them out of this world by interrupting to find out where the TV remote is (for example) it's like pouring cold water over their head. You may get an answer in the short term, but in the long term these little interruptions block the creative process. Fortunately these episodes of intense focus don't last forever. It's difficult to deal with if your partner seems to spend more time at their craft than they do with you. It sends all the wrong signals in a relationship.

However, not all production or performance preparation flows easily. A lot of times it's a case of the artist slogging it out with hard work. They feel like they are making no progress and it's a discipline for them not to just give up in sheer frustration. Every instance of the creative process is different. Every project is different, and it's difficult to predict which ones are going to be easy and which ones are going to cause heartache.

> So to find something that really touches and addresses my attention, I have to do a lot of hard manual work ... but why shouldn't my work be hard? Almost everybody's work is hard. One is distracted by this notion that ... it comes fast and easy. And some people are graced by that style. I'm not. So I have to work as hard as any stiff to come up with the payload.[21] - **Leonard Cohen**

There is an upside – when an artist is in a struggle to bring a work to life, they are easily disturbed and are more likely to be drawn into what's going on around them - with family and friends. The downside is that the frustration makes them moody and preoccupied. While away from the work or the project, they will be turning the problem around in their heads. Sometimes being away from the work is just what they need, and the break gives them a new perspective – a new perception. When this happens don't be surprised if they rush off and apply what they think might be the answer.

More frustration.

> We work in an unorthodox fashion and regularly drive producers, engineers, assistant engineers, studio managers and anybody else who happens to be around to distraction ... it takes an awful lot of stamina ... to work with us. - **Larry Mullen Jr.**

> U2 work very hard, they're perfectionists, but work expands to fill the time available to do it ... that was the writing on the wall. It was kind of gruelling and nobody seemed to be having much fun. - **Paul McGuiness**

> We basically worked the guts out of nine months ... but the songs were getting nowhere, or in some cases getting worse.[22] - **The Edge**

U2 are open about how the production phase of their creative process is so tortuous. *How to Dismantle an Atomic Bomb* took eighteen months to compose and record, and was a difficult and laborious experience. Of course the end result was brilliant[23].

Production Gets Blocked When:

- Skill and technique are insufficient.
- There is lack of self-discipline.
- There are too many distractions.
- We lose passion, motivation or depth of feeling.
- There is no time or space.

Production Gets Activated When:

- Skill and technique are up to the task.
- We can exercise self-discipline.
- Distractions can be removed.
- There is motivation, passion and feeling.
- There is sufficient time and space.

TALENT AND TECHNIQUE

It's not what you are, it's what you don't become that hurts.[24] - **Oscar Levant**

When it comes to the creative professions, people attach a lot of significance to this one little word – talent. Who can say exactly how much of an artist's accomplishment or a performer's achievement is down to their innate talent, and how much to hard work?

If you ask an audience they will say - talent. If you ask the artist they will say they worked incredibly hard. Think of talent as the innate potential to become accomplished more quickly. However, moderate giftedness can be turned into something amazing by adding hard work and experience to arrive at the same place. Actor Robert Downey Jr. was once asked where he thought his talent came from.

Experience, I guess. I don't even know. I think the talent thing is kind of a ... I don't want to be a schmuck about it, but I think ... you could literally walk out on the street and point at somebody and say, "I want him or her to be a fully formed, gifted actor or actress inside of six months." And if I was training them, I'd be like, "Please. That's a no-brainer" ... It's very rare that I have been working on a character or been on a set or in a location and said, "Boy, I feel so darn inspired today, I just feel talent pouring through me." Instead it's more of the groundwork; what it is to be an actor on a movie set...[25]

If we think of experience and skill in a creative profession as being like the vocabulary of a language then the whole picture makes more sense. The language of an art form is just far more symbolic than a normal language.[26] The bigger your vocabulary, the better you are at speaking the language. The more 'words' you know and the more practised you are at using them, the more nuanced your communication can be. Artists aspire to communicate complex ideas with nuance. During the production phase it is easy for the artist to lose sight of the big picture because the subtle or specialized use of technique is what they focus on.

One by-product of great technique is that it makes creative accomplishment look simple – although of course if it were simple anyone could do it.

Having technique alone doesn't make you creative – nor does having talent alone guarantee success. In the same way, the creative process demands a certain kind of discipline. The creative mind must understand that discipline or things can go wildly wrong in their personal world, irrespective of professional success.

The next stage of our journey in working out how to live with a creative mind means looking beyond the creative process to look inside the creative person.

1   Howard Gardner is well known for his research into the diverse nature of human intelligence.

2   Sir Ken Robinson is a British Educationalist and senior adviser to the J. Paul Getty Trust. He offered this definition of creativity at the 2006 TED conference.

3   Graham Nash is considered among the world's most successful songwriters. He was a member of two seminal bands in the 1960s: The Hollies (from the UK) and Crosby, Stills, Nash and Young (from the US). This interview appears in Paul Zollo's book Songwriters on Songwriting.

4   Coffs Harbour based visual artist Jeffrey Baker holds the view that this "order" (as he describes it) underlies every creative and performing artist's work, whether they know it or not, and all artists are working in part to satisfy their own sense of balance and order. Baker discussed these ideas with the authors in a personal interview in July 2007.

5   Sir Ken Robinson, op. cit.

6   David Byrne is the founding member of sensational 80's rock band Talking Heads. His solo career as a songwriter has extended from the breakup of that band until the present day and incorporates world music as well as soundtracks for feature films. For more of this interview see Paul Zollo's Songwriters on Songwriting.

7   Sidney Lumet was an Academy Award winning US film director with over 50 films to his credit.

8   For more on this see Eno's book A Year with Swollen Appendices.

9   John Berger made a landmark TV series Ways Of Seeing with the BBC.

10 Alan Fletcher wrote a brilliant book about creativity and design called The Art of Looking Sideways.

11 John Berger, op. cit.

12 This quote from Robert Pirsig (author of Zen and the Art of Motorcycle Maintenance) was cited by Alan Fletcher.

13 For more on this research see Kay Redfield Jamison's book Touched by Fire.

14 World renowned photographer Ken Duncan granted the authors an exclusive interview.

15 Ned Rorem is a US author and composer. This assertion was made in Facing the Night, one of his many published diaries.

16 We are making a distinction here between originality and creativity. Creativity is by its nature not necessarily original – it is often collaborative, or is often referential and derivative. Unfortunately, creativity and originality are sometimes confused. Something can be original but not creative because it doesn't have value.

17 It has been difficult to source the attribution of this quote. It can be found online at http://www.brainyquote.com/quotes/authors/a/albert_einstein_9.html

18 Lee Child is a UK author who has written 16 best selling thrillers.

19 We can find no source for this quote from Clayderman. It may be an urban myth, but if so it has circulated among the musicians that we know to the extent that it has gained the status of truth.

20 Mihalyi Csikszentmihalyi has written extensively about the concept of flow – being totally absorbed in something challenging and interesting.

21 The full interview with Cohen can be found in Zollo's book Songwriters on Songwriting.

22 Full versions of the interviews from which these excerpts are taken can be found in the book U2 by U2 (2006). The members of U2 have always been quite forthcoming concerning the difficult nature of their production process, in this case specifically the 2004 album How To Dismantle An Atomic Bomb.

23 Source: U2 by U2.

24 We could not find the correct attribution for this quote, but it can be found online at http://thinkexist.com/quotes/oscar_levant/

25 Robert Downey Jr. was interviewed on At The Movies an ABC TV broadcast on 04/5/08.

26 Neurosurgeon Charles Limb suggests that he has found neurological evidence that music is primarily an act of communication. For his 2010 presentation go to http://www.ted.com/talks/lang/eng/charles_limb_your_brain_on_improv.html

CHAPTER TWO

PSYCH 101

PSYCH 101

ALL ACTORS ARE CRAZY LEMON, AND THE MORE
TALENTED THEY ARE, THE CRAZIER THEY ARE.[1]
- JACK DONAGHY (PLAYED BY ALEC BALDWIN) IN 30 ROCK

Open any gossip magazine and stories about the instability or mental health of celebrity creative artists and performers will fill the bulk of the pages. Exploring, reporting and exposing the behaviour and psychological problems of creative people is a multi-million dollar industry. The overwhelming impression is that if you are a creative artist then you are probably unhinged in some way. Being creative has become associated with craziness, and there is a kind of universal acceptance of the correlation between mental health problems, irresponsible and antisocial behaviour, and creativity.

There is a growing body of work centred on researching creativity and mental health. For the sake of a deeper understanding of this area, we will look at the story of creative people through the highly focused lens of the psychologist and discover to what extent their findings support the ideas we put forward in this book.

Julie: When I ask groups of creative arts students if they can name creative people who suffer, or have suffered, from mental illness, now or in the past, they immediately come up with names that span the decades and cover the full spectrum of the creative arts.

- Van Gogh
- Coleridge
- Michael Hutchence
- Spike Milligan
- Anne Sexton... the list goes on

People seem to know intuitively that there is some association between creativity, fame and mental illness. Our voyeuristic fascination with the drama of these people's lives, I suspect, underpins a curiosity about what is really going on.

So are creative people more prone to mental illness or are we simply more aware of their mental illness because they are famous?

Psychologists and psychiatrists have been exploring these questions for several decades. The simple answer is yes. There does seem to be an association between creativity and some types of mental illness and our attention is drawn to it when those people are in the public spotlight. However, before you begin to slash your wrists and plummet into a depression, let's look at what this may mean.

One of the most influential researchers has been Kay Jamison, a psychiatrist and diagnosed manic-depressive. She has written a number of groundbreaking books including *Touched by Fire* and *Mania and Creativity* that have provided great insight into the relationship between creativity and bipolar disorder (manic-depressive disorder). Below is a brief description of this disorder.

What is Manic-Depressive Disorder?

Manic-depressive disorder is also called bipolar disorder. It is a condition that can be characterised by extreme highs and extreme lows.[2] Those experiencing the lows or depression demonstrate apathy, lethargy, and hopelessness, sleep disturbances, slowed thinking and movement, difficulty concentrating and memory loss and a generalised loss of enjoyment in usually enjoyable activities. The slowing of movement, speech and thinking is more common in bipolar disorder rather than general depression.

Conversely, the highs or mania manifests quite differently. People need less sleep; have expansive moods and heightened self-esteem. They have excess energy and tend to speak rapidly and forcefully and they can move quickly from one topic to the next. They hold strong convictions about their own ideas and the correctness of their position and this can contribute to poor interpersonal relationships and to impulsive and impoverished judgement and decision-making. In the manic phase, people believe they can do anything - be anyone. Mania has also been associated with promiscuity and heightened sexual appetite, reckless and extreme spending and sometimes, paranoid thinking.[3]

Most of the subsequent research[4] has supported the idea that:

- Many people with bipolar disorder demonstrate higher than average creativity; and

- Highly creative people demonstrate some qualities similar to bipolar disorder.

These findings raise so many questions.

- Why is there a strong association between creativity and mental illness?
- What comes first – does the creative process lead to mental illness, or is it the other way round?
- Do we need to embrace our insanity to become more creative?

What is clear from the research is that there are marked similarities between the moods and thinking of creative people and those who are considered to be manic.

These similarities are:

- High output and new ideas
- Rapid and interconnected thinking
- High energy and focus: needing little sleep; working intensively
- Highly sensitive and emotionally varied: an alert sensitive system

We are not saying that creative people are bipolar, however, there are resonances that can help us understand the business of living with a creative mind.

When we have spoken to creative people about some of these issues, it is like they come alive. For most of their life they have been told to 'be normal' or 'get balance', yet are still expected to create and innovate. Learning instead to manage their highs and lows makes them feel like they have been given permission to be free to be who they are. Many have crashed and burned trying to live with their extremes by self-medicating or, alternatively, trying to live a 'normal life'. Both have got them into trouble. Once creative people learn to understand and embrace their natural highs and lows, they can learn to navigate their waves of energy and emotion, rather than running aground, or never going into the water.

What We Know About Creative People

- Creative people move through a rhythm of highs and lows that is more intense than a person with lower creativity.
- In the high energy state, creative people show similar qualities to mild hypomania.
- It is this state that leads creative people to be most productive.
- The mood of high energy and euphoria that precedes creative output is an important part of the creative process.

Simply put, the common threads that emerge seem to be the phenomena of creative ego, creative energy, creative thinking, creative behaviour and creative mood.

CREATIVE EGO

For a creative person to perform or create they need to have an inflated belief in their own creativity and ability; like those with mania, they have a grandiose sense of who they are. A person with diagnosed mania believes that they are the best – in their most extreme phase a manic will, for example, overspend on their credit card, fly to LA and expect to be discovered as the next big thing.

For a creative person, the inflated ego will keep them believing their work needs to be seen or heard, despite all the odds. It keeps them creating, gets them onto a stage and is absolutely creatively necessary. Stephen Fry puts it this way:

> *This is a problem many writers and comedians face: we possess the primary arrogance that persuades us that our insights, fixations and habits are for the most part shared characteristics, that we alone have the boldness, insight and openness of mind to expose and name: we are privileged thereby, or so we congratulate ourselves, to be spokesmen for humanity ...[5]*

This can of course swing back to the negative if the necessary affirmation; acceptance or accolades do not materialize. Stephen Fry again:

> *It may be the case that my afflictions of mood and temperament cause me to be occasionally suicidal in outlook and can frequently leave me in despair and eaten up with self-hatred and self-disgust.*

The creative person therefore, has personality characteristics that allow for both an inflated ego and at times crushing self-condemnation. This may be why research describes them as having an emotionally unstable temperament, similar to those with bipolar disorder. In particular they are seen as quite sensitive, anxious, angry, depressed and vulnerable.[6]

Along with these swings of ego come similar swings of creative energy.

CREATIVE ENERGY

Creative energy is that incredible surge of activity and action where creative people can work faster, sharper and more productively. It allows them to continue to create long past when others would have run out of steam. They seem to require little sleep and have unlimited energy for the creative tasks at hand. It's also energy that appears to dissipate when domestic tasks need to be done!

It's really important when it starts to come, it's like you are in a trance and a frenzy all the time.[7] - **Rickie Lee Jones**

One successful visual artist commented on what it was like when she was working on a particular canvas. She described an intense heat throughout her body, particularly on her back. She commented on a passion and drive for the work that meant that she slept little and had unusual energy. During that period she needed little sleep and did not eat unless she forced herself to.[8]

Finding Flow

Mihaly Csikszentmihalyi[9] describes this condition as 'flow'. Csikszentmihalyi, a leading researcher in the field of positive psychology, observed that people are at their happiest when they are absorbed in an activity that challenges their level of skill in a way that is 'matched'. If the level of challenge is too great for our skill level then we become anxious. If the level of challenge is beneath our level of skill then we become bored. If the 'match' is just right, we experience 'flow'.[10]

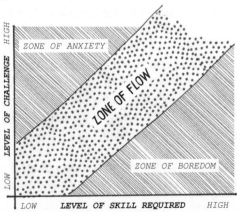

Diagram of Flow (after Csikszentmihalyi 1990)

During flow we are so immersed or involved in something that we lose track of time, and we can experience a complete sense of accomplishment or fulfilment. It is the experience of performing or working to our optimum.

*The ego falls away. Time flies. Every action, movement, and thought follows inevitably from the previous one, like playing jazz. Your whole being is involved, and you're using your skills to the utmost.[11] - **Csikszentmihaly***

Csikszentmihalyi formed the idea of flow after interviewing a lot of successful people in occupations that demanded high levels of skill – including musicians, dancers, artists and surgeons. Although the experience of flow is open to everyone, his particular interest is creativity and in the experience and qualities of creative people. Because accomplishment in the creative arts demands high levels of technical skill, we have found that the experience of flow is common enough for them to talk about in their own words – 'getting into the zone', 'getting into the groove', 'hitting the spot', or 'in the sweet spot'. Such experiences are not just talked about by artists, they are also highly prized.

*... the hardest part for me is to be there and just to turn up and something happens beyond you. It's tapping into that zone, it's going into the zone.[12] - **Ken Duncan***

Jeff: Once I was talking with some professional musicians at a gig about the experience of the whole band getting into a zone together where everything just seemed to happen perfectly on the night as if by magic. In retrospect we were talking about flow, experienced by a group together. As we talked about this kind of experience it became clear that these times were rare and cherished. They felt lucky if they had one of those magic moments once every couple of years. I didn't say anything at the time, but I realized that playing with the musicians I normally worked with at that time, we experienced those magic moments nearly every time we played.

There is an interrelationship between periods of intense energy and creative input. It seems that intense energy can bring on periods of creativity.

There are two aspects to creative energy. One is having the stamina to maintain flow. The other is being able to shift the body clock.

CREATIVE ENERGY AND OUR BODY CLOCK

Understanding the body clock is an important factor for creative people in managing themselves and their creative energy. Creative people, particularly performers, live and work to a different rhythm than other people. This has huge implications for their body clock and how they manage their inner world.

If you mess with the body clock too much, it has an impact on your mood.

There are studies emerging that suggest that stress on the body clock, or circadian rhythm, has been associated with triggering bipolar episodes.[13]

A Normal Day: The Body Clock

6:00 am: The adrenal gland, just above our kidneys, begins to secrete the hormone Cortisol. By increasing our heart rate, breathing rate and body temperature, it gets our body ready for a wake up at around 7:00 am.

7:30 am: Melatonin (sleep hormone) secretion stops.

9:00 am: Highest testosterone secretion

10:00 am: Highest alertness

2:30 pm: Best coordination

3:30 pm: Fastest reaction time

5:00 pm: Greatest muscle strength

6:30 pm: Highest blood pressure

9:00 pm: Melatonin secretion starts getting us ready to go to sleep at 10:00 pm.

2:00 am: Deepest sleep.

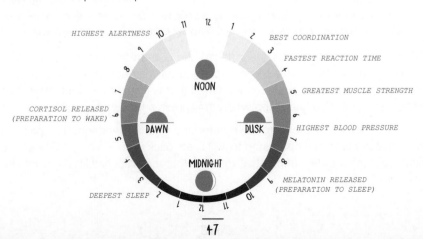

Emerging research is also confirming that each cell of our body has its own internal clock – so that even the liver and pancreas get ready to secrete insulin for the morning or evening meal.

In creative people, particularly performers, who have a different sleep/wake cycle, deregulation or difficulties in the internal body clock, may contribute to mood disorders – particularly depression and bipolar disorder. Studies are showing an association between problems in circadian rhythm as a predictor for a bi-polar episode.[14]

Research indicates that one of the strategies creative people use to manage themselves is to regulate their circadian rhythm. When they have periods of intense creative output, they need to ensure that those intense energy periods are brought back into balance by realigning and readjusting their circadian rhythm.

Also, having a lifestyle that factors in these periods of intense creative energy and activity seems to be essential for a creative person. Although this would appear to be obvious, we have seen a number of creative people who are locked into physically demanding and mind-numbing work that sucks any potential for creative energy out of them. For a creative person, not to create is to die a little.

When Michelangelo was sculpting his masterpiece, David, he reportedly worked night and day – not stopping for food or rest. This was similar to the way he worked while painting the Sistine Chapel.

> *As he became increasingly absorbed, Granacci [his servant] could no longer persuade him to come to the villa for supper; he went rarely to the meetings at Rustici's and then only if the night were too wet and raw to continue work. He could hardly concentrate on what was being said, let alone contribute anything to his friends.[15] - **Irving Stone**

Of course when he finished he crashed and burned. He had a servant who would bring him food. The contemporary artist may not have a servant but they do need to have people in their world that will help them look after their basic needs for food and sleep when they are in a frenzy of activity.

Creative people also need to have someone who understands the passion and drive but who can be trusted to pull them back from the edge. One of the distinguishing qualities of creative mania is that the artist has little insight into their energy and speed – they feel fantastic and have an over-inflated view of themselves and what is produced. This is why it is so important to have an independent person who can be trusted who will pull them back.

If you are the creative person in this scenario, then your job is to listen to your support person – even if you feel amazing, think that you are a genius and that what you are producing is the most ground-breaking piece of creative work ever.

Each of the creative people we interviewed has commented on their creative energy and how they and those around them were affected by it. For some it has been an understanding of the importance of rest, for others it has been key relationships that provide balance.

> *My friendships and family have often been put aside for creative projects. For example, I forgot my dad's 50th last year because I was rehearsing till 1pm at night. I still feel awful about it.* **- C.P.**

CREATIVE THINKING

We have already described the creative process and referred to the initial creative spark as perception. This spark of an idea – it may be an image, a concept, a phrase, a song lyric, a riff – is at the heart of the creative process. This ability to perceive the world in a new and unique way is the core of the creative person and is what defines them as creative.

> *When I get an original idea for a project, it's like a bolt of lightning travelling through a cloud right above my head. It communicates to me more than just an image, there is weight, smell, temperature, colour, sound, emotion and experience. In that moment, on so many levels, the idea comes ... then almost goes! You are just left with the imprint, that's like a still photo sometimes, other times it's like a part of a movie. It is, though, an imprint with all the information in it for the story ...[16]* **- D – a film maker**

What D does here is use the word 'imprint' to articulate the perception phase of the creative process. He also powerfully expresses the importance of that moment of perception and what happens after it.

> *... preserve the imprint, then, find the right time to deconstruct or expand on it. It is most unwise to try and formulate or fashion a creative idea if you cannot give*

your whole mind to it. You've got to find a football field to kick the idea around in, see where it goes, how it travels, what's it's weight, how much force does it need, what are the limits. Imagine the same journey in a crowded one-way street with taxis driving up and down, and the noise of traffic either end, you're not going to see how far it goes. If it's work, a client will either pay for the hire of the field or tell you that you only have the back alley. The real artist will run down to the football oval that afternoon no matter what the budget, and work back from there.

It is crucial to recognize what is happening to the creative mind at this point. In psychological terms, the creative mind needs to engage in unique types of thinking activity to allow the creative process to flourish; it is called the flight of ideas. This type of thinking forms the basis for the perception phase of creativity.

Julie: When Jeff is performing is the time I particularly see this flight of ideas. When he is tired and his inhibitions are reduced, anything can come out of his mouth. I am particularly conscious of not saying anything significant or having an argument before he gets on stage because he is likely to say anything in his flight of ideas.

I remember once, as a good psychologist, asking him what he was thinking as we were driving together. He must have been annoyed with me at the time because he actually told me all the thought fragments in his head. I remember thinking how similar to manic thinking it sounded, and so got a little concerned and stopped him. I also decided not to ask him ever again.

The primary difference between being creative and being manic is the way that creative people sort and control their flight of ideas.

One of the best examples of the flight of ideas emerged in an interview between James Lipton and comedian Robin Williams. Lipton commented on Williams' mental reflexes and asked, "Are you thinking faster than the rest of us? What the hell is going on?" Williams' response was to jump to his feet and begin by miming opening up his skull:

It comes from a deep part inside myself that was actually looking for my momma ... but when she looked up at me, and I said, "Okay I'll be funny for her that's fine, work that way" – but when I came out from there I just want to be accepted.

I can be trained. I can show you how intelligent I am – I can use big words like delicatessen and know what it means; or invertebrate or invenerate, degenerate and all of that is – all part of a brain that just flows like it. Because I realize that the human brain is a 350 lb [sic] gland that pumps neurons constantly and deals with itself by responding to stimulus and that is what we are supposed to do – evolving slowly – respond to stimulus and Darwin's going, "I had hopes, I had such high hopes!" It's all part of it, because I think the human mind is adapting and evolving; but I am trying not to speak all that fast cause eventually ... you ... have ... to ... catch ... up. But the brain is not really working all that well because you know that you – cough, you breathe, you come back, she's about to pass out (indicating a woman in the audience laughing uncontrollably) but the ideal is to create something different, something that moves with the times, new motion – crouching dragon – hidden CD (mimicking tai chi moves) move out away from the moment, take microwave – open the door. When you realize that no one at the MTV awards ever thanks Vishnu ... I want to thank Skinny G. Ghandi; the man who said that when asked, "What do you think of Western civilization?" said, "I think it would be a wonderful idea ..." [17]

Although it is difficult to accurately translate that moment into text we are sure you get the idea. From this fluency of ideas comes new perception. As Williams himself put it, "...the ideal is to create something different..."

This difference between the flight of ideas that somehow make sense and the flight of ideas that are nonsensical forms the difference between creative thinking and manic thinking.[18]

CREATIVE THINKING AND MEMORY

As an artist I am taking in colour, light and shapes constantly. It is as if I have a built-in computer system that sorts and files making sure the ideas are sorted in order of the original ideas.[19] *- AK*

For fluency of ideas to have any success the creative mind needs resources they can call on. This comes in the form of a memory bank of experiences, impressions, sensory imprints from which they can draw; we called it the well in chapter one. Memory is linked to creative thinking in the following ways.

The storage and categorization of material relevant to a creative discipline such as sounds, light, colour, texture, emotion or characters.

The ability to rapidly retrieve relevant information: Creative artists seem to develop a shorthand that allows them to remember musical forms or sequences; dance phrases; character pieces – this is called chunking.

The ability to select relevant from irrelevant information. As we have seen, it is this quality that separates the manic from the creative mind. The manic tends not to be able to separate the logical and sequential from the irrelevant.

The ability to synthesise stored memory in different and unexpected ways to create something new.

So never play music trivia games with a musician. Never play movie trivia games with actors and directors.

Preserving Memory

We are beginning to get a picture of a creative mind that is constantly seeking out and storing new information: a mind that is thinking rapidly and making unique connections and associations. These demands can often be at odds with the pressure to preserve, synthesize and process the often overwhelming input of sensory information.

I need time alone. I need to accept that I need time alone. I need to accept that time just sitting quietly or walking ... is part of the creative process. I need to say no to people even if they don't understand. My life is full of people and if I don't have the balance of time alone, I cannot create, I cannot get out of me all the things that are in me and so I become blocked by too much input and not enough output.[20]

*I never feel like my family or friends understand or would give me grace because I am creative. I'd say I keep everything inside until I am on my own where I write and draw etc. - **L.B.***

COGNITIVE ENERGY

Have you ever tried to get the attention of a creative person when they are focused on some creative endeavour or their new toy?

It seems to work something like this – when creative people see, sense or experience something novel or new, their attention immediately becomes focused on what is new. Along with this focus comes the ability to learn faster and retrieve memories faster. In fact, attention may be a key to the creative process.[21] Initially a creative person may be unfocused and disengaged, memory processes not activated – but when there is something new or novel, focus is increased and their memory and speed of thinking is increased and they begin creatively 'sparking'.

This may be why creative people seem to have superior problem-solving ability[22]. If we think of the creative process being about creative problem-solving, particularly in the discovery and production phase, then the ability to give unique and heightened attention to the creative problem combined with the ability to specifically search and locate memory, added to the skill of absorbing new information, makes creative people ideally suited to finding creative solutions to problems...or this can be what you tell your boss –

In fact one researcher described the type of power thinking that happens in the mind of a creative person as unique cognitive energy.[23] However, just talking about a creative person's energy and thinking is not the whole picture. What we believe and feel influences our behaviour. It is this area of mood and emotions that can provide both the primary fuel for their creativity and also be their Achilles' heel.

CREATIVE BEHAVIOUR

RISK-TAKING

Robert Luketic, a film-maker who directed *Legally Blonde* and *Monster-in-Law* (among other movies) described a visit to Chinatown in Sydney when he was in his late teens. While highly risky at the time, it was this experience that informed his direction of 21 (a story about college students who developed a system to win at blackjack).

> *There were little clandestine gatherings, quite friendly community things, nothing that would suggest organized crime in any way. But they were little competitive blackjack games and mah-jong ... I would have been about 17 or 18 going out. I was what you'd call a very adventurous young man. It's a miracle I'm alive, to be quite honest. There wasn't anything I wouldn't try, there wasn't anything I wouldn't do. I was out all night.[24] - Robert Luketic*

From our understanding of the creative mind, this makes perfect sense. The creative person has to push the boundaries of social convention through experience, and in doing so, store up memories, images and personalities that will become part of the creative frame of reference that they will operate from in the future.

Marina Prior in her interview with us, spoke about her risk-taking being in the form of challenging herself to take risks in her art. She continues to accept characters and work that push her out of her comfort zone. As an experienced professional, this is probably one of the most adaptive ways to continue to take risks while not threatening physical, emotional or relational health.

> **Jeff:** *You are currently performing in the play, The Hypocrite, where you are acting and not singing. Do you like the idea of the challenge of being just an actor and not bursting into song?*
>
> **Marina:** *Part of who I am as an artist, and actually part of what has kept me going as an artist in this country for twenty-five years now, is the fact that I almost compulsively have the need to push my boundaries and go into areas of discomfort for me as a creative person. I find that that's when I actually break through into new ground. So, immersing myself in the culture of the Melbourne Theatre Company, where it's all straight actors ... I have almost a safety zone of singing, and in a musical you still have to act of course, but you have another level you can go to which becomes song and then dance. When you're doing a straight play you still have to go to all those levels that you go through to make a full theatrical evening, yet you can't rely on bursting into song or, you know, bursting into flight through dance. So therefore it's much more complex and challenging as an actor because you are only relying upon the characterization and the spoken word and the purely dramatic. It is definitely a different skill and a different shape that you bring to the piece. It is purely through one discipline, and that can be scary, and that's why I like doing it! I like pushing my boundaries and constantly doing things that challenge my perceptions of what I can do ... let alone anyone else watching.*
>
> **Julie:** *How have you continued to be a risk-taker without letting it be a self-destructive thing either personally or relationally?*
>
> **Marina:** *It's a choice that I make. Most creative people that I know are risk-takers and I have a huge number of friends that have been drug users, have broken relationships, or have lived dangerously where they put their health or their soul*

in danger. I think it's just an innate sense – that is actually the way that I'm made; to take risks. I think what happens is ... you start taking risks with the wrong stuff. I think we're created to take risks. I think I'm wired to take risks creatively. I think that if you haven't got your body, mind and spirit together then you start taking risks with the wrong bits.

Julie: *What you're describing is the taking of risks specific to your art ... but one of the things that I have observed can kill creativity is a sense of boredom ...*

Marina: *Oh absolutely. And you've got to be with somebody who will live an exciting and brave life. That's different to a dangerous sort of unwise life, but yes absolutely. I'm about to go to work with a lot of people you've just described – who are risk-takers! But the interesting thing is that being a creative person, I am drawn to these people. They're my tribe and I'm drawn to them and I understand them, and I get bored when I'm surrounded by people that actually are not sort of a little bit wild, a little bit edgy and a little bit out there. I mean, generally drawn to people that use that in their work. Generally the people that sabotage their personal stuff actually also do very brave extraordinary work. Sometimes there's something about ... there's a fractured quality that certain performers have that they bring to the stage which is really compelling. It actually comes out of a brokenness and for some reason the audience finds it compelling to look at. Judy Garland ... had something extraordinary about her, and I think it was that ability to be able to pour their brokenness into what they do on stage ...*

Risk-taking is essential behaviour for the creative person and requires an artist, either consciously or unconsciously, to make decisions about how that drive will be expressed.

As we have explored before, artists take risks to build up a memory bank of sensory experiences from which to draw on to create new and original ideas. This needs to be balanced with a rich inner world; the world of our imagination. Creatives throughout the years have also taken risks with their inner world to fuel their imagination.

RISK-TAKING EXPERIENCES — INTERNAL

*This capacity to focus intensely, to dissociate and to realize an apparently remote and transcendent 'place' is one of the hallmarks of the creative personality when in the midst of the creative process.[25] - **Nancy Andreasen***

The creative person draws from a rich inner world, and their ability to focus - perhaps even to dissociate, is a necessary part of their ability to produce art. Because of this rich inner world of imagination creative people take risks in expanding their awareness. The English poet Samuel Coleridge was a frequent user of opium as a way of risk-taking. When he wrote the extraordinary work *Kubla Khan* he was most certainly under the influence of this mind-altering drug.

The Beatles similarly employed hallucinogenic substances to push their internal boundaries, although some of John Lennon's substance use may also have stemmed from the need to numb emotional pain. Creative people have also used meditation, prayer and eastern mysticism to explore their inner world and fuel their imagination. In fact, The Beatles became famous for their exploration of Eastern mysticism as another way of pushing their boundaries.

The following is an excerpt from an interview Garry McDonald generously granted with the authors in 2008. In the interview he spoke about his introduction to meditation and how this has positively impacted his emotional health.

Garry: *...My first foray into spirituality was extraordinary.*

Jeff: *Can you talk about that?*

Garry: *Yeah, I just wanted to learn how to meditate. I was interested in learning how to meditate for years and I kind of put it off. A whole lot of things happened in my life. I'd come to the end of Norman Gunston and so I thought I'd learn how to ride a surfboard and I'd learn how to meditate. I just happened to tell a friend. This friend was up in Sydney and he said to me, "That's why I'm in Sydney; I've come up to do an introductory program." ... There were quite a few people there, a lot of actors – hell of a lot of actors. Then Swami came on, he was European; shaved head, he had a red dot, and I thought that this was laughable. Then he* *opened his mouth and he was American, which was even worse. He did his talk, and I thought he was trying to be funny. So then he said we're going to chant a mantra from yoga for five minutes, and then we'll silently meditate for ten minutes, just repeat the mantra in your head. And so I thought well I've bloody well come here to do this, so I'll do it. So I sat down and I did it and immediately, when I went into the meditation, started to feel something – coloured lights and all that stuff.*

He opened up for questions afterwards and, of course, I never shut up. So I asked lots of questions and I said to my friend, what do I do now? It had been pretty wild. He said just go to the intensive in ten days time. Once again, I thought, "What is this?" But then I really got a full blast that day, went right off the planet. Full Kundalini trip. So I suppose I am sensitive in some ways. I mean I don't turn around and say to someone, "Wow there is a lot of shakti here today". But afterwards I might say to someone, "God – there was a lot of shakti there today". Others may call it the Holy Spirit. So I suppose I'm sensitive to those sorts of things. There was a woman there from England, called Charity Jones. She was High Church of England and I remember reading an article by her and she said she could go into a church and she knew when there had been communion. She knew when it had been blessed – amazing. Some people are just much more sensitive.

Jeff: *Just a bit beyond cognition is right.*

Garry: *I kind of like the mysterious quality of it too. I like that you don't try and explain it or understand it. After '84 I'd stopped doing it because I'd gotten so ill. It's very hard to meditate when you're depressed. But once I got back into it again, I slowly put my foot back in again, and then I started to realize what I was doing wrong. I'd been trying to avoid the real world by meditating stuff away – blocking things out, rather than allowing stuff to come up and dealing with it. So then that was a huge leap forward for me. It's interesting. There are periods where I get slack. I meditate about once a day. It should really be twice – I feel so much better when I meditate twice. And if I'm really good, I'll be doing like silent praying, I'll do the mantra ... and it tops up the bank. It is still possible to suddenly turn within yourself and go to that spot, and you feel really good. You can feel the warmth start in your stomach. But you need to nurture it, that's the only thing. It's no good only meditating when you need it, you've got to do it all the time – you've got to be match fit.*

Creative people seem to need to explore beyond themselves. Finding ways of doing this in a healthy, positive way forms an integral part of how to manage a creative mind.[26]. Garry's interview raises the question of how essential it is for a creative person to explore transcendent experiences, particularly in relation to their creativity, and how to do this without risking mental health through mind-altering substances or by blurring the lines between reality and fantasy.

Given the need to take risks and push boundaries both externally and internally, the attraction of drugs is a powerful one for the creative person. The downside is that substance abuse has some unfortunate long-term side effects. One of these is the deterioration of the ability to categorize and memorize the tool kit of sounds, images, colours and so on. It is an irony that the act of trying to 'fill the well' in this way impedes and damages the very mechanism that is meant to retain all these wonderful new experiences. This problem is compounded by the euphoria that masks the bad side effects. The artist is sabotaging their ability to be creative, but remains unaware that it's happening until much later.

> *All of us thought ... "Oh, man, I'll take some of this whatever the hell it is, and now I'll write some far-out s**t." And it's hogwash ... it actually gets in the way. The reason I believe this is ... as the increase of drugs curve went up the amount of songs and creativity curve went down at the same rate. Until it got to the point where I wasn't writing at all.* [27]
> **- David Crosby**

It is also reasonable to suppose that there is another attraction of using substances that impart the high. Amphetamines such as cocaine and others, mimic the natural high of the creative 'manic' experience.[28] Using amphetamines, the creative person may be trying to artificially induce a dopamine high when under pressure to create or when perception has dried up.

After the natural high, with its buzz, energy and rapid thinking, comes a natural low where the mood is more subdued, the energy flat and the 'sparking' creative thinking just isn't there. It is easy for a creative person to panic and try to artificially create the high by self-medicating to fuel the imagination. Stephen Fry alludes to this in his autobiography.

> *After twenty or thirty minutes we did the same thing again (taking a line of cocaine). And then a third time. By now I was buzzing and garrulous and wide-awake and happy. I did not know it but this was to mark the beginning of a new act of my life. The tragedy and farce of that drama are the material for another book.* [29]

"I have been feeling flat and low this week and I thought it was just me," a talented young filmmaker said to us one night. Helping creative people to better understand the impact and rhythm of their moods may empower them to choose risk-taking behaviour that will fuel their creativity not just in the short-term but also over the long distance.

CREATIVE MOOD

As with ego and energy, creative people experience natural mood highs and lows. What does this look like?

Adrian has just come off stage knowing he nailed opening night. The crowd was with him and he knew that he had them with him the whole way. It was electric. He is buzzing, feeling the euphoria of the release of pressure and tension that built up before the performance. Smiling and elated; his friends are laughing at all his jokes. He is thinking, "I am so good." He stays up until four in the morning. Performance number two is the next day but he doesn't want to lose this feeling. Plus he is young, full of energy – he can make it happen.

Next day, during the second performance, he misses a cue, stumbles over a line and his leading lady makes a comment as they pass each other on the way to the dressing room: "What happened to you tonight?" The applause was not quite as electric as last night. Adrian begins to feel a little sick in the stomach, like he is losing his grip. That old black doubt creeps into the back of his mind and takes hold: you are a fake, you knew all along you never had real talent, they're going to get rid of you, they're probably all in the pub now talking about how terrible you are. What starts as twinges of doubt is reinforced by some old thoughts and is soon developing into paranoia.

Adrian's mood plummets. Suddenly he is obsessing over small aspects of the show. He phones a friend and makes them come round and rehearse a scene over and over. The smallest details are issues for him. Adrian has become hypersensitive. Self-assurance has become self-doubt, and he starts looking for little clues in the way others react to him that will confirm what he now dreads but secretly believes is true – it's over for him. He is depressed.

Emotions are irrevocably linked to our physiology and thinking. They influence what we do. Emotions are very important to a creative person, because, as we are beginning to understand, they fuel the creative process. Understanding a little of the physiology of emotions can help the creative person gain control over their emotional world rather than feeling like a victim has fallen into an emotional maelstrom.

The Anatomy of Adrian's Emotional Journey

As Adrian began to build up to the performance on opening night, his brain began to register a demand – the demand of performance. Two hormones were released, adrenaline and cortisol. These are known as the stress hormones and have the effect of increasing our breathing and heart rates; redirecting our blood flow away from our digestion towards our leg and arm muscles as they tense in readiness to either fight or run away; heightening alertness, so we take in and process information more rapidly; and speeding up our metabolism.[30]

Following his opening night success, Adrian's social brain began to register acceptance, value and appreciation for his performance. The neurotransmitter dopamine increased and his mood became expansive and elevated – tied to the belief that he is loved, valued and appreciated.

Noradrenaline, the hormone associated with rest, was activated as the adrenaline and cortisol in his system finally diminished. Adrian's normal circadian rhythm was looking for some rest and sleep but owing to his extended partying, he arrived at his second performance still sluggish and tired.

He missed a cue and registered the imperceptible disapproval of his fellow actor. This triggered the emotional memory of fear within the *amygdala*: the pea-sized structure imbedded deep within the brain that has an emotional override mechanism.

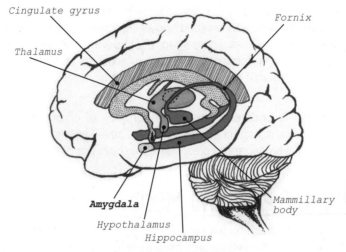

Cingulate gyrus

Fornix

Thalamus

Amygdala

Hypothalamus

Hippocampus

Mammillary body

THE LIMBIC SYSTEM

Normally, we *see*, then *think* and then *react*. However, in some circumstances of threat (or even just perceived threat like disapproval or rejection) we see then react before we can even understand why we are reacting. Our social brain, because of its links to the fight/flight/freeze response of the amygdala, is wired to perceive and react to negative emotions such as rejection more quickly than to positive emotions.

Adrian's rush of fear, brought on by the release of adrenaline and cortisol, is like a flood of physiological reactions preparing him for either fight, flight or freeze. He begins to tremble, his voice becomes uncertain and, as all the blood flow leaves his digestive system, he starts to feel nauseous.

The fragments of beliefs, such as: *I won't be loved if I make mistakes* that hover at the threshold of consciousness are called implicit relational schema. These form the foundation of Adrian's sense of self. When the second performance is over, the self-doubt and self-critical thoughts sweep into his consciousness, overwhelming him. Serotonin is released and Adrian starts to become flat and depressed.

To be human may be to have vulnerability toward shame, guilt and depression.[31]
- Louis Cozolino

As a creative professional, this roller coaster of emotions was destructive for Adrian. His performance diminished and will continue to diminish while the depressive mood pervades. Learning to recognize the early warning signs of negative mood, and understanding the negative beliefs about his identity will be essential for Adrian if he is to prevent himself from repeatedly falling into these patterns.

It is impossible to underestimate the importance of emotions for creative people. In fact, some writers and psychiatrists have suggested that there are unique emotional pressures on creative people because of their susceptibility to pain.

EMOTIONAL PAIN AND MOOD

As we have listened to, and read about, well-known creative artists, we have been struck by how frequently they have experienced pain or trauma in their past. Many of them have commented on the extent to which this has shaped them and defined their art. John Lennon's mother left him in the care of her sister. Billy Connolly's mother left his family when he was young and he was later sexually abused. Billy Crystal, Paul McCartney and Bono all suffered the death of their mothers at age fifteen. Childhood trauma does not make a person creative, but the high incidence (anecdotally) of early suffering in creative artists has led us to explore the impact of personal pain on shaping the creative artist and fuelling individual creative efforts.[32]

Two questions arise from this:

- Do creative people experience more emotional pain?
- Do they need this intensity of pain in order to create?

Do creative people experience a greater intensity of emotional pain or is this a myth?

No, it is not a myth – they feel their own pain more intensely and feel others' pain as well. This is also based on the belief that creative people are not only better able to describe their own emotions, but they feel other's emotions more intensely.[33]

Skinlessness

When I was a kid, I felt like I was this skin-covered antenna, and I could never get this antenna down. I was so aware of everything around me. I would watch people looking for signs of danger all the time. It was so acute that I really was able to jump into other people's skins. From this vulnerability, came opportunity. When I was 13, I parlayed that passion into a means of escape. **- Ryan Reynolds (Actor)**

The term *skinlessness* seems most appropriate in describing the quality that makes creative artists more susceptible to emotional pain. British author Leslie Stephen (Virginia Woolf's father) first coined this term in describing himself.[34] American Poet Sylvia Plath later wrote about herself along similar lines.

It's as if neither of us, or especially myself, had any skin. I am afraid. I am not solid, but hollow. I feel behind my eyes a numb, paralysed cavern, a pit of hell, a mimicking nothingness.[35]

Skinlessness is best thought of as a hyper-acute sensitivity that can manifest itself in many ways. UK psychologist Gordon Claridge has observed that "skinlessness can appear in nightmares, in sensitivity to bodily complaints, [and in] hyperawareness to sensory stimuli."[36]

Dr Anthony Clare, the psychiatrist who treated the brilliant and prolific author/comedian Spike Milligan also used the word skinlessness to describe Milligan's unique sensitivity. He quoted the American psychiatrist who first used the term in a psychiatric context.

From the very beginning, they seem to lack the 'protective shield' and the constitutional buffering between themselves and the world around. The hypersensitiveness that permits such free exchange between outer experience and the psychic interior may conduce to two outcomes: 'breakdown' when the primitive content takes over and allows the milieu of irrationality and unrealism to prevail without constraint, and an upsurge of creative productivity delicately controlled by the ego.[37] **- E. J. Anthony**

Friends and family also described Milligan in similar terms.

... he seems physically to feel pain when he reads of distressing events affecting children, animals, the planet. At times, as he talks, he sounds like a man who has been stripped of the normal rough, protective layer on which most of us

unthinkingly depend, the layer that enables us to cope with the constant, relentless, often disturbing bombardment of sensory images impressions illusions.[38] *- Norma Farnes*

We have had many visual artists, musicians, actors and performers speak about how sensitive they are to the emotional pain around them. Most people become aware of the same circumstances but simply detach from them. Creative artists seem to take in more sensory material.

The way we understand this is by referring to something called the Cocktail Party Phenomena which describes how we 'tune in' to different stimuli. Say you are standing at a party listening to one or two people and someone else nearby mentions your name in another private conversation. Immediately you tune in to that conversation. Our senses take in much more information than we actually attend to. We have an internal filtering mechanism that blocks out unimportant information.

Creative people take in more sensory information, particularly in the area of their art form, and they are filtering it less. This makes perfect sense now that we understand that creative people are constantly storing sensory material in their memory banks for that moment of perception. Learning how to recognize and manage this is essential for a creative person's mental health.

Think of the Internet like an epic cocktail party, filled with chattering 24/7 conversations. Our goal shouldn't be to ignore everything beyond earshot – that would inhibit our creativity, and keep us trapped in a very narrow world. Instead, we should keep on searching for those smart voices, so that we can remix the right data inside our head ...[39] *- Jonah Lehrer*

So now we can see that heightened sensitivity to stimuli, particularly those associated with the relevant art form, relates to sensitivity of perception. This is reflected in an increased intensity of experience, so that the artist is, as Robert Lowell described it, ... *seeing too much and feeling it/with one skin-layer missing.*[40]

Brooke Shields, speaking at Michael Jackson's memorial service, described him in terms that closely resemble what we have just been describing. Shields observed that Jackson's "sensitivity was more extraordinary than his talent ..."[41]

The image that comes to mind is of a human with antennas out all over their body – a bit like a human hedgehog. However, a creative person has twice the number of antennas than a person with less creativity. This is an incredible gift, but it requires careful management.

It appears the ability to feel things deeply and to continue to 'click on' to those strong emotions is a major factor in being successful, but this places creative people in a position of emotional vulnerability, which they need to manage for their psychological health. In fact, Sydney academic Mark Seton has recently highlighted this issue for actors. At the time of writing he is conducting research into what he describes as post dramatic stress – a condition arising from the personal vulnerability required to deliver high-quality performances. Seton cites Heath Ledger, Daniel Day Lewis and Robert Downey Jr. as being seriously affected by the mental exhaustion of playing 'troubled characters'.[42]

Here is a story of how one visual artist, with a troubled and traumatic upbringing, learnt about her skinlessness and how to manage it. But, more powerfully, it shows how she uses all that is within her to create great art.

As a child I became highly aware of what was going on around me in order to survive in a world of few spoken words and much danger and expectation. I had to be skinless to be constantly aware of changes in the people close to me. I had to be aware of what happened around me so I could quickly adjust, change and adapt to whatever was expected of me.

My ability to survive depended on my sensitivity and other survival mechanisms, which developed as part of my personality, because I needed them from when I was a very young child. I didn't even know that I did this because it has been part of me for as long as I can remember.

It has been both my strength and my weakness. It was a helpful survival technique but in my twenties it became my weakness as it was too overwhelming to be constantly aware of other people's needs, expectations, moods and even sounds and colours. Because of this all my senses became overloaded. Good places have the same effect because it's about the senses getting too much input. I was too skinless for a world full of constant information. The bucket was full, no space left.

I remember how I just couldn't cope; pictures, sounds, people's pain and smells; it was a constant input without a filter. Being a person of few words, not much came out either. Going into town wasn't bearable; it was like being hit by a bus every day. I was overloaded with information as soon as I left home.

After a journey of getting to know myself and heal, I have learnt to live with my skinlessness. How did I do this? By trial and error! I have read psychological books, had teachers helping me, had counselling and basically recognizing and acknowledging the fact of my own skinlessness. I learned to listen to my own body, recognize the signs of tiredness and stop to rest. Most of the time I was already past the stop sign as I woke up. I didn't know what it felt like to feel rested. I had to break my strong habit, which was to always keep going and to do as I was told.

Boundaries and learning to say no were new concepts to me. Being so good at observing, I learnt from other people how to set boundaries. I went on a long healing journey to deal with and change the consequences of the past. This changed my way of relating to myself, and others.

My constant state of being hyper-alert and aware of what was going on around me also kept me awake at night, which made the sensitivity worse during the day. It was a very hard cycle to get out of. Just using earplugs helped to simply block one of my senses. Other than that, I needed to process old locked-up emotions and face the demons of the past. I am getting stronger every day in doing that and learning that the world is not dangerous anymore. This new growing trust helps me in not having to observe and be on guard at night so much anymore.

Since I have been able to sleep I am much more able to filter information. Exhaustion is the worst thing for skinlessness.

Other practical adjustments I made:

I am careful with the music I listen to or the movies I watch.

I don't go into galleries or shopping malls when I am too tired.

I believe that any quality in people that might be a weakness can become a strength. I see that my skinlessness has caused me pain but it also makes me a better artist and a caring person to others. I have lots of empathy and that, combined with boundaries and healthy balance, is very helpful with people. Also in my teaching, I pick up quickly if my teaching is helpful or if I have to change my approach.

As I have become aware of my skinlessness I have started to understand why I have so much inside of me to put into my artwork. It's been like I have a huge *storeroom inside of me where I have been storing lots of information. I never seem to run out of ideas! Learning skills has helped me to express myself better as an artist and to come to a good result in my artwork. It gave me more tools to express the gathered information. I feel better when I create and express myself in visual ways. It's even more satisfying when the work turns out well, it's like finally finding a shape to say what I needed to say. It's an outlet for where words couldn't say enough.*

The unfiltered stored information had become more than I could express in words I guess. I had to find a way to express myself in a more creative way. I reckon for me it is, like people say: 'a picture speaks more than a thousand words'. Colour, texture, shapes, materials etc. all express what I've experienced and stored inside of me ... this makes me the artist I am today.[43]

Understanding the psychology of a creative person, and in particular their skinlessness, makes it easier to grasp their complexity, as well as the reason they may self-sabotage, self-medicate or self-destruct. Furthermore, it highlights the basis of difficulties that arise for those living or working with creative people.

However, understanding why these complexities exist does not provide solutions for how to successfully manage them. Let's return to the work of Mihaly Csikszentmihalyi for some further insight not only into what the problems are, but also into what the answers may be.

CREATIVE PEOPLE AND COMPLEXITY

Csikszentmihalyi conducted a study of 91 creative individuals who were all over the age of sixty.[44] The reason he chose artists over sixty, we imagine, was to look for those who were successful creatively and personally; those who had learnt to manage their creative energy, creative thinking, creative behaviour and creative mood. From his observation of this group, he developed the term 'complexity' to describe how creative people possess qualities that are normally seen as opposites. In a certain set of attributes, the opposites are held together in a kind of inner tension. A more conventional mind tends to find a zone of equilibrium between the opposites rather than having both. In actuality, circumstances of family, education and vocation mean that most people come to possess either one or the other of these qualities.

Csikszentmihalyi found that there were ten aspects to creative complexity in his sample of 91 people. In summary he proposed that successful creative people tend to:

1. Have high levels of energy, but to be often at rest
2. Be smart and yet naive at the same time
3. Be playful and yet disciplined
4. Alternate between imagination and pragmatism
5. Be extroverted and simultaneously introverted
6. Be humble and proud at the same time
7. Be somewhat androgynous – the men are more feminine and the women more masculine
8. Be rebellious and yet traditional
9. Be passionate and yet objective about their work
10. Be sensitive to both suffering and joy.

Our observations tend, independently, to bear out much of Csikszentmihalyi's framework, particularly the notion of the possession of opposite qualities. Our experience of working with over a thousand creative artists, primarily from a younger demographic range (18–35 years) has been contextualized in contemporary expressions of music, acting, dance, visual media and film production. As we shall see in the next chapter, in some cases our model of the creative mind intersects with Csikszentmihalyi's thoughts, but our observations have led us to describe many of the attributes that are subject to complexity in different terms.

IN SUMMARY

Creative people are by definition those who see, sense, feel and perceive their inner and outer world more intently and more intensely. They take in more sensory information, which becomes the fuel for their amazing creativity. This information becomes part of the memory bank of sensory experiences from which the creative mind draws to produce the moment of perception.

This produces two opposing forces that act on the creative person: firstly, their sensitivity to pain and, in particular, their sensitivity to the pain of their world; and secondly, the pressure to take risks, to confront, to challenge and to experience.

> *I, myself, alternate between hiding behind my own hands, protecting myself any way possible, and this other, this seeing [and] touching others. I guess I mean that creative people must not avoid the pain that they get dealt ...*[45] *- **Anne Sexton***

Notions of routine - predictability, the pedestrian and boring, are not part of a creative person's world. They will run from anything that resembles an ordinary life. Instead their world is one of extremes. They move from a state of boundless energy; intense focus; little need for sleep; almost manic thinking, rapid association and fluency of ideas, all the way over to a state of stillness as their body rebounds from the frenetic energy of creative output. They also experience extremes of emotion. They will move through euphoria, expansive ego, great joy and fulfilment to self-condemnation, despair and depression. These natural lows, following the highs of creative euphoria, can productively provide a critical voice for the creative person that helps them access a more analytical and detailed mental facility. They provide a counterpoint to the mania.

Creative people live with opposites. At the core of this tension is this opposition of moods of mania and depression. The mood of mania, in its mild form, can fuel creative energy. The creative person's unique sensitivity also allows them to see and feel what others don't. From this place comes a voice that can touch the hearts and souls of millions. It is a compassionate and resonant voice, which connects to our humanity in a way that the manic voice never can.

Friends, family and work colleagues look on and espouse a life of equilibrium, balance: something more normal. But this does not work well for the creative person in the long term. Without new experiences and input their creative well becomes dry and empty. On the other hand, the out-of-control roller coaster can lead to personal, emotional and psychological breakdown and ultimately the breakdown of relationships.

ThE PSYChOLOGY OF BEING CREATIVE

To be creative is to think, feel and behave differently. These differences fuel the creative process.

Perception:

- Novelty – new things stimulate rapid, fluid thinking
- Creates unique cognitive and perceptual connections

Discovery:

- Requires risk taking, exploratory behaviour to fill memory bank (well) in order to make unique discoveries
- Unique sensory input helps to fills memory banks (wells) but can lead to overload

Production:

- Heightened energy under creative compulsion need to be managed otherwise burnout or depression can occur.

SO WHAT NOW?

In the next chapter we are going to describe a model that explains things further – what we call *the nine dimensions of the creative mind*. It is based on the psychology that we have described in this chapter, as well as our own experiences. Our model considers the creative artist in terms of their identity, cognition, behaviour and mood.

If you are interested further in the psychology that we have outlined, we have included a more detailed summary of the research in the appendix at the back of this book.

1. 30 Rock is a comedy series created by Tina Fey that follows the exploits of the writers, cast and management of a weekly live television show set in New York City. Tina Fey plays the role of Liz Lemon, head writer and Alec Baldwin plays the part of network executive Jack Donaghy. This excerpt is from the closing minutes of Episode 4, Season 4: 'Audition Day'.

2. There are generally considered to be two types of bipolar disorder, bipolar I and bipolar II. Bipolar I is the more serious and can include the experience of psychotic thinking and behaviour, particularly during the manic phase. Conversely, people with bipolar II have greater periods of depression with occasional highs. These periods of mania are usually not as extreme as bipolar I mania and can last only hours.

3. This last excerpt was found online at http://www.geocities.com/SoHo/Workshop/4296/creativity.html but has since been removed.

4. A summary of key research is included in the Appendix

5. This quote comes from the book, The Fry Chronicles by Stephen Fry. He is a British comedian, writer and actor.

6. See Appendix.

7. This excerpt is drawn from an interview with singer/songwriter Rikki Lee Jones by Paul Zollo.

8. This observation was made during personal communication with the authors.

9. His name is pronounced "Me–high-ee Cheek-sent-me-high-ee" although apparently his friends call him 'Mike'.

10. For more on this see Flow – The Psychology of Optimal Experience (1990).

11. The full interview in Wired magazine can be found online at http://www.wired.com/wired/archive/4.09/czik_pr.html

12. This quote was taken from an interview with Ken Duncan and the authors in 2008.

13. For more on this see, for example, Leibenluft's article – Circadian Rhythms Factor in Rapid-Cycling Bipolar Disorder. Online at http://www.psychiatrictimes.com/display/article/10168/54751?verify=0 (A fee is payable for access to this journal article.)

14. The ABC TV program Catalyst reported research undertaken by Greg Murray, PhD MAPS, Senior Lecturer and Clinical Psychologist - Faculty of Life and Social Sciences, Swinburne University of Technology.

15. Writer Irving Stone sourced Michelangelo's correspondence in order to write his 1961 biography of the artist.

16. This quote from D – a film director was taken from our survey of 245 creative art students and creative artists.

17. This Robin Williams interview with James Lipton is a part of the series Inside the Actor's Studio.

18. For more on this see Carson et. al. (2003) in the Journal of Personality and Psychology.

19. This is a quote from AK, a visual artist who completed a survey conducted by the authors as part of the research for this book.

20. This excerpt is from an anonymous survey we conducted among performing and creative artists.

21. Gabora's 2002 study was cited by Schmajuk, et. al (2009) in the Creativity Research Journal.

22. An assertion made by Getzels, J. W. & Csikszentmihalyi, M. in a 1976 study also cited by Schmajuk, et. al (2009).

23. An assertion made by Wallach, M. A. in a 1970 paper similarly cited by Schmajuk, et. al (2009).

24. The full interview with Robert Luketic was conducted by Garry Maddox and published in the Sydney Morning Herald.

25. Andreasen op. cit.

26. In an extensive study of emotional creativity, the correlation between mysticism, religious experience and coping style was explored. James Averill (1999) found that being creative was closely associated with mystical or

transcendent-like experiences that are not bound by custom or authority. To be creative is to embrace the spiritual and transcendent.

27 David Crosby was a founding member of the seminal US acoustic pop band Cosby, Stills, Nash and Young. This quote is an excerpt from an interview conducted by Paul Zollo in 1993.

28 This claim is made by Rybakowski et al. in 'Psychopathology and Creativity' (2008).

29 Steven Fry op. cit.

30 Elated mood, increased motivation and exploratory behaviour have also all been associated with a part of the brain called the Dopaminergic Mesolimbic System which is what becomes activated in mania and after taking amphetamines, such as speed. This system was clearly at work in Adrian post performance. This process is outlined in detail in the 2008 study by Rybakowski et al.

31 Cozolino deals with this assertion in great depth in his book, The Neuroscience of Human Relationships.

32 Averill, in his previously cited study of creative artists, explored early trauma and creativity. He found that early trauma, such as the death of a parent, may predispose a person to 'emotional creativity' or the tendency to think about, understand and explore emotions and to seek unusual experiences that may help make sense of the trauma.

33 Hsen-Hsing Ma makes this claim on the basis of his 2009 survey of research into creativity.

34 Stephen's use of this term is documented by Brian Koehler in a 2006 article for the International Society for the Psychological Treatments of the Schizophrenias and other Psychoses.

35 Sylvia Plath is also cited by Koehler (2006).

36 Claridge is also cited by Koehler (2006).

37 Anthony is cited in Clare and Milligan's 1994 book: Depression and How to Survive It.

38 Norma Farnes was Milligan's agent for 36 years. She is also cited in Depression And How To Survive It.

39 Jonah Lehrer writes for Wired Magazine. The full article is available online at http://www.wired.com/wiredscience/2010/09/are-distractible-people-more-creative/

40 Ian Hamilton cites this quote from Lowell in his 1983 book Robert Lowell – A Biography.

41 For the full Memorial Service for Michael Jackson go to http://music.rightcelebrity.com/?p=2700

42 Mark Seton's work was reported in Joyce Morgan and Garry Maddox's 2010 article for The Sydney Morning Herald: 'Actors Search for the Light after Dark Roles'.

43 This testimonial is from an email sent to the authors. The correspondent wishes that their name be withheld.

44 For more detail on Csikszentmihalyi's notions of complexity see his 1997 book Creativity: Flow and the Psychology of Discovery and Invention.

45 Anne Sexton is a US poet. This excerpt is cited in Anne Sexton: A Portrait in Letters, 1977 book by Linda Gray Sexton and Lois Ames.

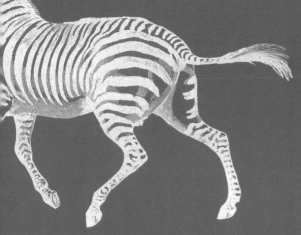

CHAPTER THREE

DIMENSIONS

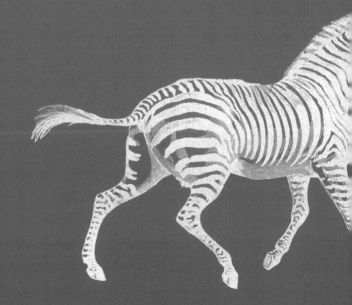

DIMENSIONS

*THERE'S A CERTAIN CHAOS TO OUR PROCESS
THAT BUBBLES ON THE SURFACE ... BUT IT'S ALL
UNDERPINNED BY A SENSE OF DISCIPLINE.[1]*
- RICHARD TOGNETTI

The creative mind is complex! No matter
how much we might like creative people
to be just like everybody else, they can't
because the qualities that enable them
to engage with the creative process also
make their experience of life different.

Everyone who knows Billy [Connolly] is aware of his considerable, albeit unusual, intelligence. However, he does not process information the same way that many others do.

No doubt Billy was viewed as an ornery child. He is still disorganized and oppositional, the former being a wired-in state and the latter a coping style.[2]
- Pamela Stephenson

Creative people are different. Rather than being balanced, the creative mind lives at the extremes. Rather than being in a comfort zone, the creative mind lives at the edge. Rather than being happy in one place, they are happy in two different places.

The secret to understanding the creative mind is to understand that they must possess certain qualities that are normally opposed to each other. To a normal person this appears to be a contradiction. In fact it's a paradox. To live with a creative mind is to live with a paradox.

DIMENSIONS AND POLES

Lets think of any of these qualities as being like a continuum. Lets call the opposites of the continuum – the paradoxes - poles (like the North and South Poles). Now we can refer to the whole thing as a dimension. Now we have a way of talking about these attributes.

Most people cope with the ambiguity and chaos of life by creating rules about the world that become like a formula. However, the creative mind is wired to notice change, build memory banks, make metaphors and embrace contradiction. Uncertainty and unpredictability are not just okay, they are important.

You're going hunting, but it's not for something to eat – it's for a moment of truth. I mean something that's real.[3] **- Don Was**

Both of these musicians are articulating something of what it means to live with a creative mind. To be able to nurture contradictions is to make a space for the creative process. Building on the previous two chapters we propose that there are nine crucial dimensions to the creative mind that we need to understand. These nine dimensions are key to comprehending their unconventional nature and are vital to the creative process.

THE NINE DIMENSIONS OF THE CREATIVE MIND

The nine dimensions that are the hallmarks of the creative mind are the dimensions of *ego, attitude, thought, sense, focus, emotion, energy, space,* and *action.*

Ego and **attitude** are dimensions of identity. Primarily they are a reflection of what we believe to be true about ourselves.

Sense, focus and **thought** are dimensions of cognition – or in other words, the way we think.

Energy, space and **action** are all dimensions of behaviour and can be thought of as outward manifestations of our beliefs.

Emotion is the one dimension of mood, and it acts as a unique bridge between our inner world and outward demeanour.

It is essential that we understand how these dimensions affect the creative mind, and those that live and work with creative people. Each of the dimensions has two poles (or opposites), and part of our understanding rests on how they facilitate the functioning of the creative mind, engage with the creative process and how each of them generates different stresses and pressures as by-products.

The nine dimensions are not exclusive to creative people; everybody has them. The vital difference between the creative mind and everybody else is that a creative mind must be able to inhabit both the polar opposites of each dimension regularly in a cycle. In effect, the creative mind must live with the paradox that they are a contradiction. They are both black and white – not one or the other or any of the shades of grey in between.[4] The idea that they can be balanced like others makes sense to conventional wisdom, but not to a creative person. To a creative person there is no such thing as a life in balance, but there is a life where the opposing forces seem to pull against each other, sometimes productively, sometimes destructively.

This is why the idea of the zebra appeals to us. It represents the paradox of being these opposites, either white with black stripes or black with white stripes simultaneously.

All great truths seem to have such contradictions inherent in them, and yet we would prefer these truths to be singular and uniform. So it is with the creative mind. It actually needs equal measures of the extremes, equal weight of each of these nine contradictions to function fully.

Artists who live a long and productive creative life have demonstrated that they have learnt how to manage the highs and lows productively. We have found that long-term success comes to artists who do not become fixed on either pole – for better or for worse. Instead they maintain a kind of elasticity between them, and utilize both extremes to help and strengthen them as an artist and a person – rather than letting them run out of control and become alternatively productive and destructive. We will call this kind of way of dealing with the nine dimensions *the creative tides*.

Creative Tides

The elastic way that successful creative artists live is what makes it possible to be both opposites together. The opposite poles of the dimensions are like ocean tides, which ebb and flow from one extreme to the other in a regular cycle. All of the nine dimensions function tidally – it is physically impossible to be both opposites at once. The creative mind swings from one extreme to the other, in much the same way as the tides go in and out. In some dimensions the tidal flow is swift and sudden; an artist can move from one pole to the other so quickly it may seem almost simultaneous – it is often unnerving. In other dimensions the tidal flow is more predictable.

Timetable is always unpredictable. Therefore every relationship is always placed upon with extra demands. This is the hardest part of my life. - HS

The secret to coping with tides is to learn that you can't fight them. Instead you must learn to take advantage of them. The elastic life of the creative mind is a response to understanding and navigating the tidal flows in each of the dimensions.

*I dwell deeply in my lows. Not till recently have I tried to push through my depressing states I get myself in - but I feel like I am still a bit creative in my depressing lows. It's more of a dry lonely state of creativity, but it's definitely a dark time. - **DH***

We believe that the creative mind has to maintain a tidal kind of life in order to be productive, successful and have longevity. However, the temptation to give in to one or another of the poles causes them to become either self-destructive, or destructive to others. When an artist tries to fight the natural cycle, or stay at one end of a dimension, they become a victim or they victimize others.

*I am so melancholic – and if I'm not careful can drag my friends down those ridiculous steep paths of darkness that grab me for a couple of days due to an unfortunate experience or bad feedback. - **JD***

In order to understand this better, we need to look at each of the dimensions individually.

THE DIMENSIONS OF IDENTITY

The First Dimension: Ego

Recap: As we discussed in chapter two, creative people and those with bipolar disorder shy, which is one way of trying to describe the changing nature of a creative person's ego. It also corresponds to observations that creative people are both introvert and extrovert, proud and yet humble.

The dimension of the ego defines your view of yourself (i.e. your self-image) in particular your own measure of your value to the world and to those around you. At one end of the scale is a person who is inflated, who possesses a disproportionately high sense of self worth. At the other end of the scale is a person who is deflated, one whose self-image is so poor they believe that they are worth very little. Such a person, like Adrian (in the last chapter) is at the mercy of the smallest change in circumstance.

Winston Churchill spoke about a lifelong personal battle with what he described as 'the white dog' and 'the black dog'. The white dog was what reinforced in him the belief that he had something in him that the world desperately needed. The black dog was a deep depression that threatened to overwhelm him with the belief that he was worthless and that all other notions were fantasy. The creative person fights a similar battle.

> *I heard that that Tony Hancock became inconsolable just after he had done his brilliant 'blood donor' sketch ... he was in his dressing room with his head in his hands moaning "How am I going to follow that?"*[5] - **Billy Connolly**

On the one hand it is necessary to have a huge self-image. The creative mind must inflate itself in the belief that it has something that everyone else needs. Without this an artist does not have the confidence to make or perform something they believe others should want to see. On the other hand, artists are insecure, because there is always a doubt – a feeling that what they have created and what they do isn't worth anything. Or worse, that it was a fluke and they will never be able to do anything like it again. The making of a work of art or a performance is an act of faith. Faith and doubt are constant companions. Without this doubt, without the possibility that they might be worthless, a creative person will not have the drive to pursue the creative life. Furthermore, doubt keeps the artist open to the possibility of new things.

Those who work with creative artists commonly adopt one of three strategies in dealing with the ego of their colleagues. One is that they throw up their hands in disgust and frustration, confront the artist and tell them that they are out of balance and then bail out. Another is to believe that the artist is totally out of balance, but to pander to them in the hope that they will come to their senses and then 'get better'. Eventually this person leaves too – but without the confrontation and often without having articulated his or her own frustrations. The third strategy is employed by those who come to terms with the fact that their creative colleague might be one kind of person on one day and completely opposite the next. They find ways of insulating themselves from the roller-coaster experience, without pandering to the ego fluctuations.

The Second Dimension: Attitude

CONFRONTING ◀▬▶ **ATTITUDE** ▬▶ CONFORMING

Recap: Creative people are supposed to see the world in unique and novel ways – this means they should be confronting established ideas, ways of doing things, and precepts, yet their emotional fragility and vulnerability means that there is a corresponding yearning for acceptance and community. They have often been described as rebellious yet conservative.

The dimension of attitude defines the way we orient ourselves towards our social groups. While attitude is an aspect of self-belief (like ego), it is more to do with how we define the way we relate to our society and the communities around us. At one pole of attitude is someone who we would define as confronting a society or group. At the other pole is someone whose posture is conforming. In general we adopt a position or a posture towards any group we become a part of. Most of us either adopt a conforming posture or attitude, or we leave. Conforming to a group dynamic provides a sense of safety and identity. Those who are attracted to a group, but wish to change aspects of it, adopt a confronting stance. It is the burden of leadership to hold a confronting attitude, as leaders are often in the process of taking the group somewhere that may be uncomfortable for its members. In fact there is no change without some kind of confrontation. Artists too are burdened with adopting a confronting attitude because their creative process (specifically perception and discovery) generates new ways of seeing and thinking about things. This may include challenging the culture within the prevailing social order. An example of this is the way the Beatles and their music confronted society in the sixties. It may also include confronting culture and dynamics within specific groups and organizations.

Confrontation is an uncomfortable thing for all concerned. Therefore, people who confront the social order, society or a group can find themselves held at arm's length by those they confront, particularly if they don't hold any formal leadership. The cost of activism is to give up acceptance and approval, unless of course their confrontation proves successful, whereupon they often achieve not just acceptance but recognition for their courage and integrity.

People who conform, however, will escape social rejection. In fact, a group that is experiencing criticism from one of its own normally tries to reinforce and strengthen its position by rewarding conformity in the rest of the group.

The dimension of attitude is easy to grasp once we understand it in these terms. We can see it in operation in small groups of friends, and on a broader social scale. In fact the entire sphere of political power in a democracy is a gigantic exercise in the dimension of attitude. For the creative mind, however, attitude is a minefield. In order for an artist or performer's work to be seen or heard, it has to be judged worthy by the gatekeepers of the culture. To achieve this the artists and performers have to gain acceptance. In some ways they have to hold a conforming attitude. At the same time, conformity is death to a creative person because it kills the creative process by imposing social limits on perception. In fact, it is often in opposition to group or cultural norms that the perception phase of the creative process occurs – the artist makes connections between things and ideas that other people have not made.

However, holding and maintaining such a confronting attitude comes at a price – either social isolation or the sense of social isolation. It makes you feel as if you are someone who is outside the group – other than the norm. American poet Charles Bukowski expressed his sense of otherness often in his poems, and described a kind of isolation that was a consequence of his perception of the world.

> *I am not like*
> *other people*
> *other people are like*
> *other people.*
>
> *they are all alike;*
> *joining*
> *grouping*
> *huddling*
> *they are both*
> *gleeful and content*
> *and I am*
> *burning in hell.*
>
> *my heart is a thousand years old.*
>
> *I am not like*
> *other people.*[6]

The dilemma is that while the creative mind needs to confront a culture or a community, it also needs to be approved by it. Despite Bukowski's own sense of isolation and despite the myth of the 'lone artistic genius', creative artists do not actually function productively alone. They do not exist in a cultural vacuum because they need others around them who will promote their work, distribute it, and ultimately they need to communicate with an audience within the culture. Despite his sense of being different, Bukowski's poems were published by a mainstream publishing company and were read by the general public. There is a delicate tension that must be held when confronting a society, and where that tension is held comes down to the individual artist and their beliefs.

By way of illustration, compare the work and experience of Soviet artist Aleksandr Gerasimov and Soviet author Alexsandr Solzhenitsyn. Gerasimov produced paintings that were heroic in nature and idealized the communist leadership of Soviet Russia. His work was an example of art being put to work to serve the interests of the state. He was lauded as the high watermark of Soviet creativity and his works were widely reproduced within that society.

He can be described as an artist who chose a solely conforming attitude to his society. In contrast, Solzhenitsyn was imprisoned by the Soviet government for his confrontation and the criticism of Russian communism in his novels. Solzhenitsyn wrote uncompromisingly of the dark underbelly of Soviet Russia, in particular the savagery of the labour camps that were used as a means of 'rehabilitating' dissident thinkers. His work was widely distributed in the West during the last twenty years of the twentieth century, but this was not so in Soviet Russia, where it was banned as subversive. Solzhenitsyn clearly adopted a confronting attitude. This tale of two Alexsandrs is a graphic illustration of the implications of the dimension of attitude. It has, like most tales, a cautionary aspect. While Gerasimov did not suffer in his conforming, today his work is more of historical interest.[7] Solzhenitsyn, on the other hand is regarded as a legend.

THE DIMENSIONS OF COGNITION
The Third Dimension: Thought

FLUID ◄—— **THOUGHT** ——► SCHEMATIC

Recap: We have described in detail how creative people are renowned for their thinking, which is rapid, fluid and uncensored. However, what distinguishes them from the manic is their ability to rapidly draw on associated memories, to filter out relevant from irrelevant information and creatively problem solve. In short: to have an internal, logical schema for rapidly processing and integrating new information.

The dimension of thought is about the two extremes of thinking adopted by creative people in order to successfully create. At one end of the scale, thought is fluid and at the other end it is schematic. Schematic thinking is rational and planned rather than the flight of ideas that characterizes fluid thought.

Fluid and schematic are labels that cover lots of different terms that have been traditionally used to describe thinking processes. Fluid thought includes divergent, sensual, imaginative, metaphorical, questioning, intuitive and constellatory thinking.[8] Schematic thought, on the other hand, incorporates convergent, conceptual, reasoned, literal, asserting, rational and linear thinking. These two lists make the dimension of thought easier to comprehend. They are neither positive nor negative, but they are different and serve different purposes.

Fluid thinking is more suited to making new associations between things. Schematic thinking is more suited to precision. You would expect a poet to operate more often in a fluid state, but you would prefer your airline pilot to be very schematic when landing the plane at night in bad weather.

Divergent **-X-** Convergent

Sensual **-X-** Conceptual

Imaginative **-X-** Reasoned

Metaphorical	-X-	*Literal*
Questioning	-X-	*Asserting*
Intuitive	-X-	*Rational*
Associative	-X-	*Linear*

At one end of the spectrum, fluid thought is how the creative mind makes connections between things that others don't – as illustrated in the extract from Robin Williams in the previous chapter. It is as if he is joining the dots on the page, but not joining them in the order that normal people would do. The creative mind looks at the night sky and makes new constellations.[9]

The artist and performer need to be able to think fluidly during perception and discovery and then be able to flexibly transition between fluid and schematic thought in the production phase, where things like the structures and rules of an artistic discipline come into play. Whether they break the rules, bend them, or adhere to them, the pure execution of the disciplines of a craft, is much more aligned to schematic thought. It's as if they have to be both artist and accountant, performer and critic, maker and validator.

I love songwriting. To me, there's all these elements that are mixed into it ... as I said before, children's games ... science ... I like to bring all these things together so it's all one. You can draw from any source.

I find that it's more like a problem that's unsolved. My mind will wander back to it if I'm in a good frame of mind. I'll say, "Well, that last line just isn't working" or "That just doesn't seem to be the right thing," so my mind will wander back to it.[10]
- Suzanne Vega

The Fourth Dimension: Sense

Recap: The unique ability of creative people to take in unfiltered sensory information has been described in detail in chapter two. Similarly we have also explored the distinctive empathic and emotionally heightened qualities of the creative mind. What has not been researched or described is how creative people psychologically manage this sensitivity.

*Effectively my guts are a transformer to amplify what's going on in my skin. - **K.N.***

The dimension of sense is to do with how deeply we feel or experience the sensations of life - how sensitive we are to stimuli, both physical and emotional. At one pole is the state of being entirely insulated, with the senses wrapped in a protective shell. The other pole is the state of being skinless, as typified by Spike Milligan and Sylvia Plath (see the previous chapter), with a totally open vulnerability to stimuli. When skinless, sometimes a person feels and senses so much that they periodically find themselves overwhelmed. We have borrowed the word from those who have described it before us. The term 'sensitive' is already used too widely, and is suited someone who is vulnerable to stimuli, but not in the extreme.

*What is happening to my skin? Where is that protection that I needed? Air can hurt you too.[11] - **David Byrne***

The creative life demands that an artist or performer be skinless and yet incredibly thick-skinned. Without openness and vulnerability there is no way that the creative mind can experience the perception that sparks the creative process. It is when creative people are shut down that they stop creating. On the other hand, to live the creative life is to have to cope with rejection constantly. Rejection of an artist's work is simultaneous with acclaim, as everyone's opinion will be different. Additionally, an artist whose work involves adopting a confronting attitude to social or moral norms must count rejection as the first sign of effectiveness. It takes an unusual person to be able to maintain vulnerability while simultaneously being thick-skinned.

Those who work with creative artists need to become skilled at reading the non-verbal signals from their creative colleagues and avoid arousing the severe emotional reactions of the artist being skinless. Inevitably there will be individual preferences and techniques for sidestepping the skinless-ness. It's a matter of learning what works on an individual basis. Insulated and skinless states are not experienced together at the same time. Rather the creative artist moves from one to the other, although sometimes the shift can be remarkably rapid. Mature artists have learned to be self-controlled and are able to make disciplined choices about their vulnerability.

*I tend to be very sensitive to my environment and have to have a certain environment around me... - **Marina Prior***

Experience teaches, for example, not to read reviews as they can be too assaulting. The creative mind needs to be skinless at the right times, and move to being insulated at other times.

The Fifth Dimension: Focus

WIDE ANGLE ◄— **FOCUS** —► *ZOOM*

Recap: One of the distinctive cognitive characteristics of the creative person is their focus and attention particularly when confronted by the new. This attention allows them to employ their creative problem-solving ability to work through creative obstacles.

The dimension of focus defines our field of attention. At one end of the scale is an ability to perceive at a wide angle the large scale and how things relate to one another in the big picture. At the other extreme is a narrow focus, which seems to zoom in on the detail, on the minutiae and the fine distinctions that make for subtle nuance. We have borrowed these terms from the writing of Brian Eno, as mentioned in chapter one.[12]

The creative mind must have both kinds of focus – wide angle and zoom. A wide angle is necessary in order to be able to make new connections between things, but the ability to zoom in to the detail is often critical to adjusting and manipulating a work at the micro level – fine details that may escape the conscious attention of an audience.

This is particularly true in the production phase of the creative process; where it is essential to be able to shift between seeing the big picture of their work and the tiny detail. The difference between good and great in a creative work often comes down to the nuances, the subtle things. More often than not the achievement of subtlety is buried in the detail of the work. It is also true that the pursuit of perfection, while holding a zoom focus, can take away the beauty of a work that you only see by stepping back and looking with a wide-angle focus. Mature artists are mindful of both and of the necessity of being able to operate at both poles of this dimension with flexibility.

Colleagues can inadvertently create conflict by misreading which pole of focus is in play at any given time. We referred to the concept of flow in chapter two. Flow and zoom focus are often synonymous. It is important to let flow run its course without interruption!

THE DIMENSION OF MOOD

The Sixth Dimension: Emotion

Recap: In previous chapters we outlined the power of emotions within the artist's creative world. Research has identified creative people as more emotionally mercurial – moving between different emotional states. We understand that the unique empathic nature of the creative mind allows them to feel deeply, feel empathically and potently express these emotions in their creative works or performances. The psychological strain of constant heightened emotions places a heavy demand on the creative person – only by learning to find the emotional 'off' switch can the creative person rest their emotions.

Now at this point it would be easy to assume that the two poles of the dimension of emotion should be 'euphoria' and 'depression' – reflecting the ways in which the creative mind often manifests itself emotionally, and also reflecting the similarities with bipolar disorder that we discussed in the previous chapter. Rather we have identified one pole of the dimension of emotion as intense and the other as calm. The reason for this distinction is that the experience of strong emotions, whether positive or negative, is critical to the creative process and therefore a significant component in the operation of the creative mind.

We discussed mechanisms of emotion in some depth in the previous chapter but, in simple terms, emotion can be thought of as the interplay of a spontaneous internal feeling or state of mind and our outward physiological response. So when we experience feelings in our inner world such as anger, happiness, betrayal, frustration or joy there are physical manifestations. Emotions register particularly in our faces but our tone of voice is affected, our tear ducts are affected, our heart rate and breathing are affected, levels of various hormones change and so on. We have described how a lot of the physical response to emotion is involuntary – our bodies react before we have time to think about it.[13]

The pole of intense emotion is a state of being where all the emotions are felt deeply and passionately, so sadness is intense grief, happiness is ecstasy, anger is fury and so on.

The pole of calm emotion is where we are no longer agitated by our emotions. They may have strength but calm emotion lends us a pliability that allows recovery from emotional intensity; in the same way that a resilient tree can recover from intense storms. This implies a level of self-control.

> *The second I get into the car (after a show), I just switch off. I put on classical music and just totally switch off... I don't obsess about the show during the day at all.* - **Marina Prior**

For most of us, the conventions of our culture and our social circumstances will serve to influence all but the most powerful emotions, and so we would place ourselves closer to the calm pole on the dimension of emotion – but allowing ourselves some room for the occasional unrestrained outburst here and there. Therein lies the problem for the creative mind because it is the experience of intense emotion that all too often accompanies perception. Intense emotion is often the direct consequence of skinless sense. Risk action, confronting attitude, manic energy and inflated ego can also contribute to a 'perfect storm' of intensity of feeling. While the notion of the 'tortured artist' has achieved mythic proportions, it is strength and depth of feeling that fuels the creative motor.

Intense emotion can be either euphoria or depression. It can be up or down, anger or triumph but it needs to be intense. When intense emotion is occurring it is almost never a dimension in isolation, but a dimension in resonance – it is the product of a number of the other dimensions vibrating on the same frequency, so to speak.

Without intense emotion, there is nothing to drive the creative process. Without a driver, there is no creativity. Conventional people frequently perceive the same things that creative people do, but without the intensity of feeling that drives them to create. Emotion is impossible to manufacture, but we believe that the perfect storm occurs inside the creative mind when enough of the other eight dimensions and the creative process align. The extremes of the other eight dimensions not only fire up the dimension of emotion, they are also to a large extent given greater potency because of the fuel created by emotion. Intensity of feeling and the motive power of strongly held beliefs and convictions, help push the creative mind to the poles of the other eight dimensions. Bukowski also wrote eloquently about emotion and the creative process.

if it doesn't come bursting out of you

in spite of everything,

don't do it.

unless it comes unasked out of your

heart and mind and your mouth

and your gut,

don't do it.[14]

Perhaps one of the greatest enemies of the creative mind is indifference, because the deep resources of emotion and passion are where the stuff that drives the creative mind emerges. Emotion itself is not enough to be creative. Convictions and passions alone are not enough to spark creativity, but the combination of them is like turning on a switch. In fact, we know that one of the common attributes of creative people is the depth of feeling. Without it – whether outrage, ecstasy, betrayal, joy, hunger or love, whether brought about by a moment of pain, or the product of deeply held convictions – the creative mind will not create. Even when the visible signs of emotion may have passed, the emotional memory will still lie beneath the surface to become the hidden flow of underground lava that forces things to move and shake.

Conversely, intense emotion is exhausting, and cannot be maintained on display for long periods of time. While necessary to drive the process, it is unhealthy to stay stuck in a state of intense emotion. The creative mind is best served by channelling intense emotion into the creative process – directing the energy – burning off the fuel so to speak, and then swinging over to calm emotion once the passion is spent. If creative people don't 'burn the fuel' on the creative process, then the intense emotion will begin to consume them and damage others. Intense emotion is there to be used. Additionally, in longer episodes of discovery and production, calm emotion is required in order to apply the disciplines of the craft to the task of realising a work, or rehearsing a performance. Production demands patience and order, which is why calm emotion is the preferred state for the creative mind during this phase. It's hard to be patient and disciplined when you are angry, frightened or depressed or whatever it was that lit the fire in the first place. If there is a perfect storm of intense emotion interacting with skinless sense, risk action, confronting attitude, manic energy and inflated ego, then the state of calm emotion is also the product of a cluster bomb type of interaction with insulated sense, safe action, conforming attitude, still energy, ordered space and schematic thought. In short, the pole of calm emotion provides a zone of safety and security that is necessary to advance the creative process beyond perception and discovery.

The importance of calm emotion was highlighted in a Michael Parkinson interview with singer/songwriter Sting, who revealed some of the source material for his compositions – including the fact that *Every Breath You Take* was about being stalked by his ex-wife. Parkinson then asked what it was that Sting felt when he was performing his songs. Sting seemed shocked at the question and answered that he felt nothing. Parkinson expressed his surprise, given the volatility of some of the source material. When Parkinson pressed the point further, Sting noted that if he were to allow himself to feel what the song was about he would not be able to perform it. All of the intense emotion had been directed to the writing of the song, but Sting needed to maintain some detachment from the emotional intensity in order to execute the disciplines of performance.[15]

The ability to move from intense to calm emotion demands that we have resilience. Resilience is that quality that helps us to bounce back when pressure has been applied. In the dimension of emotion developing resilience allows is to access intense emotions and then finds a pathway to swing to the calm pole. Resilient creative artists work on developing their ability to go to the pole of calm emotion, almost as if it is a physical place that they can visit when they need to. They practice going to it, to make it easier to return there under pressure. Resilience in emotion sometimes requires periods of feeling numb or detached in the short term.

The Sting/Parkinson interview highlights the dichotomy of the two poles of the dimension of emotion. No doubt Sting's professional detachment is a discipline he has arrived at as a way of coping with the fact that the songs are about intense episodes in his own life.

THE DIMENSIONS OF BEHAVIOUR

The Seventh Dimension: Energy

MANIC ◁—■ ENERGY ■—▷ STILL

Recap: Along with the mania of creative energy comes the need for stillness and rest. Creative people have been observed as exhibiting both high energy and listlessness. The ability to move between these two poles is necessary to re-establish a healthy circadian rhythm and avoid the psychological repercussions of unfettered manic energy.

The dimension of energy describes what kind energy state we are comfortable with when we approach our work. At one end of the scale is a manic energy level and at the other is still: Manic energy approaches projects at high speed and tends to operate in a whirlwind, creating a wake of turbulence. When at this pole, people are most comfortable when things are verging on disaster. At the other end of this dimension, those at the still energy pole operate in a measured and carefully paced fashion. They can rarely be persuaded to function without pause and deliberation. While most people find a flexible zone between these two poles, the creative mind operates at the extremes because the creative process typically involves episodes of stillness and episodes of mania. The still energy creative mind does not indicate that nothing is happening, rather that things are going on beneath the surface. This is more likely to be related to the discovery phase. Manic energy creative mind episodes are associated more with either the perception or production phases, when there are flurries of seeing, or surges of producing or where the creative mind is in flow.

> *I once did write 10,000 words in one day, like Balzac! I was pressured inside. I couldn't sleep. I just wrote and wrote. I couldn't stop, I couldn't control it ... in all the state lasted about 48 hours. All I could think of was the book. I didn't think of time.[16]*
> *- Spike Milligan*

The opposites on the energy dimension exhibit one of the strongest patterns of tidal flow. The creative mind can swing rapidly between the two poles, and so may appear to have only two speeds – fast and stop. Part of the reason for this is that both energy states are essential to the creative process.

Firstly, movement and activity create their own kind of momentum and this is not only an antidote to predictability and boredom, but, more importantly, a high level of energy output produces a more chaotic environment. As we shall see when we look at the dimension of space, what others perceive as chaos is not actually chaotic to the creative mind. The manic energy of an artist is, in reality, the creative mind harnessing unpredictability and fluid thought in the hunt for something new. Frequently they demonstrate the manic end of the dimension of energy when they have seen something new, or have made some kind of breakthrough. Sometimes there is an urgency to turn that perception into something more substantial before it is forgotten. Sometimes the environment just seems right to tug on the thread of an idea. Sometimes that timely tug produces something wonderful that might not have been found at any other time.

On the other hand, creative people also need to engage the still energy pole in order to mull things over, or just to wait for stuff to come emerging from the well.[17] Still energy can be a state of recuperation if the manic state has been particularly intense, however, it is over-simplifying to think of it just as recovery. Still energy is often a disciplined choice on the part of the creative mind in order to allow discovery to bubble along beneath the level of consciousness. The creative mind is working when it doesn't seem to be working. This notion may seem unnerving to others. However, seasoned creative professionals not only expect it to happen but have intuitively developed the discipline to engage that part of their mind, or at least have developed the patience to wait for it to process.

When that idea stops, I stop. I don't force it. If it's not there, it's not there and there's nothing you can do about it. Neil Young[18]

The Eighth Dimension: Space

Recap: While there has been no specific research that underpins this dimension, it is implied in much of the cognitive research into the creative person. In the same way that the creative person's thoughts oscillate between both fluid and schematic thinking, so the way they engage and interact with their creative space is a reflection of their inner creative world. There is, we believe, an implicit dichotomy about the chaos and the order, both internally and externally. Others, alluding to this dimension, have referred to both the playfulness and the discipline of the creative.

This dimension defines how the creative space is organised. Creative people relate to their space, and manage it in diametrically opposite ways. At one end of this dimension is an environment of chaos and at the other is order. We referred to the idea of chaos in our discussion of the energy dimension because there is an innate relationship between these two dimensions. It is important to think of the dimension of space as the total environment, the emotional, the spiritual, and the physical. Space also encompasses the notion of time since these two are inextricably joined.

There is an apparent lack of structure and planning at the chaos end. The opposite pole is characterized by meticulous and obsessive structure. As with the energy dimension, chaos and order are not held together simultaneously, but the creative mind swings between the two poles, needing both to function productively.

Chaos space is akin to manic energy in that they both provide an environment that enables fluid thought in the creative process. What normal people think of as chaotic, and therefore frightening because of a lack of certainty, is actually an environment of excitement and exploration to the creative mind. A certain kind of chaos is complementary with the creative process and is therefore energizing to the creative mind.

It is conventional wisdom to try to .maximize certainty in any endeavour. However, by doing this we are deliberately limiting the scope of new possibilities in order to make management easier, while inadvertently making life uninteresting for the creative mind.

In order to enable perception and discover the new, the creative mind craves uncertainty and unpredictability. The 'not knowing' coupled with the pressure of having to produce something forces the creative mind to engage in the creative process to discover something innovative. Of course the idea of this kind of pressure and uncertainty is terrifying to most people, but Dame Judi Dench describes how she deliberately sets up a chaos space in order to generate a sufficient creative challenge.

> *I don't ever read scripts; not because I don't enjoy reading, but I like to push myself to the fear level of going to fall right off the cliff ... there is something about the fear that is absolutely wonderful. When I played Cleopatra, people used to look at me and say, "What are you going to do?" And I'd say "Cleopatra." They used to look at me and say "Really?" The fear of it was such a challenge. Perhaps that's what I need.[19] - **Judi Dench**

For a normal person, risk minimization is the appropriate way to manage fear of the unknown, but the creative mind becomes bored when the space is predictable. Boredom is such a creative killer, that the creative mind will actively seek to undermine the predictable in order to avoid it. In many ways the avoidance of predictability is the essence of why chaos is crucial to the creative mind. Of course, in practice, this plays havoc with everyone else's schedules and systems. The danger is that it can be difficult to draw the line between what is selfishness and immaturity – the legendary self-indulgence of the creative temperament – and what is the instinct of the creative mind to stay in a zone of stimulation and new possibilities.

Conversely, the creative mind needs ordered space to provide the anchor for productivity. While chaos space is necessary for perception and for a certain amount of discovery, the order space of a creative discipline facilitates the production phase of the creative process. A close examination of productive creative people reveals that there is always space in their world that is almost obsessively ordered – how the paints and canvasses are stored, how the studio is organized, the care and maintenance of the musical instrument or the strict regimen of physical warm-ups. There is a space that is untouchable in terms of chaos because in that space, chaos is unproductive.

> *It is very rare that he will use the same sound in 23 songs. The guitars are set per song with their output levels - they're dedicated for that song and that guitar level. He sets his effects to receive that guitar level in a particular way.[20] - **Dallas Schoo, (guitar tech for The Edge, describing how each song has it's own guitar and set up for a U2 concert.)**

For Billy Connolly it is the sanctity of his home and family. The ordered space is sacred to the creative mind because there is nothing worse than going into the studio, or the rehearsal room to produce something only to find that someone has borrowed your equipment and not brought it back, or has used your amplifier and changed your settings, or left your guitar with a broken string. The creative mind relies upon order space to be able to produce and function in the disciplines of the craft.

R: *I have to have the desktop on my computers completely bare – I just want to see the drive or a folder with miscellaneous. I don't want a scattered desktop. The whiteboard in the office, once the data's gone up and been copied down, it has to be cleaned. Guitars in the corner, the desk has to be in the corner of the room. The guitars can't be at an angle, they've got to be flush against the wall. I demand that order from those who share my space, otherwise I'm going to slash my wrists. It's borderline obsessive/compulsive; my son's like that as well.*

Jeff: *All creatives, particularly musicians, have got to be a little obsessive/compulsive.*

R: *Desktop's simple, office is simple. I don't like a lot of stuff going on. But here, you've talked about the order, but the chaos is in my mind.*

Jeff: *So you can have a chaotic mind, because everything else is in order..*

R: *That's how I live. It's the chaos that creates the edginess.*

The Ninth Dimension: Action

Recap: Openness to experience, the quality of temperament most closely aligned to the creative, implies the drive for risk and risk-taking. In chapter two we looked at risk from an internal and external perspective. We love the saying, "Everything is sweetened by risk", yet risk without some safety leads to physical, psychological and relational damage.

The dimension of action defines behaviour, but in a specific way. This dimension is primarily concerned with openness to new experience, and the lengths someone will go to in order to pursue it. At one end of the dimension social behaviour is characterized by risk. At the other, behaviour reinforces personal and social safety. In chapter two we described risk-taking behaviour and the dangers it posed. In order to offset the risk, creative people also demonstrate a drive for security and safety, which at it's extreme, can become obsessive and present a different kind of problem.

Safety and risk are two sides of the same coin, driven by a common force in creative people – the need to preserve and protect the individual's creativity in the face of things that appear to shut it down. Whether it's self-medication for emotional distress; an attack on boredom or a way of generating an alternative set of experiences, risk is all about energizing the creative process. It is rare, however, for a young artist to be able to articulate this as their motivation for taking risks.

The need for risk has to be harnessed and directed productively. Seasoned artists do this. Comedian Billy Connolly prefers to go onstage with no prepared material and believes that such an approach makes for a better show. His psychologist wife describes it as "an accelerated state of magnified consciousness".

> *Billy believes the catalyst for … electric hilarity is a particular kind of tension. [He] attempts to create it spontaneously every time he goes on stage … [and] on those heavenly nights when he successfully puts himself out there on a limb, something happens that rehearsed material can never instigate in a million years. On those magical occasions he knows he's flying.*[21] - **Pamela Stephenson**

What she describes is Connolly's need for risk. However, there is a cost to this kind of lifestyle that is often borne by friends and family as well as the artist. Stephenson described herself as being terrified by Billy Connolly's pre-show nerves as he was "quivering in the wings" at the Apollo Theatre in Hammersmith before a show. She wondered if he was going to freeze when he got on stage, but of course, he did not.

Those who live and work with creative artists can find both risk and safety unpredictable and distressing. We have already described how misdirected risk behaviour can have destructive effects on those around the artist. Safety-driven behaviour can also be difficult to cope with. Reckless behaviour is most often destructive to the creative person, but preservation-driven obsessions tend to be damaging to those around them who are forced to accommodate the various compulsions.

WHAT DOES IT LOOK LIKE?

Like this...

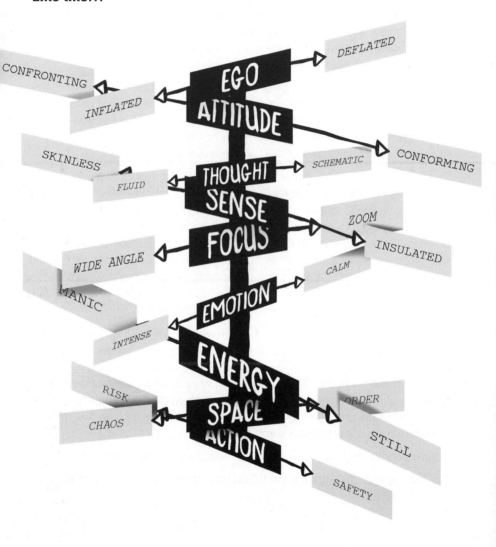

HOW DOES IT WORK?

The creative mind requires the extremes of the nine dimensions to be productive. This is not just because of the need to notice change, build memory banks, make metaphors, tolerate ambiguity and embrace contradiction. It is also because the demands of the creative process can't be fulfilled without powerful driving forces.

Most creative ideas seem logical in hindsight, and most people recognize creativity when they see it. Some people who are moderately gifted in an area will even think to themselves: Oh yes ... I could have done that myself. The reason they didn't may not be a product of their lack of giftedness – it may well be a product of having a more conventional mind.

The extremes of the nine dimensions create driving impulses that make those with a creative mind spend their time differently to others. The creative mind spends hours in the studio – spends hours doing things that don't make sense to others, spends days or weeks swinging preposterously from high to low, going flat out and frantic and then slowing to an absolute stop – behaviour that frustrates everyone else. Yet it is from that kind of wild improbable internal environment that an artist produces something, because the creative process in film, writing, music, dance and so on is full of obstacles. If it was easy, anyone could do it, and therefore everyone would do it.

However, creativity turns out to be hard work of a kind where there are no immediate tangible rewards, the possibility of even producing what is imagined seems remote, and where ultimately there may be no recognition, no reward and no future. That kind of hard work is difficult to undertake and continue unless there are powerful drivers at work. The extremes of the nine dimensions produce the driving forces that enable the creative mind to pursue making or performing something.

Do we need to embrace our insanity to become more creative?

No, but we need to embrace the difference by embracing the creative tides.

LIVING WITH THE TIDES

The secret of living with the creative mind is twofold.

- Accept that the optimal state for the creative mind is to function at the extremes of the nine dimensions – they drive the creative process.
- Recognize the need for a tidal life – inhabiting the opposite poles by navigating the inevitable cycle of highs and lows.

The qualities of each of the poles either serve the creative mind or dominate it. Any single one of them will dominate when it is unrestrained by its opposite. The poles become the servant of the creative mind when their qualities engage the creative process and bring about productivity and longevity. The poles serve the creative mind best when they restrain each other and combine together for a positive creative life.

Because the productive and positive qualities of one pole naturally counteract the negative and destructive qualities of the other, each of the poles acts as a restraint on the other, and each of the poles acts as a complement to the other. Think about it as: Buddy I've got your back. Each pole has naturally got the 'back' of the other – so the opposite poles protect us from ourselves as the tide goes in and out.

High Tide and Low Tide

We have made reference to bipolar disorder and creativity in the previous chapter. Rather than cause confusion with the actual disorder by using related clinical words, we will use the terms high tide and low tide to describe the polar opposites. One extreme is similar to mania (the ocean has come rushing in) and one is more closely associated with depression (the ocean has gone rushing out). The idea of the tides also avoids the positive and negative connotations that are attached to many of the clinical terms in widespread use.

As a generalisation, creative people are often attracted to the high tides of the nine dimensions because they tend to be more euphoric, and because they mostly have more fun there. High tides are good fuel for driving perception and some aspects of discovery. High tides are also good for letting off steam, for getting energized and for the process of making memories. High tides often produce the heady cocktail of brain chemistry that resembles a drug high. Low tides are just the opposite, which means that creative people are not always attracted to them. However, low tides are good fuel for the creative mind. Some aspects of discovery only occur when the low tide makes space for internal reflection. Just as importantly, the production phase of the creative process depends a lot on the drivers of the low-tide poles. Even more importantly, the low tides ensure that the creative mind gets a good dose of essential things like rest and safety. Low tide is the haven that the creative mind needs but may not always crave. Low tide allows for recovery and forces the creative mind to confront reality in a different way.

Euphoria and mania alter our perception in ways that drive the creative process. Low tide is the wake-up call that gives the creative mind the chance to take on board different and more sobering aspects of life. But a life at low tide lacks high points and exuberance. It's the combination of the two that is critical.

Nine Dimensions and Creative Tides – What This Can Look Like

Imagine an artist or performer – let's call him Dave. He has a creative mind and has learned how elasticity allows him to flow with the creative tides. He is allowing the high tide and the low tide to fuel his creativity rather than negatively dominate his personal and relational contexts.

> *Dave is confident without being overbearing and arrogant, he is insightful without being obnoxious, and feels things deeply without exploding all over everybody else. He thrives in a rapidly shifting environment without losing track of how to get to the finish line, and is able to see the big picture without losing the ability to focus on the details when needed. Dave also has apparently boundless energy, yet can rest at the right times in the right way. He seems to have mastered the art of improvising in the midst of chaos, and yet he has a place for everything, and everything is in its place. Dave is adventurous and spontaneous and will live life right on the edge, but he will never put at risk the things that are the most valuable and important to him.*

Ask any creative person about their best days and they will talk about themselves in the same way we have just described Dave. However, ask the partner or friend of a creative mind who has gone adrift at high tide or run aground at low tide, and they will paint a picture of their partner that matches what we have come to accept as a portrait of the artistic temperament – the selfishness, the narcissism, the tantrums, the depression, the mania, the swirling vortex of an out-of-control life that sucks in everyone who has to be around it.

It's Not About Balance

Balance is a concept that conventional minds strive for. Creative tides are not a matter of balance. Balance inhibits creativity because it means a creative person can never go to the extremes.

Navigating the flow from high to low tide is about realizing that there are cycles and rhythms to everything.

> *Anyone who has learned how to sail knows that the art of sailing is about using the winds, currents and tides to your advantage – because you can't change them. Recognize the tidal flows and use them to move forward. It's not just a matter of going with the flow, so to speak, which may see you end up on the rocks. When the tides are running high, the creative mind should use that part of the cycle to best advantage, and, when the tides are running low, the same applies. When you sail you learn to adjust everything; the setting of the sails, the position of the crew, the heel of the boat, the angle to the wind – in order to make the best headway. Sometimes the conditions mean that you have to compromise speed through the water in order to keep on a heading – sometimes it's the other way around. When the tides are really low, you have to sail slowly and carefully in shallow waters – or you will run aground.*

Navigating the Creative Tides

Navigating the creative tides is about slowing down when it is time to slow down, letting go of intense emotion when it is time to let go, changing your perspective when you've become too focussed or fixated, and so forth. Because there are natural cycles to this, the creative mind must learn to identify his or her individual patterns – or tides. Being able to do this is truly a matter of self-awareness and the willingness to work with a life that ebbs and flows rather than trying to push on regardless, or stay unmoved regardless.

Creative tides produce the kind of rhythm that allows creativity to flourish, as well as making creative people easier to live with. Healthier relationships and a long productive life, make for a better outcome than an early burnout and a trail of damaged relationships.

Before we look at the 'how to', however, it is appropriate to look more closely at what goes on to undermine a person's creative tides and innate elasticity. There are forces at work that force creative people to be cast adrift, or run aground.

BUT...

Not every creative person lives in the extremes of all nine dimensions.

For some, the extremes are experienced only in a few dimensions, and not all. For some, they experience the extremes relatively infrequently, for others it is nearly every day. Performers major in some dimensions, and geeks, writers, and artists – major in others. The dimensions don't all act simultaneously, nor do they always function alone. Frequently they interact with each other in clusters that are unique to an individual.

Some dimensions only emerge as critical on rare occasions; some are frequent, some are constant and some set off chain reactions.

Treat every creative mind as a unique individual – get to know them and find out how the dimensions function in them.

1   Richard Tognetti is a violinist and artistic director of the Australian Chamber Orchestra. This interview was also broadcast on the same ABC TV program as the Don Was excerpt.

2   This is an extract from Pamela Stephenson's 2002 biography of her comedian husband Billy Connolly.

3   Don Was is a US music producer who counts Bob Dylan, the Rolling Stones, B.B. King and Elton John among his lengthy credits. This interview was originally broadcast on ABC TV as part of the series Access All Areas.

4   See our previous citation of Csikszentmihalyi's notions of complexity in chapter two.

5   This excerpt is from Stephenson's book previously cited.

6   This extract from Charles Bukowski's poem *Displaced* can be found in the 2003 volume of his poetry entitled Sifting Through the Madness for the Word, the Line, the Way.

7   Gerasimov's painting V. Lenin on the Tribune is one such example.

8   Constellatory thinking is not strictly speaking, a word. We have included an accompanying note in explanation.

9   The ancient Greeks named our constellations, frequently after animals or figures from legend, although there are earlier records from ancient Babylon and Sumer of people describing constellations. When you look at the night sky you may discover that the constellations don't actually look like what they are meant to resemble. This is not surprising since the constellations are a product of the imagination. Long ago somebody looked up at the stars and joined the dots (so to speak) in a unique way, but in a way that made sense to their imaginings. They thought to themselves – 'if you joined this one to those it might look like the outline of a scorpion: Scorpio.' This happened all over the world, and astronomers from India and China invented their own different constellations. It's the joining up of the dots in a unique way that is interesting. The creative mind looks at the world and draws constellations – makes connections between things that other people don't.

10 Paul Zollo's interview with Suzanne Vega can be found in his 1997 previously cited.

11 This excerpt is from the song Air by Talking Heads front man David Byrne. It was originally released on the 1979 album Fear of Music.

12 Brian Eno op. cit.

13 The hit TV program Lie to Me explores how even the most disciplined of us reveal our emotions in 'micro expressions'.

14 Charles Bukowski op. cit.

15 The authors saw this specific episode (S02E15) of Parkinson when it was rebroadcast on Australian Television. It was originally broadcast by the BBC 17/12/1999.

16 This quote from Milligan is from Clare and Milligan's 1994 book previously cited.

17 We have described 'the well' in chapters one and two, where we outlined how the filling up of memory banks with sensations and experiences is essential to creativity.

18 Young's interview can be read in full in Zollo's 1997 book previously cited.

19 This extract is from an interview with Dame Judi Dench by Andrew Zuckerman in his 2008 book Wisdom.

20 Dallas Schoo was interviewed in the documentary It May Get Loud.

21 Pamela Stephenson op. cit.

CHAPTER FOUR
UNDERCURRENTS

UNDERCURRENTS

I THINK FEAR IS A VERY POWERFUL DEPRESSANT.[1]
- MARY WELLS

Artists who self-destruct early give in to forces that inhibit the natural creative tidal flow. Four main forces work to push the creative person away from these natural rhythms: *Fear and anxiety; insecurity; rejection;* and *spin*. They are like undercurrents – dark, dangerous and unseen.

Jeff: My father grew up near a beach in the Eastern Suburbs of Sydney. As a young kid heading for the beach every day in summer, he got used to the ways of the surf and became expert at spotting the hidden dangers beneath the waves. I can remember him, in turn, teaching me on my first trips to the beach how to spot the small tell-tale signs of the various currents – the longshore drift, the rip, the undertow. Some of these currents can sweep you out to sea in a matter of moments; some just pull you away from safety gradually. All of them can be dealt with. I remember it was hard to spot the currents – they didn't really appear to be doing much on the surface, but I also remember how powerful they were even though they were out of sight.

An undercurrent is a good way to think of something that undermines us, and our ability to trust. The four undercurrents drag us away from where we want to be. They set off negative cycles of thinking or belief.

CHAIN REACTIONS

An artist will instinctively try and avoid anything that threatens to shut down their creativity. When undercurrents occur they make the creative process harder. To solve the problem the creative mind reaches for whatever is at hand to try to suppress the frustration. Self-medication is one well-known tactic – so is avoidance. While these are immediate and produce an almost instant sense of wellbeing, they are costly over the long term because of the damage they cause.

It may seem simplistic to blame the famous artistic temperament on just these four undercurrents, but they work together and reinforce each other. Rejection generates insecurity. Insecurity generates fear. Insecurity forces us to create the illusion of success and then to maintain it with spin. Spin creates a bubble of unreality. This in turn creates the climate for further rejection, insecurity and fear – and so it goes on.

- Fear closes us down, constricts us and shut us up.
- Rejection isolates us from social networks that help us with insecurity.
- Isolation makes our insecurity worse.
- Insecurity makes us more vulnerable to fear.
- Spin denies us the ability to think honestly and objectively. We begin to believe our own PR.
- They act together negatively. The end result – the creative mind becomes fixed and inelastic, and is therefore prevented from going with their tidal nature.

THE CURRENT OF FEAR

*.... so we can all agree – can't we? – that no matter how confident we may appear to others, inside we are all sobbing, scared and uncertain for much of the time. Or perhaps it's just me.[2] - **Steven Fry***

Fear is a response of the autonomic nervous system, and arises as a reaction to the perception of a threat, even if it is imaginary. When our brain perceives that we are under threat, a number of automatic responses are triggered in our brain, in particular in the *amygdala*: the centre of strong emotion.[3] The threat can be physical and direct – a threat to our personal safety, our finances or our friendships. Or it can be more emotional and abstract – a threat to our identity or security, a threat of rejection or abandonment. Fear in one specific situation also tends to generalize, spreading like a virus to other situations.

Fear triggers a flood of biochemistry, known as the fight, flight or freeze response, which prepares us for instant physical activity. Remember Adrian in chapter two? His fight, flight or freeze mechanism was triggered by his fear and anxiety about his performance. This response is rapid and involuntary. It bypasses our normal reasoning process. We are hard-wired to respond to danger without thinking and to anticipate and protect ourselves from any threat whether physical or emotional. If you have been fearful in a social situation, your brain remembers the imperceptible relational cues as warning signs of danger and will trigger your defences in similar situations. It is like the type of learning that occurs when we are learning to ride a bike: the pain of falling off teaches us to avoid another tumble.

We Can't Think Fear Away

The *amygdala* responds to the inner and outer environments faster than our conscious awareness: it bypasses our thinking. This explains why we can't 'think the fear away' and why fear doesn't need to make sense. The amygdala is formed before birth, so fear is one of our earliest and most defining emotions. It retains learning from early experiences and so helps to shape the way we perceive later on. It functions to resist the triggers of fear being extinguished. Unfortunately, it also means that we are hard-wired for negativity and to anticipate danger.

In modern life the biochemical cocktail of fight-flight-freeze is overkill when you consider the circumstances that actually make us afraid. Most of the time fear is produced by our own imaginings, or by anxiously chewing over the things that might never eventuate. A lot of fear centres on our social environment. When our fear is over something more serious like financial or health worries, the biochemistry is still unsuited to helping us cope. That's why the fear response frequently appears unreasonable and irrational.

Fear makes us focus on the threat, rendering us unable to take in new and important information.

It makes us defensive and expectant of danger, rather than on the lookout for new possibilities.

It gives us tunnel vision and can often lead to a cycle of anxiety as one fear triggers another in a downward spiral.

It leaves us transfixed and immobile in the face of overwhelming circumstances.[4]

Stage fright and writer's block are familiar ways that fear strikes to disable the creative mind.

Just because fear is common to our experience doesn't mean we can dismiss it. It is so much a part of our primal brain that the creative mind must learn to harness it, rather than be disabled by it. In time, we can even come to love the adrenaline that makes us ready to be amazing rather than turning us into a helpless mass of quivering jelly.

The Impact of Fear on the Nine Dimensions

DIMENSION	IMPACT	DESCRIPTION
Ego	Self-condemnation	Fear forces the questioning of identity.
Attitude	Isolation	Fear isolates.
Thought	Rigid Thinking	Fear constricts, therefore important cognitive connections can't be made.
Sense	Sensory Shutdown	Fear stops the natural input of sensory information, become thick skinned.
Focus	Fixated	Fear shifts focus into *zoom* – but only in terms of fixating on the problem.
Energy	Driven	The natural cycle to find rest is overtaken by the fear-induced driven-ness.
Space	Obsessive Behaviour	Fear feeds the driven need to impose order and control in order to have something to rely on.
Action	Risk Avoidance	Fear does not let you take risks.
Emotion	Numbness	Fear kills other emotions like nothing else – particularly kills passion and empathy within the creative person.

The diagram below shows how this works in the dimension of 'Ego'.

The undercurrent of fear pushes the creative mind out of the normal tidal flow and into self-condemnation. The low tide state is circumvented for something more unhelpful.

Jeff: I remember playing in a band in an environment where the form of the songs was improvised at the whim of the vocalist – much like a jazz gig. In this one instance, the singer turned to the band-leader/music director (MD) about eight bars before the end of the section and called for a key change – up a tone. The MD turned to the rest of us, and gaining the requisite eye contact established that we were going up a tone into the next part of the song. He made eye contact with everyone except for one musician who was through fear, fixated within his narrow world – resolutely focused on performing his part as rehearsed in perfect detail – head down, unshakable. Seeing this, the MD tried to call off the key change but it was too late. The new section was upon us. The vocalist launched confidently into the new key. The MD (on guitar), conscious of the impending harmonic disaster, shrugged his shoulders and followed the singer. Both the bass player and myself on keyboards, on the other side of the stage, followed the key change. But because we could hear our fixated pianist, ploughing on in the original key, we both became unsure if the key change had actually occurred. We alternately switched back and forth between the two keys trying to work out which was correct. This went on for nearly half a verse of a song – a long time to be playing so dissonantly – before our colleague, wondering why we were all playing in the wrong key, lifted his head and looked around at us. It was a musical catastrophe, and for the rest of us in wide angle it felt like we were watching a train wreck in slow motion, but not for our piano player – he was fixated within his own narrow world.

ANXIETY

Anxiety is closely related to fear – a similar biochemical cocktail is involved, but instead of a sudden response to a perceived threat, anxiety is actually a state of mood. There may be no immediate threat, but instead it's a long-term worry about a future that contains problems that appear to have no solution. It is less predictable and the triggers are far more difficult to identify. It is believed that anxiety is centred in a different part of the brain than fear,[5] which can begin and end quickly. Anxiety, however, can persist over a long time. Some people live with a heightened sense of anxiety for years.

The hallmark of anxiety is *rumination*. An anxious person is consumed by cycles of negative thoughts that go round and round, over and over again. The physical symptoms are similar to fear but last longer, are more persistent and can lead to chronic stress symptoms such as sleeplessness, nausea and chest pain.

Anxiety Is the Silent Killer of Creativity

Actor Garry McDonald talked with us about his struggle with anxiety. He is currently the public face for Beyond Blue, an organization assisting people with anxiety, depression and bipolar disorder.

Garry: *My problem...was coping with the idea that I was failing as I was doing something – that was always my problem.*

Jeff: *So you're doing something and then as it goes on, is it the anxiety of having to produce it at the same level night after night?*

Garry: *No ... once I'm on it's all right. It's working up to it, I get very bad anxiety. That's when I used to try and meditate it away. And it would go, it would leave me, but it would come back again in an hour's time. It would leave in a big rush and it would feel so good ... but you wouldn't do anything about it. So I guess the way I deal with it now is CBT (Cognitive Behaviour Therapy).[6] If I feel like I'm getting into a stressful situation – I won't turn to meditation, I'll try and deal with it then and there – work out what I'm telling myself, and try to get support. I'm okay now that I know early enough – I recognize the signs quite early. It never gets out of hand ... well, it hardly ever gets out of hand.*

Julie: *You have talked before in a previous interview about not stuffing things down. Does meditation generally help with anxiety?*

Garry: *What I find is, if you do it every day, it just kind of evens you out. Some people might find that a bit weird. It's quite nice to have the highs and lows – well not the lows but the highs are quite nice, but evening you out means you don't get so anxious so easily.*

Jeff: *You don't plummet downwards so quickly.*

Garry: *I just find if I do that, it really helps calm me. I think your best work comes out of when you are calm anyway.*

Anxiety shuts down most of the high-tide poles. We become trapped inside the closed-in space of our worry – our accompanying thoughts become narrowed. The more we are anxious, the more we ruminate on the problem. The more we ruminate – the more we become convinced our view is right! The creative mind may well struggle with anxiety differently than other people. Combine a cocktail of rapid fluid thinking, a vivid internal imagination and a high tide of emotion and you have a recipe for the perfect storm of anxiety. This cluster of qualities means that creative people have a unique ability to imagine the worst kind of "what if" scenarios in colour and 3D. Fluid thought allows them to generate imaginary catastrophes complete with a cast of characters, a script, and ever more dire consequences that accelerate as the rapid flight of ideas propels them onward. Just like an out of control fast train, this combination can lead to anxiety of "epic" proportions.

The anxious mind also contracts to become self-focused as they become consumed by the negative possibilities. Because there is no mental space for anything but the looming disaster there is a major side effect. Anxious creative minds lose their compassion and empathy for other people's issues. They even feel justified about being like this at the time. Anxiety doesn't just cause a kind of mental paralysis; it may cause creative people to become socially withdrawn.

When Anxiety Drives Us: A Case Study

Julie: Rachel came to me for counselling, presenting with a long history of managing depression.[7] Her adoptive mother had recently died and her adoptive father was dying and she was looking to the therapeutic process to help her manage her grief. She was an actor and singer, with more than twenty-five years experience of performing. At the time she was using her performance skills sporadically in a highly demanding hospital setting.

Rachel had been adopted at birth into a beautiful, caring and conservative household. As a young child she was very petite, very attractive, very talented and very skinless. She had felt completely alienated in the small Australian country town in the 60s and 70s. Her adoptive parents gave her love and security and a strong protestant ethic, which stressed humility, denial of self and hard and selfless work. She escaped the confines of the country town and moved to a capital city where her natural mania collided with her skinlessness. She returned to the safety and security of her home several years later after suffering her first breakdown.

Now in her mid-forties, married to a performer and with a small child to care for, she had developed strategies to manage her natural lows. These included medication, exercise, meditation and a personal commitment to self-development and self-awareness. As we began to monitor her natural highs and lows, a pattern seemed to emerge. Increasingly, Rachel had been asked to perform or speak and, despite the difficult and painful process of working through her complex grief, she would strive to meet everyone's expectations of her, including her own, and then she would crash. When she crashed her thoughts would ruminate in a cycle of self-loathing and she would become angry and destructive in relationships as she tried to push people away.

As we began to understand this cycle, a pattern of increasing anxiety emerged as she felt an expectation to meet the demands that she and others put on herself.

Some of her core beliefs were driving her:

- As an adopted child I must earn the right to exist.
- I need to work hard at pleasing others generally (and within work) in order to be valued.
- Creative work isn't real work. The only real work is selfless work helping others.
- Rest is not allowed.

It was her skinlessness that made her an incredibly insightful performer, but it was also her skinlessness that placed a unique demand on her psyche. When she denied her skinlessness and responded to the increasing expectations, it tipped her into a driven-ness and anxiety that triggered the crash and then the self-loathing.

The first step was to recognize and understand when her physiology and her emotions were becoming overwhelmed – when there was too much demand.

We then looked at realistic expectations of what she could achieve – taking account of the unique demands of her skinlessness and exposing the driven aspect of an unrealistic work ethic. This led her to accept some gigs and refuse others.

She then gave herself permission to go to her still energy place. This was a spiritual, meditative, restful place that enabled her to nurture, re-energize and re-group.

So the next time she had a challenging performance demand, or high stress life experience, she left free space in her schedule afterwards. She began to recognize the post-performance flatness as the need to re-energize and nurture – not as the early stages of depression. She made decisions to nourish her soul: walks on the beach; meeting with a caring friend and avoiding high maintenance friends; constructive and self-esteem building retail therapy; regular meditation – finding her spiritual zone. In a couple of days she was able to move out of the post-performance flatness, regroup and manage the normal challenges in her life.

Anxiety was the destructive force that shifted Rachel's natural manic energy to driven-ness and then depression.

As anxious ruminations push a natural high to driven-ness, the body's physiology is forced beyond what is healthy for a creative person, to a place where they are 'running on empty'. This lack of self-care can easily reinforce self-loathing – leading to depression.

Anxiety Shuts Down the Creative Process

It is impossible to engage the creative process when gripped by fear and anxiety. It is impossible to perform well when terrified. Not only is it exhausting, anxiety uses energy that the creative mind needs to be directed towards production. The intense flood of hormones that prepares us to face danger means that we lose the fine motor control of the musculature necessary for playing an instrument, portraying a character or singing. Further more, because anxiety creates tunnel vision, perception and discovery become severely limited and the creative mind is unable to shift away from the low tide poles.

For skinless people, one of the greatest fears is that of being socially excluded. This leads us to the next undercurrent.

THE CURRENT OF REJECTION

*The hardest part about anything is starting ... the biggest thing that stops them is their fear of rejection. 'What will the people...?' Forget it ... you just go for it. - **Ken Duncan***

The creative life involves rejection. There will always be failed auditions, lost competitions, critical reviews, unhappy clients – people who don't like your album, audiences who don't get it, or drunk and abusive crowds.

*It's a business of rejection - things are getting killed off all the time. You start working and you kill ideas for yourself; you show it to your partner – he or she kills a few ideas, you show it to your client and the client kills a few ideas, then you show it to some people in the focus group and they kill a couple of ideas. And then you come back again and show it to the client, and he decides he doesn't like it after all 'cause his wife saw it. That can sometimes take a year that process – it can take a year. It's very stressful and depressing to have those ideas killed and so there has to be a nurturing environment around...because people have to get themselves up off the floor and do this again.[8] - **Jeff Goodby***

The creative mind has to take steps to cope in an environment that constantly reminds them they should have given up and gotten a real job. This is particularly so for those involved in the performing arts. Rejection in these fields is so immediate. Actors, singers and comedians know straightaway what the audience thinks.

How do creative professionals cope with the rejection they experience as a part of their job?

Jeff: We rationalize the criticism. We take into consideration any adverse circumstances we were facing and we also know that certain people or critics are always negative. We secretly demonize critics/producers/managers and write their opinions off because they know nothing about the art or the craft. We don't read the reviews – or rather we don't read the bad reviews. Sometimes we have friends who read all the reviews and only pass on the good ones.

We band together in adversity and develop a close social circle of like-minded individuals – comrades in arms, a tribe. Our professional tribes cling together because we are united by the common experience of our work, and because we are bonded together by the common experience of rejection. We have legendary stories of how audiences or managers snubbed us, even though we were great.

We have a code of language and behaviour that identifies who is part of the tribe and who is not. We have little tribal rituals that work the same way. These include things like after-show drinks or meeting at a certain bar or café to celebrate our uniqueness and togetherness.

We develop a devastating and often cynical sense of humour that is born from the shared agony of being vulnerable and being exposed to rejection night after night.

We focus on our moments of success and acclaim, and hold onto those as truer indications of our achievement and self-worth than negative reviews or opinions.

We develop a pride in our skills and ability in our chosen field. Our technical skill is a tribal badge of honour. We all recognize that the people outside the creative tribe can offer criticism but we would love to see them try and do what we do – because they can't.

You can see the same kinds of patterns in occupations where colleagues feel outnumbered or misunderstood, or where they face emotional stress on a day-to-day basis. Police departments worldwide are like this. Camaraderie is created by the knowledge that no one else understands their situation. Operating theatre nurses have a famously tough brand of humour that helps them cope with the reality of their work. Fortunately, their patients never witness it.

The creative mind must learn to rationalize rejection in the professional sphere in order to be able to survive. Creative professionals do as others do; they believe that the rejection is ill informed and therefore unimportant.

Rejection is tough in the professional domain, but when it comes from within the artist's primary social groups it's far more damaging. The social network is a refuge - a means of coping with the brutal honesty of the creative working environment. The creative mind desperately needs a social network where rejection is rare and affirmation is high. Their community is a safe haven of acceptance in a world that doesn't get them.

Professional rejection is also generally obvious – the bad review, or the drop in sales. Social rejection takes many forms but it's mostly more subtle. When people reject someone socially they are rarely open about it - it happens covertly so that it's plausibly deniable. By the time we reach adulthood, most of us are pretty good at reading social signals – we understand the hidden messages in body language and other non-verbal cues that tell us if we are in or out.

Covert Rejection

Cliques or sub-groups within a group are often a means of covert rejection. The fact that somebody is excluded from a clique might never be spoken of, but it will be acted on anyway. There may never be any overt exclusion, but there will always be an understanding in the clique about who's who. The people who are in - know they are in, and the people who are out gradually get the message. Covert rejection gets the job done without anyone ever having to confront the guilt of causing pain. Tribes of creative artists that form together use cliques to exclude non-artists as a means of evening the score. We reject them – they reject us.

Consequences of Rejection

Our brain does not differentiate between physical or emotional pain – it reacts by employing the same physiological responses. Being rejected socially feels emotionally like being hit physically, and produces similar protective behaviour in us.[9] Also the part of the brain that manages empathy is associated with rejection. A skinless person, doesn't just feel their own rejection, they feel others' rejection as well.[10] There even appears to be a positive correlation between acceptance and belonging and improved immune response and better physical health.[11] The reverse is also true. So there are three outcomes of rejection: short-term numbness, loss of empathy and long-term loss of self-esteem.

> *The initial response to social exclusion may often be shock, marked by an emotional numbness or lack of feeling* [12] ***...Roy Baumeister (et al)***

Just like physical pain, the first thing that happens is a numbing of our feelings. Numbness is followed by anger, and combined with a lack of empathy this gives us reason to retaliate in ways that we might not normally. If you can't join them – beat them.

> *The whole emotional system seems to shut down (temporarily at least) in the wake of rejection. Excluded ... [people] ... show less emotion than other[s] ... Likewise they seem to lose their capacity to empathize with other people. The loss of empathy helps explain why rejected people cease to help others and why they become more aggressive than others. Empathy promotes treating others well and without it, people become less kind and more cruel.*[13] *- **Roy Baumeister***

The spate of mass shootings in US high schools by social outcasts is an extreme example of this. While most of us don't go around with an AK-47 blowing people away after we've been rejected, we often attempt to 'even the score' on a much smaller scale by retaliating in some way. Rejection from our social framework also means we become willing to take more risks, because we are now outcasts and have nothing to lose. So the pattern goes: rejection followed by anger and recklessness. It's easy to see how these immediately impact the dimensions of sense, emotion, attitude and action, eventually leading to detachment, emotional callousness, isolation and self-harm.

Rejection and Identity

The long-term effects of rejection affect our identity and self-esteem. People with low self-esteem are widely known to be more prone to depression and anxiety – as they feel powerless to change their circumstances. Thus rejection is an undercurrent that reinforces other undercurrents. The loss of self-esteem is so significant that one researcher has proposed that it be used as a gauge to measure how much rejection people experience.[14] Rejection when we are young can also inhibit the healthy functioning of the part of our brain that processes our self-image and thereby hamper our ability to integrate and process future rejection – insecurity.

The impact of rejection depends on how important that group is to the individual and how vulnerable they are to the feelings of others. This is a double whammy for a creative mind. As you will read in future chapters, social groups are essential for maintaining creative tension. We already know that the creative mind is tidally skinless. Therefore, rejection of a creative person from a group that they consider to be of high value is incredibly destructive in both the short and long term.

In every case, the undercurrent of rejection produces a driven-ness in the creative mind that is unhealthy. Qualities that normally move the creative process forward become relentless. There are four dimensions that are particularly vulnerable to rejection; they are sense, attitude, action and emotion. The table below outlines how these dimensions are impacted.

DIMENSION	IMPACT	DESCRIPTION
Sense	Detachment	Rejection causes the skinless person enormous emotional pain as their sensitivity and empathy go into overdrive. The only coping mechanism is to retreat and become detached, which is a form of protection. This is where they disconnect their ability to process and integrate emotional and cognitive material

DIMENSION	IMPACT	DESCRIPTION
Attitude	Isolation	You reject me so I'll reject you. Rejection isolates causing a creative person to become withdrawn because they no longer feel as if they belong.
Action	Self-Harming	They can cast off all restraint and take self-harming risks, partly in order to make a statement.
Emotion	Callous	Rejection is such a powerful shock it can dominate and drive our emotional expression. Frequently the anger remains at the intense pole. Thus becoming emotionally calloused.

The diagram below shows how this works in the dimension of 'Emotion'.

Rejection has such an impact on our sense of self it is only natural that our next undercurrent is to do with this.

THE CURRENT OF INSECURITY

Insecurity is a direct attack on identity, is largely invisible on the surface and is incredibly dangerous.

> *I know some actors, who when they're not working, it's like they cease to exist. They panic; they're heart actually palpitates if someone says, "What are you doing at the moment?" And they have to say, "Nothing." They'd rather not go out to have to answer that question. It's that caught up with their identity.* **- Marina Prior**

It is the rip current that pulls artists into the dangerous waters of doubting who they really are. Because the work of an artist involves making the imagined become real, self-image is fundamental to long-term productiveness and to the maintenance of great social networks. The creative mind needs anchors. The dimensions of ego and attitude produce important drivers for the creative process and they are all about identity. Therefore, anything that undermines the quest to live with one's own inherent contradictions can cause the creative mind to not move from their high or low creative tides. Ego and attitude extremes that should drive the creative process finish up driving the individual, making life difficult for everybody.

> Julie: Stacy was an effervescent young woman with a beautiful singing voice who enjoyed singing and performing. She had an older sister who was tall, lithe and attractive, but not as accomplished as Stacy. Both were part of a community where they sang regularly, but the community placed a higher value on looks than on talent and so Stacy found herself sidelined while her older sister was given position and accolades. Although she was not overweight, she was stockier than her sister and she came to blame her weight for the fact that she was being snubbed. Stacy became fixated on her self-image and on losing weight. It haunted her. She ruminated about it and began a cycle of destructive eating and negative self-talk. She lost her joy and found herself too intimidated to perform. Eventually she stopped singing altogether.

> In our narcissistic, self-image driven world, a performer must regularly manage insecurity around the issue of their self-image. I have counselled the most attractive young men and women and have been surprised by how insecure they are about their self-image. However, insecurity has little to do with appearance and more to do with identity.

WHO ARE WE?

Eventually, we come to realise that all of our actions and beliefs stem from who we think we are. As we live and grow we construct a mental model of ourselves. This self-image is really nothing more than a set of beliefs that we hold about ourselves: what we are good at, what we are bad at; what we deserve, what we don't deserve; what we think we are like to be around, and so on. These beliefs are central to how we live because they affect the way we see ourselves and our expectations of the way the world should see us. [15] Some of these beliefs are pretty solid and some are open to change.

Our identity is vulnerable to insecurity precisely because it is not set in concrete. Our 'self' is a lived character in the unfolding drama of life. It is constantly being updated. We are also vulnerable to insecurity because our self-image may not be totally based on actuality.[16] This uncertainty is why we need good friends – people we can trust.

> Jeff: Try and recall the last time you met someone who devoutly believed something about themselves that was clearly false. I once knew a great guy who thought he was a wonderful musician and singer. The reality was quite different, but he was blissfully ignorant of his lack of ability – until he entered a talent quest. It was an excruciating evening for everybody. He couldn't play in tune, or in time, and his voice sounded like a cat being strangled. There was no applause. Tough you say. Well, I had been made a judge of the talent quest at the last minute – and he was a friend. It fell to me to deliver the bad news. Did I say he *was* a friend? Yes – past tense. I was as gentle as I could be, but he was deeply offended. Not an easy moment.

> Like any set of beliefs; some of our identity beliefs are objectively true, some are subjectively true and some are fantasy. For example, the belief that I am 186 cm tall is objectively true – it is verifiable by measurement. The belief that I am good-looking, however, is only subjectively true. It's more a matter of opinion – there will a few who think I'm good-looking and others who think I'm not. If I were to say that I am a hot athlete, this would be a fantasy - because my poor bat and ball co-ordination has achieved legend status among my friends. Fortunately, my self-image includes the view that I am bad at sports but good at other things.

We also construct our identity by exploring the world around us. We form our own view of what is right and wrong, partly on the basis of experience and partly on information we get from people we value and trust. Therefore, our self-image is derived from both intrinsic sources (an idea of who we are from within us) and extrinsic sources (our experience and what others say). By the time we reach adulthood, our identity should be pretty well formed, but it should undergo change as we grow older and learn more. Neither the intrinsic or extrinsic sources of identity are infallible – so we have a kind of internal dialogue where we weigh up what we have experienced with what other people are telling us.

We can also equate maturity with identity. The more mature we are the more accurate our identity is. If we go back to the story of Stacy, we see her sense of self was eroded by extrinsic sources at a young age. She allowed her mental model of herself to be battered by comparison with others – siblings are a particular favourite – and by culture and values within a community.

Symptoms

There is nothing quite as difficult as dealing with someone who is chronically insecure. To start with, nothing you say or do seems to be able to change their position. Everyone and everything is seen, felt and heard through a filter that reinterprets every word or action as a negative. Insecure people spend their lives compensating for what they *think* they lack. This compensation is at best socially awkward – someone who is always too loud at parties, or the person who is always apologizing. Sometimes it can be painful to watch, or even destructive, like the person who is always getting angry too quickly, or who is manipulative, or constantly obsessing about their weight and appearance.

AUTOBIOGRAPHY

We rely on our identity unthinkingly, but it is subject to assault. Because it is not a one-off, one-time thing, it is better to think of it as an unfolding discovery – and we can reflect on it. Self-reflection turns out to be an important tool for managing the creative mind. Anything that undermines our ability to be self-reflective ultimately undermines our ability to maintain a life of creative tides.

Liken it to writing your own story. That's why we refer to identity as a self-narrative. We are playing the central role in the movie of our lives and the script is always open to revision – our identity becomes more accurate as our insecurity becomes less.

When circumstances or people challenge our self-image we are initially unsure how to react, or what such a challenge might mean. It is here that the practice of self-reflection can help us.

Is this new information about myself something that I need to take on board?

Are these events part of a larger picture or just circumstantial?

Have I been wrong about myself all along?

Is this new information something that will make me feel better about who I am – or does it threaten me?

Is it coming from a reliable source? Or does this other person have a vested interest in putting me down?

Are they trying to gain an advantage over me by making me doubt myself?

Are they looking to promote themselves and need to make me look insignificant?

Am I in a competition for something that I am unaware of?

Is everything here as it seems?

Are they being cruel to me for sport, or is it a test of my resilience?

AND SO THE CREATIVE MIND

Insecurity may be a problem for most, but it is particularly so for creative minds because they already live with the extremes in the dimensions of ego and attitude. The tendency towards deep insecurity and yet to present with high self-esteem is a hallmark of the creative mind. The tendency to be critical of the very group they want to belong to is as well. For the creative mind, insecurity is situation normal. Adding more insecurity to this mix is almost a crime. Additionally when they are at skinless sense they will be profoundly more vulnerable to insecurity than normal, because of the heightened awareness of emotions.

A controversial biography of actor Peter Sellers explained how this aspect of ego functions professionally, or at least how it did for Sellers. Biographer Robert Lewis thought that Sellers was such an imitator with an exceptional ability to read people - then adapt himself to mimic them, that in later life he never demonstrated an actual identity – he was incapable of being the real person.[17] Film director Jonathan Miller independently observed the same thing, but not just in Sellers.

> *There are a lot of people in the theatre who don't have personalities. That's why Sellers was such an astonishing creator of different personalities – he didn't have one of his own. Peter Cook had a lot of that. I never really had a conversation with him unless he adopted an accent.[18]* - **Jonathan Miller**

Performers have to learn to live with an abnormal level of insecurity but the problem is compounded for actors because their job is to believably portray some other imaginary personality night after night or take after take.

Insecurity and Technique

Even though we have already discussed the importance of technique in chapter one, we should take a moment to revisit it because of the link between technique and identity in creative people. Artists place such high value on technique that their sense of self and their technical competence become intertwined. For many, it becomes synonymous with identity. Not just that they spend so much of their life to acquire it, but because others use it to define them – colleagues, critics, fans and so on. When so many people think of you as a great artist, it is difficult for you not to see yourself in these terms as well. This is particularly true for a performer because their technique is so immediately and constantly on display as they work. Audiences pass judgment on how good they think the artist is. We reject an artist on the basis of their technique – say it is not personal – and wonder why they are distressed. To them it is very personal.

We have found that this is most painfully the case for singers, dancers and actors – where their body is the instrument. At least, with a musician, an instrument stands between them and the audience. For an actor, body shape and age serve to define a cluster of possible characters they may play. For a dancer, body shape is critical to how their technique is perceived. A dancer must become used to the constant striving after physical perfection and fear of ageing. Some of them are tormented by the need to stay thin. Anecdotal evidence from dancers suggests that eating disorders occur in the dance community two hundred times more than in the wider population, so powerful is this link. We have found that the most pressing issue for dancers is to separate what they do from who they are - so they find value as human beings independent of their work.

For singers it is not just the appearance but it is the sound of their voice. There is nothing so uniquely defining than the sound of one's voice. Singers agonize over how they sound.

Insecurity – Externally Driven

Artists make something out of nothing, and they are professionally dependent on the opinion of others. It's tough enough feeling insecure normally without the added lack of security that comes from not knowing whether people will like your work - or want to see the next thing you do. Most creative minds try to battle insecurity in their professional lives with their technical competence[19] and by trying to do the best possible work, as an insurance policy against unemployment – so the thinking goes. At the extreme, this turns into a drive for perfection, a quest that is doomed to fail because it's impossible.

The drive for perfection is a sign of insecurity.

Insecurity – Internally Driven

The artist must battle insecurity for themselves. It is effectively a battle for the very existence of the artist's individuality, uniqueness and their particular vision – the things that make their work original.

> *... there is only one of you in all time, this expression is unique ... if you block it ... it will never exist ... it will be lost.*[20] *- Martha Graham*

If they give up this battle, then all the work that we can expect from them in the future will be robbed of originality. Negative self-talk quenches the willingness to take risks and be unique. It undermines the confidence they need to feel - in order to be different.

Unrelieved insecurity forces them to construct rigid mental or emotional defence mechanisms – to prevent their identities being damaged. Staying within a rigid mental defence destroys the elasticity they need to move with the creative tides. By using such defences to shore up a self-image, freedom to swing from high tide to low tide in a dimension is lost.

Insecurity following trauma

As we mentioned in chapter two, an insecure self-image is thought to be the result of the accumulation of negative criticism, particularly from authority figures such as parents. Such circumstances require courage and determination to overcome.

> *Billy's story is an utterly triumphant one. Not a day has passed since I met him twenty years ago, without my shaking my head and marvelling at his miraculous survival of profound childhood trauma. His ability to sustain himself beyond those days is equally impressive, for once he was known to the world, another challenge presented itself: to survive the trauma of fame ... When I asked the essential, penetrating question of how he always managed to summon the resources to turn trauma into triumph ... what I got was: 'Well, I didn't come down the Clyde on a water biscuit.'[21]* - **Pamela Stephenson**

What makes people resilient in the face of early trauma? Three qualities are thought to be key: humour, creativity and spirituality. [22]

Creative artists have within them the ability to constructively work on their self-narrative, as Billy Connolly clearly did, to prevent the early part of their narrative from limiting the whole story.

The good news is that insecurity can be conquered. Rewrite your narrative. Recognize the parts of your story that are keeping you in a mental or emotional prison. Find a community that will believe in you differently and thus reinforce your new narrative. Change the way you speak about yourself, when it comes to those areas where you are insecure.

Do some things you've never done before, but expose yoursel to new experiences in a gradual fashion, so that you can demonstrate to yourself that you are able to grow and develop. Make goals and start working towards them. Try out new things away from your normal social context so that you can do them without the implicit judgment of your peers. Be honest with yourself about your strengths and weaknesses and make your plans about how and where you can grow and change. Above all – don't give up.

Insecurity and the Dimensions of Cognition, Mood and Behaviour

Insecurity causes stronger, more frequent and unhealthy fluctuations in the poles. The oscillation between high and low tides is driven by neediness and the need for approval. Rather than allowing truth and creative exploration to drive the creative process, it is propelled by approval and therefore makes the creative mind fearful of trying new things.

DIMENSION	IMPACT	DESCRIPTION
Ego	See-saws between Narcissism and Self-condemnation	Questions of identity drive the ego dimension into extreme cycles from high to low, depending on external circumstances: if you are loved you become inflated; if not affirmed: deflated.
Attitude	Sycophancy	Need for approval, rather than creative identity drives the conformity to sycophancy or the flattering and fawning behaviour. Easily used by people who feed off the flattery.
Emotion	Unstable	Emotions become driven by external forces alone and are prey to every little circumstance.
Action	Perfectionism	Beyond the pole of safety action lies the quagmire of trying to achieve perfection as a means of ensuring that risk is eliminated.

The diagram below shows how this works in the dimension of 'Action'.

THE CURRENT OF SPIN

Whether a creative person is lied to, or whether they are lying to themselves; the process of putting a spin on the truth causes loss of trust, can undermine identity and also block perception.

> MORPHEUS
>
> Unfortunately no one can be told what the Matrix is. You have to see it for yourself.
>
> NEO
>
> How?
>
> MORPHEUS
>
> Hold out your hands.

In Neo's right hand Morpheus drops a red pill.

> MORPHEUS
>
> This is your last chance. After this there is no going back.

In his left, a blue pill.

> MORPHEUS
>
> You take the blue pill and the story ends. You wake in your bed and believe whatever you want to believe.

The pills in his open hands are reflected in his glasses.

                    MORPHEUS

          You take the red pill and you
          stay in Wonderland and I show
          you how deep the rabbit hole
          goes.

Neo feels the smooth skin of the capsules, with the
moisture growing in his palms.

                    MORPHEUS

          Remember that all I'm offering
          you is the truth. Nothing more.

Neo opens his mouth and swallows the red pill.[23]

What Spin Is

Deception covers a broad variety of concealment – it is rarely an outright lte, more often a subversive twist of the truth – so we have decided to name this last of the four undercurrents spin. Spin is reality customized by ideology. Spin is reality version 2.0.

Spin is what allows people who are normally highly moral to be evasive with a good conscience. Spin is the product of a process of rationalization – we convince ourselves that there is a less unpleasant, less confrontational approach to interpreting events. Spin enables us to make the facts fit our view of things, rather than have to change our views to fit the facts. Spin is somewhere between an explanation and an excuse. Spin is commonplace, convenient, slippery and almost impossible to pin down in one place. It is subtle, smooth, ingenious and hardly ever obvious – even to the person who is creating it.

I did not have sexual relations with that woman...[24]

Spin is when we put ourselves in the best light.

Spin is when we are selective with the information we divulge.

Spin is when we allow others to draw conclusions based on partial information.

Spin is when we take a bad situation and make it sound good.

Spin is when we reinforce our own illusions, or the illusions of someone else.

Spin is when we weave a fabric of illusion around our lives to create a halo effect.

Spin is when we deny even to ourselves the downside of something.

Spin is what PR companies and politicians do for a living.

Spin is what we imagined we wanted something to be.

Spin is a web that entangles us as much as it mesmerizes others.

Spin is attractive to the creative mind, because imagination is their metier.

Spin and the Creative Mind

Spin is such an issue for the creative mind because of the manic qualities of the creative person. Remember how euphoria and a grandiose self-belief were integral to the creative mind? This leads to a tendency for artists to use hyperbole, embellishment and hype as primary messages.

How many times have you heard something like: *Please welcome to the stage, ladies and gentlemen ... the one ... the only ... fresh from a sell-out tour of Europe ... the legendary ...*

Legendary rock band Pink Floyd even recorded a song about this phenomenon. Composed by bassist Roger Waters, the following lyrics of *Have A Cigar* reflect actual phrases spoken by record industry executives to members of the band.

We're just knocked out,

We heard about the sell out.

You gotta get an album out

You owe it to the people.

We're so happy we can hardly count.

Everybody else is just green,

Have you seen the chart?

It's a hell of a start,

It could be made into a monster

If we all pull together as a team.[25]

The creative professional is forced to live in a culture of spin. The world of arts, media and entertainment is one where everyone is competing for airtime, audience share, or just the next gig. The inflated ego needs to self-promote in an environment where everyone else's inflated ego is self-promoting. The only solution is to get louder – egotistically speaking.

Unless there are definite strategies in place to manage this embellished world, then it can be as destructive as a culture of fear. There are two challenges to spin. The first is what happens if we start believing our own spin, and the second is the challenge of maintaining trusting relationships, personal integrity and credibility in a world that depends on spin to achieve success, or at least the illusion of it.

The legendary mockumentary, *This Is Spinal Tap*, alludes to this in an 'interview' between the characters of director Marty Di Bergi and band manager Ian Faith.

DI BERGI

Last time Tap toured America they were booked into 10,000 seat arenas, 15,000 seat venues, and it seems that now on the current tour they are being booked into 1200 seat arenas, 1500 seat arenas. I was just wondering, does this mean that the popularity of the group is waning?

IAN FAITH

Oh No. No no. No no no. No no. Not at all. I just think that their appeal is becoming more selective.[26]

Victims of Spin

What happens to the creative person over time when they live in a world of spin? When people find out that they have been a spin victim, there is an immediate feeling of betrayal. We realize that we have been victims of manipulation. You will often hear artists use the term *disillusioned* to describe how they feel once they understand that spin has been in operation to make them conform, or to do something they would rather not.

This is an excerpt from an interview with SR, a creative person who was involved in a culture of spin within a creative team led by a charismatic individual named Tony.[27]

> *[He said] that not everybody else on the team was big enough to take it, so it was a charming, flattering, encouraging justification all the time. "You gotta understand you're my best, you gotta understand you're a cut above the rest, that you are special, you've got to understand it. And so-and-so can't take it, and so-and-so can't take it, and that's why I do it." Because it felt sincere and it felt good, it was always enough to cancel out the disappointment or the embarrassment.*

SR talked later about his disillusionment and loss of trust.

... because you're acting then, you're being a pretender. I've felt like I was pretending with Tony. I never really felt like a lot of it was sincere. I felt like it was all a show, a game.

The greatest long-term impact, however, was on his creativity.

I'm living more protected now. I've actually sacrificed the creative journey, the flow, for the sake of protection. And I'm aware of that by the way, I'm aware of that socially ... in myself.

The creative mind works in the realm of ideas; therefore truth is vital to them. All creative product or performance comes from the interplay of perception with what we believe to be true. Once an artist learns that the very ideas they thought were true are unreliable, they lose trust in those who brought those ideas to them.

Spin sucks the creative mind out of a community. When key relationships prove untrustworthy, we are unwilling to remain committed to them. Under better circumstances, that group might have been relied upon to mediate and help the creative mind stay elastic.

Spin is a key reason why many creative people go from one social group to the next. They are searching for what is authentic and real. While this may seem like the impossible dream – given that everybody spins – there are limits to what can be considered genuine differences in perspective and what amounts to being deliberately misleading. Those limits are tighter for creative minds than they are for politicians.

Yeah. It rattled my confidence and funnily enough the person who brought that to my attention was D, he said, "Mate, you talk yourself down. You gotta understand something – you're absolutely fine, you don't have to make apologies for who you are – it's creativity." He used to say that to me. But I was so rattled. - SR

The costs for the creative person to live in a world of spin are the erosion of confidence in knowing what is right and true, and the loss of trust. The magnitude of this problem will be explored in later chapters.

Dealers in Spin

There is a different cost to the creative person when they are perpetuating the spin.

Lets detour quickly into the world of celebrity. While most of us are not part of that world, there is an increasing yearning for attention and value – the very things that fuel the cult of celebrity.

> *I suspect the enduring appeal of celebrities ... is that we envy the attention they receive and look to them for clues about how to attract attention ...*
>
> *What we want is to be important to someone, to be noticed by someone and celebrities are a signpost to that possibility*[28] ... *- Hugh Mackay*

Imagine how attractive the cult of celebrity is to the creative person, particularly the performer who lives for attention.

The Cult Of Celebrity

The image of the celebrity is mostly manufactured – it's a myth. However because celebrity is powerful, the myth must be maintained and protected in order to keep the power. Very few people are strong enough to resist the seduction of the five-star lifestyle. When everybody is agreeing with you, when your every whim is satisfied, you enter an unreal world. It's a world that lures you into self-delusion – you begin to believe your own publicity, because no one is correcting you, or disagreeing with you. You have become the victim of your own spin because ultimately it's a world of your own making. If you weren't powerful and couldn't afford the cost of paying for the entourage of assistants, you would be thrust back into the normal world very quickly.

The myth of celebrity is reinforced by the power of celebrity. When the celebrity at the centre of things offers an opinion, right or wrong, there is enormous pressure on those in the inner circle to agree - even though the fact of just voicing an opinion does not necessarily make it the truth. However, the very sound of the words begins to convince them that it could be true. It only takes a few repetitions of those ideas for them to begin to believe their new and improved version of the truth. Reality 2.0. This is particularly so when what has been said seems at least plausible.

The next step occurs when people in the next circle out repeat those words back to them, particularly in slightly different contexts. This further reinforces reality 2.0. If they are saying it beyond the entourage, then it must be right.

Even though you may not achieve true celebrity status, the inflated ego combined with charisma, thirsts for attention. Positional power can create mini-celebrities within various creative communities – the professional theatre; the local theatre group; the band or music group and, dare we suggest it, even the glee club.

The climate around celebrity/mini-celebrity is therefore a self-reinforcing climate. Much of the impulse for everyone to agree springs from the need to hold on to membership in the magic kingdom – and to maintain the magic kingdom itself. Therefore, associates and assistants, who have a vested interest in keeping the celebrity (or mini-celebrity) happy, will reflect the celebrity's own spin back to them. Thus the power of celebrity is reinforced by the myth of celebrity.

> *Many years ago there was an Emperor so exceedingly fond of new clothes that he spent all his money on being well dressed ...*

The fable of the Emperor's new clothes is the definitive example of how spin can infect an entire group of people. In a destructive group culture, it is not uncommon to find that the cult of celebrity has run amok.

Believing our own spin

As we build the narrative of our own life we can fall into a trap that makes our identity dependent on our own spin. We judge ourselves by our intentions, but we judge others by their actions. We mentally relive past events selectively in order to make ourselves feel better about the way we acted, or the way things turned out.

We naturally hate to admit that we are in the wrong, but spin can help us take this to a whole new level. We can get to the stage where we are often in the wrong but we have developed a philosophy or a one-sided self-narrative that makes our wrongs appear perfectly justifiable.

Spin: Our Defence Against Depression

One of the challenges for the creative mind is managing the low moods. In chapter two we talked about the tendency for creative people to have mood swings. Depression can be so familiar to the creative mind that it becomes like the Dementors in a Harry Potter novel. To avoid this, an easy tactic for creative minds is to build a bubble of spin around themselves as a protection against the growing black. A culture of spin forms a permanent patronus charm[29] of happy thoughts. What a relief to have people who will always tell us how wonderful we are; who will bolster our self-image and help us reinforce our inflated ego. Kind of like our own *Truman* movie. It is very tempting for the talented creative person who is trying to defend themselves against the 'black dog'. But what impact does it have on the creative process?

If we surround ourselves with people who tell us only what we want to hear, then we condemn ourselves to a prison of misinformation – of our own making. In fact, we condemn ourselves to a life that is not real because reality 2.0 keeps us from experiencing actual reality. We have the means to create a parallel existence through the power of our words.

This is why elasticity is so important and why both high and low tides of the nine dimensions are important. Pain is as crucial to the creative process as euphoria, but we like it much less. It's important to be skinless; to feel and experience fuels our creativity. The low tides are as constructive as the high tides. If we assemble an unreal world of spin, it creates a dissonance with our skinlessness and we begin to detach and dissociate our feeling and sensing parts. Gradually our creativity dries up.

The following diagram illustrates how spin affects the dimensions of ego, attitude and sense. Spin is a little more than an undercurrent though; it is in fact the active avoidance of certain aspects of the creative tides.

DIMENSION	IMPACT	DESCRIPTION
Ego	Narcissism	Spin and celebrity are temptations for the inflated ego – feeding the grandiose self-image and providing protection against the deflated ego.
Attitude	Illusion	Communities built on Illusion and deception, replace authenticity. The culture of spin ensures that the group always conforms – it breeds a cult of celebrity, where the illusion must be maintained at all costs.
Sense	Dissociation	Dissonance between the deceptive quality of spin and the skinless sensitivity to truth and beauty causes dissociation. This is the disconnection between understanding and the sensory and empathic information the creative mind is receiving. The only defence is to dissociate.

The diagram below shows how this works in the dimension of 'Sense'.

The dimensions of identity are the most vulnerable to spin, but there is a domino effect. Ego and attitude forge links between the other seven dimensions in ways that the others cannot, because ego and attitude are concerned with core beliefs about our relationships and ourselves. If one undercurrent can undermine and destabilize those beliefs, then every other dimension will be destabilized – often by the creative mind trying to compensate.

In order to fight the effects of all the undercurrents, we must now turn our attention to the three strategies that underpin a life of creative tides. Without them, the creative mind cannot withstand the currents that will drag them into becoming fixed at one or the other tide, and away from being productive.

1   Mary Wells was the creative director and founding president of Us advertising agency Wells Rich Greene. The observation made here was in Doug Pray's 2009 documentary *Art & Copy*.

2   Stephen Fry, op. cit.

3   See chapter two.

4   This recapping of the fear response is based on the work of Louis Cozolino who we have cited in earlier chapters.

5   According to Cozolini (2006: 249) researchers believe that anxiety arises from the *Bed Nucleus of the Stria Terminalis* (BNST) as opposed to the *amygdala*.

6   Cognitive Behaviour Therapy is a popular psychological tool to assist people manage distressing and overwhelming thinking and beliefs. It has been found to be particular effective with anxiety and depression. For more on this see Grazebrook et al. http://www.babcp.com/silo/files/what-is-cbt.pdf (accessed 29/1/11).

7   7 Rachel is a real person who gave us permission to use her story. Her name has been changed to preserve her privacy.

8   8 Jeff Goodby is US advertising executive and creative director in San Francisco based ad agency Goodby, Silverstein and Partners. This observation was made in *Art & Copy* (2009)

9   9 A research team at the University of Michigan led by Ethan Kross got hold of 40 people who had experienced recent painful romantic break up. They were asked to recall the break up, and then they were given a painful stimulation similar to pouring hot coffee on skin. On the basis of functional MRI scans taken during the experiment, the researchers concluded that the brain uses the same regions to process both physical pain and social rejection.

10 Cozolino (2006) op. cit.

11 There are two areas in the brain that are believed to be involved in rejection. The first is the *cingulate cortex*, located near the cerebral cortex, which is believed to help integrate thinking, feeling and sensing. This is the area that becomes activated when we, or those we love, experience physical and social pain such as rejection. The second area that is important in our understanding of rejection is the *insula cortex*, lying beneath the temporal and frontal lobes. This area is involved in intensifying and distinguishing our sense of self – particularly our differentiation from others. It is responsible for our self-awareness and self-insight – or lack of it. The *insula cortex*, along with the *cingulate cortex* (particularly the front part of it) is activated when we feel empathy for others. Given that empathy is a crucial aspect of the creative person, it's important not to underestimate how these two areas of the brain help us stay creative and healthy.

12 This claim is made by Baumeister et al. in the September 2009 issue of *Perspectives in Psychological Science*. A full citation is in the bibliography.

13 Roy Baumeister is a researcher specialising in social rejection. This is an excerpt from a brief 2008 journal article summarising the effects of rejection.

14 Mark Leary's idea of low self-esteem as a 'social fuel gauge' was reported in the November 1995 issue of *Psychology Today*.

15 There is prolific literature on the issue of identity. Consequently we haven't covered this issue in any detail.

16 Petersen & Seligman op. cit. p 252.

17 This contention about Sellers can be found in Lewis's 1995 biography *The Life and Death of Peter Sellers*.

18 Jonathan Miller is a renowned British theatre and opera director. This extract comes from an interview with Norma Farnes in her 2010 book *Memories of Milligan*.

19 See also our earlier remarks about rejection.

20 Martha Graham, US dancer and choreographer is considered to be one of the pioneers of Contemporary Dance. This quote is from Agnes De Mille's 1991 biography entitled Martha: *The Life and Work of Martha Graham*.

21 This excerpt from Stephenson's 2002 biography of her husband *Billy Connolly*.

22 Peterson & Seligman op. cit.

23 From the screenplay of *The Matrix*, (2002) written and directed by Larry and Andy Wachowski.

24 President Bill Clinton's carefully worded denial (on 26 January 1998) is the truth in the strictest definition of the words he used, however it is one of the best known examples of spin in the public consciousness. See it online at http://www.youtube.com/watch?v=KiIP_KDQmXs (accessed 29/1/11).

25 This lyric excerpt is from *Have a Cigar* composed by Roger Waters and can be found on the 1975 Pink Floyd album *Wish You Were Here*.

26 This excerpt is from the screenplay of *This Is Spinal Tap* (1984) directed by Rob Reiner.

27 The interview with SR was a personal communication with the authors. SR's name is withheld by request. The real name and gender of the person being discussed in this interview has been disguised.

28 This is an excerpt from *What Makes Us Tick? : The Ten Desires That Drive Us*. p24.

29 For those who have not read the Harry Potter series of books, a *patronus* is a charm that defends against dark creatures, particularly the Dementors who track their victims by sensing their positive emotions. One useful definition is online at http://www.hp-lexicon.org/magic/spells/spells_p.html#Patronus1 (accessed 29/1/11).

CHAPTER FIVE
LIVING IT

LIVING IT

*I ALSO FELT A SENSE OF PEACE AND A SATISFACTION
FROM MY MARRIAGE AND EARLY STEPS IN RECOVERY…
I TOOK FEWER CHANCES IN MY PERSONAL LIFE AND MORE
IN MY WORK. I FOUND FULFILMENT IN NEW AREAS.*[1]
- ROB LOWE

Most of the time, when creative people are experiencing difficulty or 'causing trouble' for their friends and colleagues, they have lost elasticity. They ignore their creative tides and their creative process then gets frustrated. What's worse: they are unable to articulate what is going on at the time beyond expressing their distress. Because when they get into this state they become unpredictable or even unstable, people around them experience their own frustration and dislocation. This is an excerpt from an interview with a fellow scriptwriter who worked in the same building as comedian Spike Milligan.

*He would lock himself in his office and that would be it. He'd stay there for days sometimes. People would walk around on tiptoe so as not to upset him. We used to think that was show business taking over. I don't think we understood. We just got on with the job.[2] - **Alan Simpson***

When the creative mind becomes fixed at either high or low tide - that pole dominates the thought patterns, attitudes, feelings and behaviour without the restraint of the other pole. That's when all the trouble begins. Let's tell the stories of Jack and Jill.[3] Jack won't move from high tide and Jill won't move from low tide. Let's see how they might look if this were to happen in the dimension of ego.

Jack

Jack (fixed at inflated ego) begins to believe he is set apart, a singular and unique member of the human race who is unusually gifted and therefore not subject to the normal restrictions and constraints that apply to the rest of us. He is entitled to continual approval and success.

A permanent and unreal state of supreme confidence persists, which can be rocked by external events but, ultimately, not shaken. Past defeats tend to be rationalized or forgotten and past victories tend to be amplified and referred to as evidence of greatness. Other people and their gifts and talents cease to be important unless they serve to enhance and maintain Jack's pre-eminence and support whatever it is that he is engaged in. When you meet Jack you will find yourself basking in the warmth of his attention if you can be of benefit to him, but if not, then that attention will be short-lived. It's important to remember that Jack is not immoral; he genuinely believes that he has the best answer or that he is the best answer. In fact, this belief is so powerful that to him it is self-evident. He can't comprehend why you might question his pre-eminence or would want to promote someone other than him. The idea that you would choose someone else is not just hurtful to him personally; it is evidence that you have poor judgment. The idea that anyone else might be thought to have the same kind of skill, talent, potential, wisdom or knowledge as Jack is unthinkable. He is almost certainly surrounded by and producing spin to reinforce this view.

Jill

Jill (fixed at deflated ego) believes she possesses a level of giftedness, enough to pursue a creative life, but that somehow real success will elude her. Therefore her creative processes and her sense of identity are tormented by the likelihood of rejection and failure, which appears to her to be very high. Jill knows she is not without talent but she believes she is not sufficiently talented for the world to really accept her and her work. Coupled with skinlessness, the state of deflated ego leads to constant self-doubt, fear, anxiety and ultimately to depression. Jill feels that nothing she does is ever good enough. She can be brilliant and will still be kicking herself and finding fault with her work. She interprets any information and behaviour as negative. She believes that she is not well regarded, and that won't change until she can deliver something that is perfect. Without that kind of a result, there is little hope. Thus Jill becomes driven to achieve perfection in her work as a way of managing her fear of inadequacy.

For both Jack and Jill, the overpowering sense of either monumental self-importance, or crushing worthlessness has a debilitating impact on their ability to see others around them clearly. At some level falling prey to the undercurrents and losing elasticity leads them both to regress in maturity, and in danger of becoming used to living in an almost of child-like self-centredness.

Both high and low tides – without the other - act like black holes. The people around Jack and Jill suffer as they are sucked into the gravitational pull of their extreme egos.

Around Jack, people become pawns in his schemes and they lose their own sense of identity in the process. Left unchecked, Jack will become a tyrant. Emotional damage within a creative team that centres on one individual is a clear sign that someone has lost elasticity and remains fixed at the high tide of the ego dimension. Most people eventually figure out that their relationship with Jack has become one-sided. Gradually they detach themselves from his sphere of influence and withdraw to lick their wounds. A sure sign of this dynamic at work is the progressive isolation of a creative person by their one-time allies.

Meanwhile, around Jill, her network of friends and colleagues are handicapped by her inability to see, feel and react normally to life. The consequences of being stuck at low-tide ego are worse for Jill – depression, anxiety and all that entails. However, it's also a challenge being her friend or colleague. The relationship can become more of a weight to bear than a benefit over the long term. Moreover, there seems to be no way out since the things that Jill believes will actually fix the problem are beyond anyone's grasp.

Each dimension produces it's own symptoms when the creative tides are ignored. If we were to follow the exploits of Jack and Jill getting stuck in the rest of the dimensions, we would see themes developing. There are remarkable similarities to high-tide Jack's behaviour, and the same is true for low-tide Jill. In fact, losing elasticity often occurs in clusters of dimensions, particularly where there is similarity in the way that the undercurrents impact on the poles.

While it would be fun to follow Jack and Jill's story through the other eight dimensions, we don't have the time to do it here. Look online at www. livingwithacreativemind.com and we will post some of their other stories in due course. Suffice it to say that there are patterns that emerge when the creative mind loses elasticity.

READ THE SIGNS

Being fixed at high tide produces these classic signs observed by other people – self-centredness, divisiveness, unpredictability and volatility. A Low tide condition manifests internally and produces doubt, depression, obsession and paralysis.

Friends of a creative mind fixed at high tide are affected by the unpredictability of their behaviour, their lack of concern for anyone else's wellbeing, and their intensity. They feel as if they are being sucked into an out-of-control life against their will. Conversely, at low tide, friends feel as if they are being sucked into a life of rigid rules enforced by the fun police in order to stave off the imaginary darkness.

If you are friend, colleague or partner of a creative mind, then the feeling that you are losing control over your own life is a warning sign that your creative partner might be getting fixed. At high tide, you will feel as if are being overtly controlled or dragged along unwittingly, trying to keep up with the pace of your creative colleague – only to fail eventually. At low tide, you will feel obliged to surrender control of your life in order to keep your creative friend from going under, giving up or something worse.

HOW TO BEAT THE UNDERCURRENTS

The ability to withstand the force of the undercurrents of fear and anxiety, insecurity, rejection and spin depends on three strategies that work together to anchor us against these pressures. They are

- Developing resilience – the elasticity that enables the creative mind to move naturally between the two poles. Resilience includes personal disciplines that are helpful for the creative mind to put into practise.
- Community – finding a tribe that will nurture the creative mind.
- Spirituality – a realization that we are a part of a bigger reality.

The weight of testimony from long-term successful artists worldwide, as well as our own observations, tells us that these strategies provide the basis for successful creative self-management. The implications of community and spirituality are so great that we will devote the last three chapters of the book to them – so let's turn first to developing resilience; the things that the creative person can do for themselves.

For any of this to work, the creative mind must be self-aware. The ability to be self-reflective, to be curious about your mind and soul, and able to weigh up and take on the evidence of other people's reactions to you is crucial.[4]

RESILIENCE

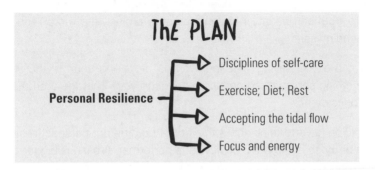

Thε PLAN

Personal Resilience

- Disciplines of self-care
- Exercise; Diet; Rest
- Accepting the tidal flow
- Focus and energy

Developing resilience enables a creative person to move with the creative tides. Resilience is the development of cognitive, emotional, physical and behavioural strength and flexibility that allows movement between high and low tide so that a creative person doesn't get fixed at low tide (depressive-like) or high tide (manic-like). Personal disciplines develop physical well being. These need to be treated with the same importance that artists give to developing technique. The body is the instrument, so is the mind. Physical wellbeing is, or certainly should be, high on the list of priorities for creative artists. Resilience is about developing a series of personal disciplines that will ultimately prove as important as the technical disciplines of practising your instrument, working on your craft and similar tools of the trade.

DISCIPLINES OF SELF-CARE

Beginning with the next section and in the following chapters we have included excerpts from some interviews we conducted with each other. Actually, it was Julie interviewing Jeff! It seemed the most interesting way to talk about these experiences.

The Therapist and the Creative Artist

Julie: Self care has been difficult for you – yet I have seen you shift from not looking after yourself physically to giving it more of a priority in your life.

Jeff: The creative tasks I have been involved with have always been bigger than myself. When the artistic endeavour is something noble and beautiful, you work longer hours for something worthwhile. The more truth and beauty I find in a creative project, the more I tend to expend myself.

Julie: Are you saying that the work is propelling you? Is the work something separate, something external to you? That the work has a life of its own?

Jeff: You have to think about this from two different perspectives and one of those is the point of view of a performer. A band is bigger than just one person. This creates a collective expectation — everyone expects it to lead to something amazing. So it automatically takes on more importance in your mind than your own self. There is a great show business saying: The show must go on. That idea permeates the culture of performance. It permeates music as much as the theatre.

I remember doing this gig with such a filthy rotten migraine, I had to lie down between each set and then go out the back and throw up, then come back and play. It was horrible.

Julie: Is that the culture in performance – that it's more important than the individual, and in the creative arts - that the work has a life of its own and is more important than the individual?

Jeff: Creating something like a song, a painting or a film has a life beyond the your life, that's one of the big things about the creative arts – the painting lives longer than you, hopefully the music lives longer than you do. So you are always aware of the fact that you're not just doing something that's for now – you're doing something that can actually have an impact beyond anything that you do ordinarily. So you tend to spend yourself in order to accomplish something beneficial because the work should be bigger than me.

This changed for me when I started to do work that was purely commercial; I wasn't so completely invested in it. You easily give yourself to it – but it's different when it's something you are being paid by the hour for. You tend to be a bit more separate from it, because it becomes more of a job.

Julie: So where have you learnt that balance now?

Jeff: I think this came out of being driven and pushed around by ruthless and selfish people. Rather than allowing for the natural creative tides these people would drive me beyond what was healthy and helpful. I've also seen people push a creative community beyond the point where they could create – that taught me to look after my creativity by looking after myself.

Here's the thing. When you are driving the work yourself you may not be all that aware of your own boundaries but you do kind of work to them. When it is your thing you naturally come to the end of your boundaries and then you quit.

I remember working on this project where we rehearsed so hard that by the time we got to the actual performance it had lost all its life. Everybody was too tired to deliver – nobody could remember the changes and everyone was so exhausted. Nobody was in a fit state to perform.

I think also that you begin to realize that you're not indestructible – which is something that comes with age and experience. You realize that you actually perform better when you are better physically, mentally and emotionally.

Successful creative artists with longevity all talk about the basics: exercise, rest and diet.

Your body is a biological machine. Just as a car engine needs fuel, water and oil to be able to function properly so too, we need to be mindful of what we put into our body. When we are younger we can tolerate insane hours, crazy diets and lack of exercise, but it all takes its toll eventually – those doctors, dieticians and physical health experts can't all be wrong.

The key is to find your natural rhythms with everything, and that includes exercise, rest and diet. There will be episodes where things just go crazy

– that is the nature of the cycle that swings from one pole to the other. However, the nature of the swing means you have to give your body a chance to rebound or risk suffering unnecessary wear and tear that will have an impact now or in the future.

Garry McDonald, talks here about finding his rhythm.

> **Garry:** *But even when there's high energy there's a stillness there. There's a ... you know ... it's just not frenetic – there's a split. I talked to Marina (Prior) about this. She said it was something like 85:15 ... how much of you is observing yourself as you're doing a play. But there's a part of you that cannot get completely lost, if you got completely lost it would just go off the rails. It would be madness. You kind of need to be watching and observing all the time. I mean, the most blissful performances are the ones where you come off and you go, 'that was effortless'. But that doesn't happen all that often – well it doesn't for me. I mean it's always enjoyable ... you get those performances where you've just sat there and let yourself go and you think, 'wow you're really flying tonight!' But I suppose I just find that the whole thing of having some sort of spiritual practice, it just keeps the lid on stuff ... calms you down and all that.*

It's amazing how awareness of these issues varies from discipline to discipline. As a general rule, dancers and actors are much more sensitive to diet and exercise than musicians, film-makers and painters for example. Dancers and singers tend to be fanatical about hydration – others not so much.

The pattern is obvious – for artistic disciplines where the body is the instrument, good training inculcates the need for keeping the 'instrument' in tune. However, there is increasing awareness of the physical toll within rock musicians and classical performers, particularly in their backs and joints from prolonged standing and rapid joint movement This is slowly changing attitudes in these artistic disciplines.

EXERCISE

Exercise is something that seems to come easier to most people than it does to many of our creative friends. Their best experiences of the gym are driving past it at 90 km/h with the music turned up loud. However, there are strong links between maintaining regular moderate physical exercise and reducing depression.[5] Given the risks associated with the creative mind, we have found that exercise makes for a clearer mind and better endurance, including the ability to cope with long distance air travel. Mix it up – don't just find one form of exercise. Try the gym – try walking, running and swimming. Keep it interesting but keep it regular.

REST

No matter how little you may think you can get away with, you need sleep to maintain good health. As we wrote in chapter two, creative people tend to play fast and loose with their body clock and push the physical demands on their body too far. Without getting into too much detail on this, you should be getting around six hours sleep before the time of your lowest body temperature, which is around 4:30 am.[6]

Creative professions are like shift workers and frequent international travellers. Performers are often just finishing work at 11:00 pm. Anyone who works in film and television has to put in long hours – rush deadlines mean long nights in post-production studios, not to mention the stress of all-night location shoots.

Creative people often find themselves doing their best work in the night. Maybe it's because all the other distractions have melted away and the mind is free to wander and play.

Jeff: I discovered that young children don't respect the altered body clock of the working musician – nor can they be made to live by it. Babies do not negotiate on their wake-up time. It was brutal! However, I also discovered that my creativity didn't depend on the hour of the day. I discovered that I was creative whenever I wanted to be – not just late at night. All I needed was the right space. The wake/sleep cycle is crucial to your ability to be creative. In the same way that travel between time zones affects the body clock, so does a few late nights at work. You have to ensure that you shift your entire body clock by the amount you work late – so that you are getting optimum sleep and waking up later in the day. This has a huge impact on the people around you, so it has to be a matter of explanation and negotiation.

DIET

The other potential pitfall in the basic self-management toolkit is that we tend to be less careful about what we eat when we are focused on projects. Late-night work and zoom focus can combine to make us suddenly realize we are hungry – then we eat any thing. Late-night pizza runs are a common fall back during post-production, mixes, late-night writing sessions, rehearsals, tech runs and exhibition set-ups. One of things about the intensity of focus is the forgetfulness about organisational detail.

Plan ahead and arrange a better solution than high-fat, high-salt fast food. Late-night work is notoriously a problem because there are fewer takeaway food choices available after midnight. Nominate some body whose job it is to look after catering – this will circumvent the late-night, bad food consequence of zoom focus.

DISCOVERING YOUR PATTERN: FOCUS AND ENERGY

The fact that there is a tidal flow to the dimensions means that you should try to recognise your own personal rhythm. There will be a pattern to the way you react that is the key to navigating creative tides.

Julie: When we first met and you were about twenty-two, I remember that you would just be awake for long periods of time; rehearsing; playing at gigs – and then you would crash. What have you learnt about managing your circadian rhythm?

Jeff: There is a rhythm and a cycle. When I was younger, I would have intense rhythms of two weeks with a migraine every two weeks; if I didn't push it so hard I would get five- or six-week cycles.

Julie: If you could time travel, what would you tell your twenty-two year old self?

Jeff: The experience of doing something creative is so wonderful and it is the product of flow, which you are not conscious of, when you are in it. I think that you have to become conscious of yourself and your cycles and know where the limits are. But even so I don't know that I would listen to that advice because playing and performing and writing is so wonderful, I was consumed by it – I would say shoot for rest when you can. But then I was shooting for stardom not longevity.

Understand how your own needs and states cycle, and identify whether there are natural pauses and breaks in your focus or your energy. Once you have established a pattern, you can work to it, ensuring that you are able to cover all the bases in your life. Deal with the practical things when you are not in zoom or manic mode.

The problem with composing, for me, is that once I start it pretty much ruins me for any more practical work. It's really not unlike drinking too much: once my head is absorbed in trying to figure out where the piece goes next, all quotidian matters, like emails I need to write, bills I need to pay, errands I need to run, fly out of my head and it's difficult to remember that I was supposed to do anything else ... so when I go into a composing period, my life becomes very disorganized. If practical duties demand my attention, I basically have to take an entire day off from composing to do them, in which case I suddenly get a tremendous amount done.[7] - Kyle Gann

It's smart to plan for a day off in your creative work here and there to be able to manage the mundane. This just means allowing for the project to take a little more total elapsed time. This can be really difficult under killing deadlines though. Zoom focus can be maintained for long periods of time if you are in flow – however, the longer you maintain it, the more compelling the need to cycle out to wide-angle will become, and the more investment you will need to make in looking after the things that have been left behind in the wake of the intense zoom.

A farmer has seasons. He has the season where he sows...[and one where] you don't really do anything... cause you're getting ready... a season of rest - and that's something I've adopted now...sometime in the year I need a month off.[8] - Chris Falson

On the one hand we are capable of expending intense energy in the excitement of the moment. But in order to recover, we need to rest. New moments of perception come from the still pole as well. Maintain personal disciplines in your craft that force a shift of focus or energy. A collaborative relationship is good for this, because you have to synchronize two different cycles together. Alternatively, you can develop personal habits that force a shift of focus – going to the gym, or answering emails at a certain time of the day. Stopping for meditation or personal reflection is another good one. Go out for a drink, a walk, a coffee – take a 'brain break'. The secret is in scheduling some time out. It's also important to be able to monitor the impact our cycles are having on ourselves and on the people around us.

You Need Flexible Work Environments

Flexibility in work and working arrangements allows the creative mind to move with their natural rhythms and regulate their body clock when necessary.

The reality is that only a small percentage of creative people manage to earn their living entirely from their creativity. So some non-creative work is usually a necessity for a creative person. Your parents, your partner or your guilt might have led you into a job that is reliable, sensible or financially stable, but it may lock up your ability to let your creative energy have expression.

Having a lifestyle that factors in these periods of intense highs and lows is essential for a creative person. While this seems obvious, we have seen a large number of creative people who are locked into physically demanding and mind-numbing work that sucks out of them any potential for creative energy. For a creative person – not to create is to die a little.

You Need Friends

Switching from zoom focus to wide angle is one of the hardest changes to make. It is very rare to find someone who can do it quickly. The creative mind should have friends who can help you pull back from zoom, or bring you back to earth from wide-angle focus. We think that artists in zoom have particular difficulty pulling back to see the big picture. Friends remind us about the big picture, but the artist needs to give permission for them to talk in ways that might otherwise be considered challenging.

ORDER IN YOUR CREATIVE SPACE

Julie: The studio where you create is a very important space for you

Jeff: I like those places to be very ordered because I have learnt that I need to know where to put my hand on a microphone, or a book, so I don't have to interrupt the creative flow to look for something. So those spaces are very productive and very creative for me and they need to be ordered. But there is also a part that needs things to be very loose and flexible in order to create.

Make Yourself a Creative Space

You need a specific environment to create – prioritizing and investing in a physical creative space is like investing in your internal creative space. In the same way, the external creative space can inform us when our internal creative space may lose the ability to navigate creative tides. When you notice your space has become disordered and overly chaotic, spend time restoring order to your external space. This will help settle your inner world and bring some elasticity back.

Perception is not bound by convenience. You might have spent four hours in the zone waiting for new connections, and then get something just as you walk out the door on your way to the next thing. Have some way to record those moments (a notebook, an mp3 recorder) so you can hang on to them for later.

Define all your spaces in terms of the ones you need for chaos and the ones you need for order. Don't mix them up. When you are collaborating you need to have a clear understanding with your colleagues which space is which, otherwise it will lead to unnecessary conflict. With your friends and family, negotiate about which spaces are okay for chaos. Your chaos can be their terror.

DO THE WORK

All the dimensions fuel the creative process, but it takes work to bring anything creative into being. One of the biggest management secrets is simply to do the work. Don't think it will be easy. There will be times that certain things come easily – but nothing good is cheap. Everything that is good really costs us.

> *That's the disease you have to fight in any creative field – ease-of-use.*[9]
> *- Jack White*

It is the stubborn, determined, dogged and persistent people who actually succeed in the creative fields. They ferociously refuse to give in to entropy and to the temptation to have an easier life. They create not because they can, but because they must.

In a nutshell, the need to develop resilience comes down to one idea: *accept it and respect it.*

1. To accept it means that you embrace and recognize the power of the creative process and the fact that you need to engage in that process in order to be fulfilled as a creative person.

2. To accept it means that you embrace the reality of the nine dimensions and the need for creative tides in your life.

3. To accept it means that you understand that to become inelastic is ultimately unproductive and inconsiderate of others.

4. To accept it means that you recognize, realize and understand the impact of the four undercurrents: fear, rejection, insecurity and spin, and how they work to make you lose elasticity.

5. To respect it means that you recognize and own your own reactions, and identify how empowerment or disempowerment of your creative process affects you personaty and uniquely.

6. To respect it means that you adjust your life to allow for the creative tides.

7. To respect it means that you adjust your life to resist the four undercurrents.

Now that we have some personal disciplines that we can maintain, in the further pursuit of staying elastic, we are going to devote the next chapter to the development of emotional resilience.

1   US film, television and theatre actor Rob Lowe has talked frankly about his journey through the up and downs of a creative life in his 2011 autobiography.

2   The full text of Alan Simpson's recollections of Milligan can be found in Norma Farnes's book *Memories of Milligan*.

3   The following stories are fictional and do not depict any actual person or event. Any resemblance to any persons who have been associated with the authors is purely circumstantial. However, Jack will fall down and break his crown and Jill will come tumbling after.

4   James Averill (1999) found that creative people were more emotionally self-aware.

5   In a 2006/07 online survey linked to the depressioNet website, about 88% of respondents rated exercise as being the most effective treatment for depression, slightly above support, counselling and medication. The results were included in Graeme Cowan's 2007 book *Back from the Brink*.

6   The time of 4:30 am has been estimated for someone who goes to sleep at 10:00 pm according to Michael Smolensky and Lynne Lamburg in their 2000 book *The Body Clock Guide to Better Health*.

7   Gann is a composer, musicologist and writer in New York. This is an excerpt from a 2007 article which can be found online at www.artsjournal.com/postclassic/2007/06/mysteries_of_the_composing_bra/ (accessed 29/1/11)

8   This is an excerpt for an exclusive interview Chris Falson gave the authors in 2013.

9   Jack White is a singer/songwriter/guitarist and member of The White Stripes. He made this claim in the film *It May Get Loud*.

CHAPTER SIX

FEELING IT

FEELING IT

*AS WRITERS WE START WITH THE FEELING AND
EVERYTHING FOLLOWS FROM THAT.* **- THE EDGE**

*DISTORTION, ANGER - THE PUNK IDEAL… GUYS WHO
MAYBE GOT PICKED ON - LIKE ALL OF US DID IN HIGH
SCHOOL. THIS IS OUR CHANCE TO PUSH YOU DOWN
NOW.* **- JACK WHITE**

*THE BEST WORK IS USUALLY DONE OUT OF EMOTIONAL
FRUSTRATION…[1]* **- RE**

Emotions. We need their heat and
passion to fuel the creative process, but
unfortunately our emotions can burn the
people around us. The answer lies in
developing emotional resilience, in the
same way that we must develop personal
resilience. Emotional resilience allows us
to feel deeply and yet direct those feelings
appropriately. It allows us to be elastic
enough to swing with the creative tides
and not be pinned to one place by the
intensity of our feelings.

We fail in our purpose as creative artists if we simply become a victim of our feelings – allowing ourselves to be blown to and fro on the winds of our mood.

The happiest people seem to be those who are producing something; the bored people are those who are consuming much and producing nothing.[3]
-William Ralph Inge

The first step towards emotional resilience is devastatingly simple and totally foolproof, but only you can do it. Create, create, create. Produce, produce, produce. Whatever you do – start doing it. If you try to keep the emotion suppressed, it will exact its revenge on you one way or another. So let the fire burn out through your work rather than burn you up.

Once you accept that your emotions don't stay level, you can respect what they are there for. By 'using the fuel' you will recover from the intense episodes more quickly.

Julie: Jeff was experiencing intense creative frustration, projects weren't progressing as quickly as he would have liked. As he shifted from intense emotion to a sense of calm, I asked him what had helped that process. He replied that he had been able to firstly vent the frustration, anger and anxiety (with me), and then he was able to begin to hear a positive reinterpretation of the circumstances.

The following four things have been found to help process emotions.

- Social support – being around people diffuses intense emotion.
- Venting negative emotion – getting the emotion out helps to give it perspective.
- Proactive coping – finding accurate information and solving problems.
- Positive reinterpretation – events and circumstances are reframed positively.[4]

Establish boundaries that you will not cross in your intense emotional phases. If you are someone who has more of a tendency to go to intense emotion because of early pain or trauma, ensure that you have an external safety net – an arrangement with a good doctor, a relationship with a therapist, or an agreement with a friend or family member.

Based on our understanding of the undercurrents, we have looked at how to become emotionally resilient as a creative artist.

EMOTIONAL RESILIENCE

The PLAN

Managing Fear ➝ Proactive Coping - Graded Exposure
Social Support - Culture of Affirmation

Managing Insecurity ➝ Positive Reinterpretation - Finding Identity
Positive Reinterpretation - Creative Maturity

Managing Skinlessness ➝ Proactive Coping - Protective Clothing
Positive Reinterpretation - Creative Vulnerability

Managing Rejection ➝ Positive Reinterpretation – Right affirmation

MANAGING FEAR & ANXIETY

Retraining the Imagination

As we mentioned in chapter four, managing fear and anxiety can also be about retraining the imagination. We like to think of this retraining as the choice of either watching endless internal movies of the worst possible catastrophes with you as the lead character, or replaying more positive, hopeful (but still realistic) movies with an associated positive benefit on your mental health. So how do you retrain your imagination?

- Recognise that an anxious imagination is just your amazing visual imagery and that this fantasy world does not tell you the truth.
- Decide that you can control your imagination, rather than let it control you. It's like deciding what movies to watch. Imagine sitting at home and watching constant reruns of disaster movies, it would not help you

relax or play or create – so change the channel and change your visual diet. If you use this "negative imagination" for your creativity (as writers or actors may) then create internal distance from your visual imagery – you don't have to be the lead character.

- Recognise that boredom or lack of creative challenges will mean that you may default to your personal "catastrophic" imagination. Maintain the discipline of taking creative risk, or the discipline of setting your own creative challenges.

- Work on developing a habitual, internal story or narrative that is positive – one that you can replay and rehearse.

- Recognise and become more aware of your anxiety. For many creative people anxiety has always been a part of their internal story - so it is unrecognised or unseen. Without an awareness of this damaging undercurrent, there is no opportunity to retrain the imagination.

Fear represents the antithesis to creativity as it inhibits the gathering of new sensory information and the making of unique connections that are necessary for perception. Fear paralyses the tidal nature of the creative person's energy, emotion, ego and focus.

Julie: Managing fear is a big issue for the creative person. I have seen you wrestle and overcome your fear of flying and then use these principles to help others. How did you overcome your fear?

Jeff: The first flight I ever took was Sydney to Melbourne when I was fifteen. I was so scared I felt that I was holding the plane up with my stomach muscles. I got off the plane and ran straight to the bathroom – my guts had turned to liquid. I knew that if I wanted to do a lot of travelling in my life, I had to beat the fear somehow. So I started to read about commercial aviation to get more knowledge. I read so much I began to get genuinely interested in it. The next time I took a flight, I was on a plane that I knew a lot about and the knowledge helped. It was a short flight as well. Gradually I found myself on longer flights gaining more experience until the fear disappeared.

Julie: I know you've used some of these principles to help students with performance anxiety.

Jeff: In my early years as Principal of an arts school, we routinely faced the problem of stage fright or performance anxiety in our students. In particular we had students who were great during rehearsals but who froze or folded during performances. In one particular instance I remember an experienced singer who was immobilized backstage, shaking and sobbing with fear at the prospect of performing before an audience. After this particular episode I resolved to change the college program to help students conquer their fear of performance. I addressed this by institutionalising three things: a culture of acceptance, encouragement and affirmation, a graded and gradual exposure to the performance environment and frequent performance opportunities in a variety of different ways and contexts.

A Culture of Affirmation

Jeff: In our culture of affirmation, failure was redefined as a necessary part of learning. This idea was presented to the student body at the beginning of every year, and reinforced by the staff at every event where a student was assessed. We adopted an approach to training performers and artists that relied on them demonstrating that they could achieve a result by the end of the program rather than at every test. This meant that you could fail the first three tests but pass the last one and still pass the course. The main thing was not how high your marks were but whether or not you could ultimately prove that you could do it – sing in public in this case. Whenever a student didn't perform to the appropriate standard, we affirmed them, noted how much they had progressed since last time, and told them what needed to be fixed for next time – then we worked with them to help them fix it.

Graded Exposure

Jeff: Taking a leaf from overcoming my own fear of flying, I instituted a graded approach to the experience of performance. Firstly, in the case of the singing course, I made changes to the program that made it impossible to come to class each week without the experience of singing with your classmates. So singers got used to singing with their friends in a closed-door environment pretty quickly. These classes over the course of the year became performance workshops – breaking down performances, rehearsing and ironing out problems. Within nine weeks they had their first public performance, but only in front of the whole student body in a classroom setting, as opposed to a stage. Within another nine weeks they performed two songs in an ensemble with their classmates – this time in a small performance space. The songs that we chose were tailored for each student so it was easy to accomplish as long as they attended all the rehearsals. This was followed after a further nine weeks by a more demanding repertoire. The final nine weeks represented rehearsal for a major production that had them on stage singing either lead or backing vocals in front of an audience of over 1000 people.

The point of this story is to articulate what it means to have a graded exposure to the performance environment. The entire program was devised to increase exposure and experience of performance over a three-year period, at the conclusion of which the average singer successfully produced and managed their own forty-five minute public recital, and also led other younger inexperienced singers on their own journey of overcoming performance anxiety. Once this program was in place there was never another case of performance anxiety like the one described above, although previously they had been commonplace.

It should be noted that a program of graded exposure by itself does not reduce anxiety – in fact, it can increase it. Linking graded exposure to a culture of acceptance and affirmation is the key. By the time the students were performing in front of less affirming audiences, the culture of acceptance and affirmation buffered them from the feedback of critics. Marina Prior offered the same insight about how the culture of the tribe helps actors deal with negative reviews:

> ... they're baring their heart and their soul and giving of their essence. And then you can wake up in the morning and read a review that says that you're just a load of ... and so there's a shared vulnerability and there's a shared understanding of when people need to be supported – at what point in the rehearsal people need to be told that they're really good and they're going to be great, which is an intuitive thing ...- **Marina Prior**

Differing Engagement

Jeff: The college program had something like forty-five different public performances a year across different disciplines – music, vocals, dance, acting and the like. Some performances were structured as intimate events with a maximum audience of about eighty people – others were open events in an auditorium that seated 1500 people. Others were in a local public theatre with seating for 400 and with professional theatre companies performing on either side of our shows. In this environment I made sure we broke down the normal barriers between artistic disciplines – we encouraged singers to work with dancers and so on. The result was that people who had no performance anxiety got themselves into nearly every show. People who suffered a great deal of anxiety got involved in performances in ways that didn't make them anxious. They worked on the production side – backstage assisting technical crew, managing front of house, and so on. In this way they began to engage in the 'scary' world of performance without their anxieties being triggered. They quickly got used to the environment without feeling threatened and began instead to associate it with fun and excitement. In fact, these performance nights developed their own community of people who made it happen, and also a regular audience. The students as a body wanted their classmates to do well. The culture of that community was one of encouragement and affirmation. As their own performances loomed, it was the fun, familiarity and the safe community they remembered, not the possibility of failure. For the bigger shows, people who were still struggling with anxiety, slotted into roles where their fear wasn't triggered. Their experience of these shows was that they were fun.

Looking back on this program, I still marvel at the power of fun in diminishing fear of performing. I still marvel at the power of simple affirmation and acceptance to create an atmosphere where this happens – and I still marvel at the fact that it is so rare in practice.

MANAGING INSECURITY

Julie: Let's talk about shooting for stardom, because I remember in your twenties you were aiming for that. There was a certain aspect of your ego and ambition that was driving that. What, then, has been the journey of your ego from that place to now?

Jeff: I remember a friend who had 'made it'– he was certainly touring with some big name bands in the US, but he was not doing well in his personal life. He said to me "We are all climbing to the top of the ladder but we must never forget to stop and look at the view from where we are now, because the view from where we are right now is pretty good." That was really sage advice that has stood me in good stead. He was always the guy who was going to make it - and he did in one way - but what he said was, enjoy wherever you are. As you mature you realize that stardom is not the outcome, but artistic longevity and doing the things you love. So you shift from being propelled into fame to having a lifelong way of doing things.

Julie: But what about the journey of your ego?

Jeff: It's been humiliated and punished. You know deep down that you have something that no one else has and something that people need, but you present that stuff - and some days it's great but people don't recognize it. But other days they do though. It is a bizarre life. You can be playing at the Entertainment Centre one week earning thousands and 'the Green Dragon' the next for a $150. You spend all these years developing your skill and talent and you play these gigs and people leave after the meat raffle.

Julie: So how do you live with the inflated and deflated ego?

Jeff: You live with the contradiction.

FINDING IDENTITY: EGO AND ATTITUDE

On the one hand creative artists believe they have something that everyone else needs; on the other, they believe that they are worthless and will surely fail. Without both of these opposites they do not have the ability to be vulnerable enough to see – to have perception. Without both they will not have the confidence to believe they can make or perform something that others will want to enjoy.

There is a parable ascribed to a Rabbi which goes something like this:

> *A man should carry two stones in his pocket. On one should be inscribed: "I am but dust and ashes", and on the other: "For my sake was the world created", and he should use each one as he has need.*[5]

The inflated ego can coexist with the totally deflated one if you use these two stones when you need to make a shift. This little table below shows you how.

WHEN IN THE INFLATED EGO	WHEN IN THE DEFLATED EGO
You think: I have something that the whole world needs. People must surely love me. I deserve the world stage.	**You think:** I am worthless and will surely fail. No one loves me. I deserve obscurity.
Remember: You are but dust and ashes.	**Remember:** For your sake the world was created.
If you don't: you will become arrogant, narcissistic and a tyrant.	**If you don't:** you will become a depressed, controlling victim.
You will need: self-discipline.	**You will need:** courage.

One key is to be anchored in the commonplace. There is nothing like changing nappies or taking out the garbage to anchor the inflated ego and the confronting attitude. You must avoid playing the *I'm a creative genius* card with your family and close friends in order to escape doing the things that normal people do. This can take a number of forms like: *I'm above these mundane tasks* or *I'm far too busy,* and other lines we can use to attempt to disengage from normal life. Don't play those games – you will get stuck at the high tide of both poles.

Ultimately, the goal is to build and maintain a secure identity.

The biggest trap for creative and performing artists is to build their identity solely on their work.

INSECURITY, IDENTITY AND CREATIVITY.

*There's also an insecurity which, to lesser and greater degrees, is in every single performer because when they are doing what they do, they're not just submitting a paper or something, you know a report on something and going where you go, they're actually ripping, ripping their chest open..[6]. - **Marina Prior***

This Is Your Life

As we wrote in the last chapter, our identity is forged in the unfolding drama of life. Our history unfolds like a story that develops with you as the central character. Rather than let events or the opinions of others totally shape us, it is important to find an identity that is secure enough to withstand the undercurrents. that will force you out of creative tension. To do this, you must find your own story, what we call a self-narrative.

It seems that our identity often doesn't fully develop until our mid twenties. In fact the human brain isn't fully developed physiologically until around age twenty two.[7] Our story in our mid twenties, is unlikely to be the same as when we were in our teens. In the development of a self-narrative, we need to see ourselves in different scenes with different characters. Having the opportunity to develop and reflect on our sense of self, away from family expectations and sibling rivalry, adds to our personal resilience that can buffer us against insecurity. Similarly, there will be some creative cultures and environments that are challenging for our sense of self. If we only see ourselves in a very narrow environment we will not be open to script changes or new information about our identity.

Remember Stacy's story in the previous chapter? For her we would begin to develop a narrative based on joy and life. Her script changes could include continuing to sing within her existing community, but then branching out to do gigs with a friend. Stacy would realize that she could light up a room with her voice and performance skills. By getting feedback in different environments, Stacy would develop a stronger identity and minimize the harm done in negative cultures and environments.

You Are Not Your Work

I'm not scared of failing because I know that the failure will not define me...and success doesn't define me either. **- Marina Prior**

Your work is not you. This is one of the hardest disciplines to accept, because in the creative marketplace the belief that you're only as good as your last gig is common and unquestioned.

Nowhere is this more obvious than in the latest version of the talent quest. TV programs such as, *So You Think You Can Dance, American Idol*, and *Australia's Got Talent* actually play to this weakness. With each new episode a performer or two must be eliminated. The lead-up to each elimination is carefully orchestrated and drawn out to extract the maximum emotional value from the moment, with pre-set camera close-ups on the losers, so that we can voyeuristically observe every detail of their nationwide humiliation. The producers of these programs know that those who haven't formed any separate sense of themselves create the best television at elimination time – tears and distress make for high ratings. They are a vulnerable group. It's incredibly hard for young artists to separate themselves from their work.

Unfortunately, these programs also reinforce the notion that creative people are expendable.

Because of the pressure to succeed, most creative people learn to derive their identity from their product. This lesson has to be unlearned. An individual has an objective existence apart from their work, in the same way that someone's work has an objective existence separate from the individual.

Navigating creative tides requires some kind of acceptance of this truth. You are yourself whether you never play another note, dance another step, or paint another painting. Your identity does not reside in how good a player you are, how good a painter you are or how good your songs are.

If your sense of self is tied totally to your performance as an artist you will find yourself condemned to a life driven and tormented by the ups and downs. Not everything you do will be great. Not everything you do will be a success. Not everything you do will be acclaimed, even if it is brilliant. Everyone has a bad day at work – for artists and performers this just means that their product does not measure up in some way. When your identity is linked to performance or acclaim, then your sense of who you are will rise and fall. The creative mind already suffers enough highs and lows as it is in the process of maintaining creativity. To add a further cause for experiencing extremes beyond those that are normal and necessary is unproductive.

In their most rational moments every artist would say that their worth and value are not measured entirely by their work. However, way down deep inside they struggle to believe it.

Artists invest so much of themselves in being good at their work and most of them never see the kind of monetary rewards other professionals, such as surgeons or airline pilots, receive for similar intense training. So it is little wonder they take their rewards in less tangible forms – like affirmation and self-esteem.

When a distinction is made between artists and their work, it becomes much easier to cope with the undercurrents of rejection and insecurity.

If your identity is no longer subject to the whims and opinions of others, or to their approval of the quality of your work, it is easier. When your work is good, you have a good day; when your work is not so good, you have a bad day – but your identity doesn't have to feel the pain.

*When I do my best performance, that's enough. If it's not enough for the win so be it. - **Mikko Salo***

There has to be a separation between your performance and your identity. I'm super hard on myself. I don't need anyone to tell me, "Hey pal, that wasn't fast enough". I got it you know ... My self-worth as a human being has nothing to do with the time on the board. Was I disappointed I didn't win? Sure. Was I *disappointed in my performance? Not a lick. When people ... comment crap on the side of it ... that doesn't define who I am.[8] - **Chris Spealler***

Athletes go through exactly the same process if they lose. Surgeons experience something similar when things go wrong on the operating table, although the stakes there are much higher. Neither can afford to lose confidence when an inevitable error of judgment occurs.

Understand that you can only be the best you are on the day – and each day is different. Endeavour to be the best you can and approach each creative situation on a day-by-day basis. Work to be better tomorrow, but don't crucify yourself for not being better than you are right now. Don't put additional pressure on yourself by perceiving that your work is your self-worth. A life where your value constantly comes from your performance is unsustainable.

All artists and performers are on a journey towards creative maturity. There are four stages to this journey. As you read the following you will be able to place yourself in one or other of the stages.

You can't do anything about the stage you're in except keep on working to progress to the next stage. There's no short cut to the final stage – like all big things in life. Anything that looks like a short cut will really only short change you. You'll miss the invaluable experience and knowledge that can only be gained by going on the full journey.

Each stage can be recognized by what you are thinking about – your main focus. We move from one stage to the next by achieving the level of mastery over the skills that each stage requires and by achieving a specific new realization at each stage.

The Four Stages of Creative Maturity

STAGE ONE – BEING RIGHT.

In this stage, the creative mind is concerned with developing the technique and knowledge necessary for 'getting it right'. For a musician this means that they are focused on playing the right notes in the right time. For a dancer it means being able to accurately and reliably reproduce the steps or moves. For an artist it's about mastering drawing, colour mixing, perspective, positive and negative space and so on. You get the picture – insert your own technique set here.

Becoming a creative or performing artist is really about learning a language – not French or Italian but the language of music, painting, sculpture, dance, theatre or film. Our creative output will depend not just on what we say, but also on how well we use the language of our discipline to say it. Think of this first stage as learning the vocabulary, the grammar and the sounds. The focus is on ourselves and on how well we can make the sounds in terms of what we know to be technically correct. Therefore, we respond to the challenge of 'being right' by imitating our mentors, teachers or role models and by practising our technical skills over and over again. In this stage there is a lot of practice and rehearsal.

We measure our success in terms of how well we did as an individual and how close we came to the standard of technical perfection we were striving for.

> Jeff: A friend was involved in a disastrous performance in which he did well individually. He came off stage feeling great, because he had done everything right and couldn't work out what was wrong with the rest of us. The same guy a few weeks later had a few bad moments but the whole night went brilliantly in spite of that. He was shattered and couldn't work out why the rest of us were untroubled.

STAGE TWO – BEING PART OF SOMETHING.

Eventually we develop enough technique and skill for it to become almost second nature. This is when we progress to stage two. Up to this point, the focus required to produce technique at a serious level takes up too much mental space. It's only when some of this space is freed up that we begin to notice that there is more to creative production than just technique and skill.

It's as if one day we wake up and realize that it's not just us and our technical brilliance that is making it happen – we are part of a group of people who are making it happen. We realize that what we do is just one part – a contribution to the whole. Our performance or product is part of a bigger community. It is not enough to be 'right' on your own – it's about the group being 'right'. This is when we discover the joy of applying our technique selectively to suit the time, circumstances and people in order to make the whole creative group look good.

For the musician, vocalist and songwriter this realisation means that the success of the ensemble is what should be paramount as opposed to the success of the individual player. For the actor and dancer, it means that the success of the whole cast or the company is more important than the brilliance of the star or soloist. Even a painter needs a community, a school or movement, to be part of – success in that community affects personal success.

In this stage the creative mind is concerned with adapting and employing skills, technique and knowledge in order to ensure the wider creative group is successful. The primary concern is about being part of something – combining with others in a common cause.

In our language analogy this stage is about being able to hold a conversation with other people, and discovering how to modify the way you use words, and even how you pronounce them to suit the people, the time and the place.

Being part of something means that your senses have become attuned to the creative dialogue – a discussion often expressed only in technique – that occurs between creative colleagues.

> *We were so comfortable playing with each other we could take it in any direction. The four members of the band had sort of taken on this fifth element ... Passion, honesty and competence: an absolute musical heaven...[9] - **Jimmy Page**

In this stage we measure our success in terms of how well the group did as opposed to how well we did as individuals. We learn that there is a greater joy and satisfaction in the group doing well. It is the first step away from an artist's individual identity being tied up in their work – because not everything revolves around what they are doing individually.

STAGE THREE – BEING EFFECTIVE.

With more experience, the higher challenges of stage two become second nature, and we realize that there is an audience out there.[10] The key realization of this stage is that the audience matters and that they matter more than great technique and more than great group cohesion. This stage redefines success once more. Our main concern shifts to getting the desired reaction from the audience. This understanding is a major leap.

The reality for professional creative artists and performers is that it is audiences that keep them alive. It's news to younger artists that how the audience feels about the work is more important than the technical skill and knowledge required to produce it. This realization means that the artist or performer focuses on moving an audience emotionally or transporting them to a new understanding. Success is redefined as getting the job done – and the job that artists do is to move an audience.

We use the term audience broadly to describe anyone who is on the receiving end of a creative work. An audience can be a crowd sitting in a concert hall, it can be people passing by an exhibition in ones and twos, it can be someone watching a video on YouTube late at night, or someone playing a computer game.

Jeff: I'll never forget when I was playing in the backing band for a talent quest for up-and-coming guitarists. All of these guys got up on stage looking the part – tight black jeans, black T-shirt and sunburst Stratocaster. They each peeled off an amazing piece of guitar pyrotechnics playing so fast it was like they were being paid by the number of notes per minute. In every case the audience was totally left behind. These guys all left the stage thinking they had nailed it, but the applause and the judges' decision told a completely different story. The guy who won was really good technically, but he also knew how to win the crowd. In the final he stepped forward into the spotlight and not only played the music, he played for effect. He had great eye contact with some pretty girls down the front and even laughed as he played. It was more than making music – it was about making everyone have fun.

In our language analogy this stage is no longer just about being able to hold your own in a conversation with other people. This stage is about being able to use the new language you've learnt to persuade people to come around to your point of view.

Each stage demands a more sophisticated knowledge and use of technical skill than the previous one. Each stage also demands more understanding of interpersonal dynamics and social awareness than the one before. The journey to professional maturity is about matching sophistication of creative technique with sophistication in dealing with people. It is a journey away from a 'self-focus' towards an 'other focus'.

STAGE FOUR – MAKING A DIFFERENCE.

Finally an artist finds that moving an audience becomes second nature. This is easy to say but not easy to accomplish. By this time, the hard-learnt lessons of the previous stages have become internalized at such a high level that beauty, excellence of form and effectiveness of outcome seem to be produced intuitively. However, in this stage making a difference in the world is the ultimate goal – beyond artistic excellence, amazing cohesion, and even beyond financial security.

With the final stage of the journey comes the realization that artistry and creativity exist to serve higher ends than our own personal drives. Even though creative people of all disciplines will invest huge amounts of time, money and energy to achieve their personal goals, deep down every one of them knows they are the recipient of a gift. Their talent – the raw potential to develop skill in a creative discipline – was a gift. The mature professional realizes that without that initial gift of talent no amount of work on their part would have made a difference.

The proper response to a gift is thankfulness. The proper expression of thankfulness is to try and give something back in return. At this stage of the journey, a creative artist measures success by how much good they are doing – irrespective of their personal technical contribution, or whether the group or community created the vibe, or whether the audience got it on the night.

It goes without saying that by this point all the other pieces are already in place – a high level of technical competence, intuitive cohesion with the group and audiences regularly moved. The difference is that artists at this stage measure success by less tangible standards. They are motivated by concerns that are ideological.

For some it is a humanitarian or charitable thing. For others it is a matter of faith or spirituality. Whatever it is, the creative product must serve a higher purpose – a bigger truth. By this stage the creative mind is able to view their work as quite distinct from them personally. This escape from a self-centred focus is truly liberating.

There is no specific time frame for getting through the stages. Transitioning from one stage to the next depends on mastery of the key aspects of that stage. The time taken to achieve mastery is so variable there is no point trying to predict it. It is dependent on talent, time, effort, willpower, opportunity, environment and so on. It's possible to find artists and performers in their early twenties who are already in stage four. It's equally possible to find artists and performers in their fifties and sixties who have never left the first stage.

In fact, it is entirely plausible for an artist never to complete this journey at all. However, we can expect artists who never leave the first stage to be self-focused and to have the greatest difficulty separating their identity from their work. Consequently, they will also never be able to successfully fight against insecurity and manage the dimensions of ego and attitude.

MANAGING SKINLESSNESS

Julie: How do you discipline your thinking so you don't get depressed?

Jeff: Almost on a daily basis I'm going up and down, so I'm not sure it's a discipline. It feels like a wave. So I'm not sure I am disciplined.

Julie: What I mean is that you may be going up and down but the people in your immediate world don't know that you are down.

Jeff: Well that's true. I think part of it emerges from a spiritual dynamic and part of it stems from a responsibility that you have to other people. It's just my values. Just because I feel this way doesn't mean I have to inflict it on others. I think others do know the ups and downs – they are closer to the real me. In every case there is a job to be done and no matter how I feel I have to deliver the goods. It is the performer's ethic, it is the ethic of the artist.

Julie: When you were eighteen you wrote poetry that was very black and hopeless, and you talked about how falling in love and having someone love you shifted that black place.

Jeff: It still exists, it is the worst part of me.

Julie: What did the experience of love do to that black place?

Jeff: It made me realize that I don't have to go there – there is an alternative.

Julie: You don't have to go there?

Jeff: But I can dip my toe in it if I need anguish.

Julie: So it's a place you can visit.

Jeff: Yes it is a place I can visit but I don't have to stay there. In the past I think I have visited it for too long. I had given up hope in a lot of areas. When you stop having hope there doesn't seem to be a reason to stay away from that place. If you remove someone's hope you remove their reason not to go to that dark place. In that dark place you can be totally reckless, full of anger, resentment and selfishness – all the things you don't want to be. I don't know why you think I am disciplined – in my thinking for me it is a highwire act.

Julie: But it is highly disciplined to be able to dip your toe in it but not go there.

Jeff: I know what happens to me if I go there – it is bad for me. The black place is a very selfish place and it feeds on a sense that you are the most important person, but my sense of responsibility for the important people in my world stops me going to that selfish place.

Having said that I have spent periods of time where I have felt very callous. My skinlessness relates not just to music but to people as well and how they feel. Most creative people are not skinless to everything but I am highly alert to what people think about me. It is wound up in ego, mood and attitude.

Julie: I have seen the callousness develop on your soul and psyche.

Jeff: It is when I have stopped being skinless. If you can no longer protect yourself and your skinlessness, you switch it off. You just switch it off and you don't go there anymore.

Julie: Tell me about switching it off – becoming detached.

Jeff: Well you are detached. It's not like you put clothing on. You have removed yourself from it entirely – it's very unhealthy I think. I have found myself where I am unthinking about people when I deeply care for people. I don't know whether the callousness is a defence or an altered state I go to. Maybe it is anger that makes me distancing … dissociative.

Julie: You are very good at protecting your skinlessness though.

Jeff: Humour is a huge part of it for me, particularly the humour within the tribe and community of musicians. It is a way of dealing with tragedy among people who get what it takes to go into places where you are not seen or valued. My spirituality as well – one event is just that, in the context of a bigger thing.

Julie: What would you tell someone who was calloused?

Jeff: Humour – start laughing. It softens you. And get among people who get you and who you can laugh with together.

On the one hand we feel things powerfully. On the other hand we need ways of protecting ourselves from these feelings, without shutting ourselves down emotionally. Detachment, dissociation or emotional shutdown is what a lot of creative people do to try to cope with skinlessness. However, it's unhealthy and has bad consequences for other people because we don't care what happens to them when we are detached. Ultimately, detachment is a strategy that means loss of creativity. Without skinlessness we don't feel. Without insulated sense we don't produce. Both sides of this dimension work together so we can be productive. The downside for skinless sense is that it's hard on you and hard on other people. Skinlessness means that outside stuff gets inside you, and inside stuff leaks out.

Protective Clothing

When our skinlessness gets too much, we need to wear 'protective clothing' – things that temporarily attenuate the feelings. Protective clothing insulates us but we need to be able to 'put it on' or 'take it off'. Insulated sense is completely different from shutting ourselves down from feeling: detachment. We detach because of the overwhelming input, or because previous experiences have caused us to be afraid of it. We can avoid the fear and detachment by putting on protective clothing – it will defeat this particular undercurrent.

To wear protective clothing means to:

- Take care of the basics.
- Channel skinlessness into your work.
- Use distraction when things are overwhelming.
- Find things that make you laugh.
- Cocoon yourself – temporarily remove yourself, or place barriers between you and the sensory input.
- Understand it's tidal. Plan for the tides and don't fight them.
- Create space for yourself.
- Embrace skinlessness as fundamental to the creative process.

A colleague who would swing very high on the skinless scale did creative work with sick or dying people – but this left her shattered, until she started looking at what constituted protective clothing for her. She began to ensure she was taking care of the basics, i.e. she was well rested and well fed. She even visualized putting on protective clothing prior to entering the distressing situation and afterwards she learnt to give herself space and time to readjust.

Have a retreat you can go to when you are experiencing sensory overload. It may be a location that is quiet and still, it may be a person who represents safety for you, it may be a regular time of the day where you meditate. The creative mind needs to structure a safe retreat.

Pain Relief

Self-medicated pain relief, in its various forms, can be helpful in the short term, but the danger lies in treating self-medication as a lifestyle choice. Drugs, alcohol, comfort foods, therapeutic shopping – all these do is numb the senses. And it turns out that the numbing effect is like anaesthesia – it numbs every input, not just the bad ones. Numbing destroys perception and that damages discovery as it dulls the senses. Ultimately, your creativity will suffer and your relationships will suffer as well.

> *... vulnerability is the core of shame and fear and our struggle for worthiness, but it appears that it's also the birthplace of joy, of creativity, of belonging, of love.*[11]
> *- Brené Brown*

Remember that feeling is the essence of being a creative artist.

For other people, it's not that you are skinless, it's that your skinlessness makes their life difficult. Channel your skinless episodes into your work – journal, record, sketch – do something at the time that gets the input from the senses translated into something you can produce from later. Also learn to work with your other cycles so you can have episodes of vulnerability and episodes of protection.

Debrief

Venting is a way to develop emotional resilience. Being able to unload your feelings and frustrations to someone else is an important part of skinlessness self care. The other party has to be trustworthy, but also somewhat removed from the situation. Close friends and romantic partners can do it, but involving them could dramatically change your relationship, depending on how great your need for debriefing is, and how intense the debriefing sessions are.

Vulnerability to skinlessness is at its greatest in the following circumstances:

- Exhaustion
- Immediately following success
- Immediately following failure
- Circadian low points
- Following rejection
- Following being ignored
- Following relationship breakdown
- During grief
- Feeling alone
- Under stress

MANAGING REJECTION

Only at this point can one begin to understand just how big, how titanic the ego of the military pilot could be.

The boys wouldn't have minded the following. They wouldn't have minded appearing once a year on a balcony over a huge square in which half the world is assembled. They wave. The world roars its approval, its applause, and breaks into a sustained thirty-minute storm of cheers and tears...

A little adulation on the order of the Pope's; that's all [they] wanted.[12] **- Tom Wolfe**

Jeff: Performers need this kind of Papal adulation several times a week.

There is something basically dysfunctional about somebody who needs to have their worth and value affirmed by large numbers of people simultaneously, but that is the dimension of ego in the life of a creative person. It is probably the case that they have to cope so often with rejection in their professional world, that the need for affirmation is accordingly disproportionate.

THE RIGHT KIND OF AFFIRMATION

The critical thing about positive affirmation is that it must be true, accurate and trustworthy. It must come from people who have gained our trust because they are close to us, or because they are professionals like us – their judgment can be trusted because they are in the same boat. From colleagues we think of affirmation as recognition. Accurate affirmation is valuable and effective because it is true feedback and not flattery. It will initially concentrate on the positives and leave the negatives for a later time. The negatives don't get ignored, but they are dealt with in a climate of analysis or critique when the dimension of emotion is in its resilient phase. Delivered in this context, affirmation directly subverts all four undercurrents: fear, rejection, insecurity and spin – but it is particularly potent at countering rejection.

Criticism in the form of the publicly expressed opinion of a cultural gatekeeper is another matter altogether. Friends and colleagues should avoid taking on the role of a critic, primarily because there are plenty of others ready to assume that role, but also because a critic is, by the very nature of their work, going to be excluded from the creative tribe and from the community of trusted friends. Think of the relationship that referees have with athletes. They can be cordial, but ultimately they are there to pass judgment.

Affirmation that is not accurate is flattery, and this is a quite different and very dangerous thing. Think of the feedback an artist gets in these terms:

- Affirmation is from family and friends.
- Critique is from colleagues, family and friends.
- Recognition is from colleagues.
- Criticism is from critics.
- Applause is from audiences.
- Dedication is from fans.
- Flattery is from sycophants.
- PR is a fiction and nobody should take it seriously.

Flattery is what happens in a culture of spin. It is given for an ulterior motive: in order to ingratiate, curry favour, or to support your illusions, and is ultimately damaging because it amplifies and empowers the undercurrent of spin.

Affirmation Is a Function of Community

Clearly affirmation is something that happens in the context of your relationships with other people, unless you just stand in front of a mirror and tell yourself how wonderful you are. We've touched on the subject in this chapter because it is your responsibility as a creative artist seeking creative tension to search out the right kind of affirmation and to filter out the wrong kinds.

It is at this point, however, that we leave behind the disciplines of self care and open up the subject of how we manage the creative mind through the powerful forces of community. The next three chapters continue this journey.

1 These remarks from Jack White and The Edge are from the previously cited documentary *It Might Get Loud*.

2 R is a respondent from our survey of creative people.

3 William Inge was a twentieth-century British author, cleric, philosopher, animal rights activist and a trustee of the National Portrait Gallery in London. This quote is widely attributed to him, although we cannot find the primary source. He is widely cited online: for example at http://www.allthingswilliam.com/people.html (accessed 29/1/11).

4 These four approaches to developing emotional resilience are outlined in the chapter entitled 'Emotional Intelligence, Coping with Stress and Adaptation' by Moshe Zeidner, Gerald Matthews and Richard Roberts in the 2006 book *Emotional Intelligence in Everyday Life* edited Joseph Ciarrochi, Joseph Fargas and John Mayer.

5 This proverb is cited by Philip Yancey in his 2000 book *Reaching for the Invisible God*.

6 Marina Prior op. cit.

7 Selecting 22 as an arbitrary "age of maturity" is based on recent neurobiological research, summarised by the Juvenile Justice Centre of the American Bar Association in 2004.

8 These excerpts are from a meeting of elite US athletes in Lake Tahoe and are available online at http://journal.crossfit.com/2010/11/roundtabletahoe-psychological.tpl (accessed 29/1/11)

9 Jimmy Page was a founder and guitarist in the seminal 1970s heavy rock band Led Zeppelin. This interview is part of the 2009 documentary *It Might Get Loud* directed by Davis Guggenheim.

10 Every artist is aware that there is an audience, but many of them never appreciate that the audience is a real participant in the act of creative communication. Some artists never treat their audiences with respect.

11 Brené Brown op. cit.

12 Even though Tom Wolfe was writing about the nature of the US military test pilot psyche in the 50's and 60's in his novel *The Right Stuff*, it seems to us that the same is true for the creative artist.

CHAPTER SEVEN

LOVING IT

LOVING IT

WE DO LIKE EACH OTHER, WE HAVE LOTS OF FUN TOGETHER, AND…I LAUGH AT HIS JOKES…THAT'S PROBABLY WHY IT'S LASTED THIS LONG, I'M THE ONLY PERSON WHO LAUGHS AT HIS JOKES…ALL OF THEM – EVEN IF I'VE HEARD THEM HUNDREDS OF TIMES. [1]

- TRUDI STYLER (ON HER 28 YEAR RELATIONSHIP WITH STING).

So, the *'living with'* part of Living with a Creative Mind was why you bought this book? This chapter was written specifically for those of you whose partner is a creative mind. You really do live with all these issues. Good, healthy relationships are critical to enable an artist to move naturally through the creative tides. They empower a creative mind to resist the undercurrents. Perhaps it's best that we start with this most intimate of relationships, and look at how understanding the nine dimensions can lead to satisfying and durable relationships.

Throughout this chapter you will hear from six new people: Anthony and Belinda, Charlotte and Dennis and Ethan and Francesca (not their real names). We asked these three creative couples to come together for a conversation about relationships. They are variously involved in design, film-making, graphics, art and music. Their ideas were so enlightening we allowed them to speak for themselves. Also, you will continue to hear from respondents in our surveys.

NEGOTIATING, NAVIGATING & RESTORING

So you enter into this place - and although you're travelling with your wife, and may talk occasionally you don't realise it - but you're so in the zone that you're not actually having quality time with your family. My wife told me this and I said, "No, look, we went on holiday together". She said, "We went on a holiday with you, but you're on your own holiday inside the holiday." And it made me really think about it. Because that's just me, I go into this place, I'm not ignoring you - I'm just trying to feel what's going on. So I've had to learn that when I go with the family, I have to do it differently, I have to switch on - off, on - off, and do it differently.
- ***Ken Duncan***

The secret of living with a creative partner is to adopt a flexible combination of three strategies – negotiating, navigating and restoring - to deal with the highs and lows of the creative mind. We are going to assume that you are in a relationship with them because you love them. We are also going to assume that you want to keep the relationship without being endlessly frustrated by it. Having got this far in the book you will already be feeling some relief, because you realize that you are not going crazy and your partner is not a selfish, manic, unpredictable, emotional child – they just seem that way every now and again.

Understanding is the key. Once you identify how the nine dimensions and four undercurrents affect your partner, the steps you need to take are logical. What you can do holistically is help your creative partner not to get pulled under by fear, rejection, insecurity and spin.

Being close to a creative artist, gives you an unprecedented opportunity to make both of your lives better by helping them maintain their ability to be tidal. This will also make life easier for everyone in close proximity, as the dynamic nature of the creative mind becomes less unpredictable. In fact, nobody can help a stuck creative mind shift out of a bad place more effectively than a close friend or partner. The special trust and intimacy that characterize these relationships uniquely empowers you to say and do things that no one else can. The dark side of this equation means that you can also betray and be betrayed like no one else. However, we hope that your powers will only be used for good.

Essentially you can live with a creative mind either by *negotiating* through the impact of the extremes to achieve a workable life for both of you, *navigating* the tidal nature of the dimensions by making adjustments according to the various upswings and downswings, or by *restoring* – that is taking some time out for yourself and re-engaging when you are up to it.

NEGOTIATING

The essence of negotiating is the realization that your life has as much value as that of your creative partner. In the face of such things as the whirlwind of creativity, talent, success, public attention and the extremes of the nine dimensions, it is easy to feel like you have been overshadowed. It is critically important to maintain a sense of your own identity in their shadow or when confronted by their ego. It's important not just for yourself but for them as well. It is unhealthy for them to be pandered to without limit.

Your Identity vs Their Ego

*Many years ago I was speaking with the wife of a lead singer in a band that was getting big. I was struck by how much she lived her life for her husband and did not have any identity or life outside of him. Several years later I heard that they were separated and it didn't surprise me. - **Francesca***

Over the years we have observed what happens when partners of creative people subsume their identity into that of their creative partners – they lose themselves. It is a potential consequence of living with a partner with an inflated ego – particularly one who has lost their ability to go with the creative tides. Marney George, the first wife of abstract artist Arshile Gorky, was one such partner who was able to articulate this particularly unhealthy relational dynamic.

> *Arshile wanted to form and mould me into the woman he wanted for his wife ... It seems the very moment we were married the battle began ... ferocious as a giant, tender as a little child ... Arshile tried to break the barriers between us. First with tenderness, then with force ... violence ... It was a tragedy for us both.[2] -* **Marney George**

Survival depends on investing in a personal and professional identity that is separate to the creative person.

> *Early in our marriage we decided how we were to be seen as a couple. Ethan would ensure I was always clearly introduced and he always articulated my identity as distinct from his. I would never accept the throw off remarks about being 'Ethan's wife'. This took work and a commitment from both of us to reinforce the same message, but it has been vital for the longevity and health of our marriage and relationship. -* **Francesca**

It requires a robust male ego to handle a wife or female partner's success and prominence. Husbands of female stars can easily begin to resent the focus on the star wife and become passive–aggressive, detached or reactive to affronts to their identity. We have seen husbands sabotage their wife's high-profile position and career as a consequence of the erosion of their sense of self.

It is our responsibility as partners to develop our identity and to continue to work on it and our personal development. It can be easy to hide behind a partner's success or fame, creative development and achievement. It can give us vicarious affirmation but it cannot replace our responsibility to develop our own identity and personhood.

NAVIGATING

The creative life means that your partner will experience an episodic or cyclical existence. They get used to it, because they are just being themselves – high-speed one day and listless the next. However, if you are not subject to this kind of inner world, then their cyclical roller coaster is not at all normal for you.

The key to navigating is to know the tides and get used to them. In the early days of a relationship it's easy to mistake the appearance of a high or low tide for permanent change. However, once you get better acquainted with your partner's cycle of ups and downs, you can figure out what is happening and where they are likely to go to next. You can encourage them to direct the fuel from these cycles into the creative process, rather than letting the poles inflict damage. Navigating is more to do with becoming tuned to your partner's processes and then guiding them sensitively and carefully. Navigating means that you can adapt your life, to some degree, to cope with the tidal changes. The difficulty that creative minds cause for everyone else is that they appear unpredictable. Once you can work out the tidal nature of their existence they become much easier to understand than everyone thinks.

Navigating should never mean pandering. Navigating is about maintaining your self and your identity by using a bit of old-fashioned give and take.

RESTORING

Being the partner of a creative artist may not always be comfortable, but it will never be monotonous. If you are a person who finds change difficult then it may be necessary for you to create your own way to retreat and restore. Some phases such as manic energy or intense emotion may be best served by leaving them to work out their processes by themselves.

The last thing you want to do is try and fight the tides that drive the creative process, so in some cases your own survival will depend on you giving your partner some space, and convincing them to allow you some as well. Sometimes this is emotional space; sometimes it's physical.

Living with a creative mind brings an intensity unlike any other; it is an intensity of thinking, feeling and sensing and an intensity of focus and energy. Creating habits of relational space will provide much needed respite. The creative mind is wired to operate at that intensity – usually you are not.

Self-diagnosis:
1. Is the creative person the centre of your world and does your life revolve solely around them?

2. Do you have a number of friendships that balance the intensity of this relationship?

3. Can you identify five ways that you take time out to breathe, recover, and replenish?

Restoring is a great strategy if you find yourself too overwhelmed to negotiate or navigate. The way to discuss it with your partner is to explain that you have been making room for them and their creativity and now it's time for them to make room for you and your need to recover. Another way of thinking about this is to consider what happens when the tides are either too high or too low for safe travel. You just need to stop. So, in those moments, it's okay for you to restore.

The Basics for You

In chapter five we identified diet, rest and exercise as being important to personal resilience. They are important for partners as well. The extent to which you can maintain your own regime of diet, rest and exercise is the extent to which you will build the necessary reserves for coping with your partner's ups and downs. Poor nutrition and exhaustion add levels of difficulty to a relationship that is already offering its own unique challenges.

Furthermore, if you can maintain a healthy lifestyle, you have a good basis for convincing your creative partner to join you in these activities. They frequently forget to look after themselves in the midst of the creative process.

TOOLBOXES

We will look at the dimensions in groups, much as we did in the previous chapter, and will include a *toolbox* for you with some practical strategies.

Processing

My art is my work ... my work is my art. The demand is always time ... relationships suffer. The demand for time is not changeable, only understandable, it's safe to say an artist can become obsessed and focused on the journey of their work, but when they come out, fall out, or walk out of that place of work, they desire to be understood. This needs work in relationships, as the place of creation may be a turbulent place, a place that takes all of their emotions, infuses their spirit and takes a toll on the physical ... this place is no less important than real life, so the artist is stepping out of one world into another, so it is important for both people to have some time to talk about where they have been. **- DK**

The skill of talking and processing emotions is important in any romantic relationship, but where one or both partners are creative, it is mandatory.

We have to watch that big time, like my partner's emotional world affects mine, we have to even say that to each other, your emotional world is affecting me ... That's a learning curve, vocalising that lets the other person know where you are without guessing ... everything sends a sign to say you might be depressed and moody or whatever but it might be something else – but one little word might actually go: 'No something didn't go quite right today,' you're processing it, and somewhere in the back ... your subconscious is processing it and you don't know how to pull it out and look at it. **- Anthony**

Often we hear about relationships between people who used to love each other but have recently stopped talking about the things that matter. Partners need to keep fostering the skill of sharing the deep issues. Emotions may be raw, and the soul may be vulnerable, therefore it's often hard, but it's what keeps relationships alive in the long term.

FOR EVERYONE

- Choose a time when you are not upset or angry.
- Choose a time when there is space for you to talk and listen to each other.
- State the issue from their perspective.
- Outline the problem from your perspective.
- Describe your feelings without emotional blackmail or manipulation.
- Describe what you would like.
- Leave space and room to hear their perspective.

Couples can develop patterns of communication that are relationally destructive without realizing it. You both need to be more positive than negative in your communication. Hurting the other person's feelings needs to be counterbalanced by overwhelmingly positive comments later. This can be challenging when the creative partner is depressed or is at deflated ego. The creative partner needs to learn not to direct their dimensional polarity at you.

Try to avoid the use of these four negative modes when communicating with your partner as research links these communication styles with relationship breakdown.[3]

Criticism: *You are never around to help with the house! You're always out whenever there is work to be done! You never help with the kids!*

Contempt: *I'm not sure you will enjoy coming to the opening. It will be full of people who appreciate the type of work I do and I'm not sure that you have the ability to really understand the depth of what I do – it would just be embarrassing.*

Defensiveness: *I have so much to do in a day I can't possibly take time out to do what you want. You have no idea how much pressure is on me to get this stuff finished!*

Stonewalling: *Yeah right … [said leaving the room and closing down the discussion.]*

FOR WOMEN[4]

Think through what you want to say and then take out all the emotive language and blame so you can begin to talk about what has been happening inside you. Your perspective is important in the relationship.

FOR MEN

Work on finding the words to talk about you, your emotions. Letting another person come close can be threatening but also rewarding. Communication is a crucial investment in your relationship. Men say they are lonely because they haven't learnt to talk about what is happening inside of them.

> *When I get asked how I feel about something I might be silent for a long time. When I have to talk about something painful, emotional or difficult, it's like I have to dig for it. It's hard for me to quickly answer questions about how I feel. My ability to express what is inside of me is not immediately available. But then I start to dig, and maybe the first thing that comes out is dirt, but if I have the right environment then I can dig deep and get out the diamond … the real expression of what is there. Sometimes you have to dig through a lot of dirt to get to the diamonds.* **- Ethan**

EGO AND ATTITUDE

Your identity is vitally important, because it is necessary ballast for your personal relationship.

*When you get married or you start to open your heart and give it to somebody, it's quite a tender area. Guys have a certain way of dealing with it, girls have a certain way of dealing with things and, when you mix your creativity in with that as well ... that's probably just as personal as how the opposite sex looks at things ...[there are] not very many people in your life, ever, that you would get to that level of 'this is my precious thing that I'm sharing with you' ... there is literally a line of respect ... like Belinda said, affirm first. Let a few of those little bridges and foundations be built before you then step out on them ... - **Anthony**

*But I think that creative people need some of the tough critique, because we can't be so emotional and we can't believe all our emotions all the time because they aren't always true. That's the biggest thing I've learnt, because if you keep living in that world of believing everything you feel, you can get completely off track ... so it's good to have some of the hard stuff... - **Belinda**

Julie: The audience are applauding and Jeff comes off stage. He is getting accolades from acquaintance; the technical team and other performers, but he comes up to me and says: "How was it?" Understanding at this point that Jeff is not wanting a detailed critique of the performance – he will get enough of that from others. What he needs is affirmation and encouragement from the one who is his soul mate. This is about managing and understanding the dimension of ego and the seesaw of inflated and deflated beliefs and self-talk.

Jeff: I think every performer needs the affirmation. I think every performer and creative artist needs it and we don't get it enough. I need it from my non-professional friends and it is different from those that are professional. Colleagues go, 'yeah, yeah, yeah' and you know that they knew it was a good gig and that would be enough, but from friends outside the profession you want a little more gushing. Really when you think about it you have spent the last hour totally vulnerable and, in my case, flying by the seat of my pants and trying to weave something wonderful out of nothing and you need to know that it was important for them.

Julie: You need to be gushed over?

Jeff: I notice the bad things later but there is a certain point in a performance where I see only good.

Julie: Do you want those close to you to keep on gushing?

Jeff: No, it's got to be real. But when you walk off stage you just want everyone to have had a great time. After, when my mood plummets, it's like everything was up, but when the adrenaline starts washing out of the system you see everything that was wrong. When I am talking about what went wrong, that is when I will welcome the more critical feedback. I look for honest feedback as tough as that can be.

Unless those close to the creative person intimately understand the dimension of ego, negative or critical comments can easily crush a creative person. We have had artists and students speak to us about parents who believed it was their job to 'take their children down a peg or two' by criticizing and never affirming them. They would mistake the confident exterior for an outsized, inappropriate ego, not understanding the fragile and vulnerable deflated inner world that was just hanging on to their positive self-image by a thread.

Those in close relationships have incredible power to assist the creative person manage the extremes of their ego. The love of a spouse or partner provides a safe refuge for the creative person to retreat to when the accolades and praise become too consuming, or when the gnawing self-doubt starts to overwhelm their thinking. Put simply, the partner can:

- Prevent their inflated ego from shifting to manic self-aggrandizement.
- Draw their self-condemnation and self-criticism away from the abyss of depression.
- Provide an affirming safe boundary for the creative ego.

For those not in a romantic relationship, parents, friends and siblings can play a vital role in this.

Sometimes I need to be careful with certain people in my life because they don't understand why I am the way I am ... but my mum understands me. **- AKD**

We should also remember how vital 'belonging' is for the creative person, yet how difficult it is to maintain a sense of community when part of what they do as creative people is to confront. Your creative partner, by the very act of creating, moves in and out of community and isolation. You can provide a pathway back into community.

I almost become a different person when I am creating something. **- JC**

I dedicate a lot of time to practice and my instrument. I fall out of touch with people, even my housemates at times. Sometimes I come from there into social situations and I feel insecure or detached. **- JB**

A partner can help 'glue' a creative person back into their community, by convincing them to come out to social gatherings, or by taking them to places where they won't feel rejected. Sometimes all it takes is taking them somewhere where they can be totally distracted.

Toolbox

Say to yourself: *My perspective is important. It is important for me to express what is happening from my perspective. It is not about right or wrong, it is about being heard.*

Feedback to your partner has to be honest and truthful. Mindless flattery does not help your relationship – it repositions you as a sycophant rather than an equal. Even if a performance or work is not their best, find something in it to affirm. This builds on the fact that you are partners. They will know when it's not been a good night, and you affirming them will help them identify where it was bad.

Julie: Recently Jeff performed and I knew he was not in his flow – the crowd was difficult and the PA not up to the task – yet I was easily able to affirm how well he had done under those circumstances.

Early criticism makes you sound like you are not in partnership with them. However, constructive comment at the right time is incredibly helpful, because it comes from somebody who loves them. If your relationship cannot withstand constructive comment, then you need to work on building trust over the long term. Timing is everything, however, and no one can tell you exactly when that right time is – it's different from person to person.

Julie: When Jeff is composing music I often ask if he just wants my positive impression or more constructive feedback. He lets me know, depending on his position along the dimension.

In a romantic relationship, a creative person is at their most vulnerable. You cannot create without engaging the heart. A spouse or partner is the closest person to that heart. The more intimate and open the relationship, the more relational power each partner gives to the other. Any power can be used or misused, either destroying the creative spark or breathing life into it.

Affirmation in a relationship works both ways – when the creative partner is cycling into the deflated ego they can easily target you for criticism and condemnation.

Ethan went through a dark period and he became really critical of me – not that I don't have faults. The pattern of affirmation in our marriage allowed me to challenge his critical beliefs as well as to deflect the hurt that would naturally have been associated with his criticism. **- Francesca**

My parents have struggled for years with how to handle my periods of depression. My boyfriend is a comedian/actor and I really struggle with dealing with the times when he gets down when preparing for shows. If we both happen to be a bit low at the same time, it can get nasty. **- JDS**

- Take time to reflect on your sense of self – how do you see yourself as distinct from your partner?
- Establish an independent and stable social life that is independent of their creative world. This means that you can negotiate your partner into your world as a way of providing social re-engagement if they've taken a beating professionally
- Establish a distinct and flourishing professional or work identity. External circumstances, such as a family crisis or career change, can have a negative effect on identity. Take time with your partner to talk through these issues to minimize the natural strains on the relationship.

- Talk through issues to do with your identity with your partner. When was the last time you spoke with them about your own need for development and affirmation? Their tendency for self-focus can blind them to your issues.

THOUGHT AND SENSE

Your creative partner has periods where they are thinking very rapidly and making associations between seemingly unrelated concepts. This can be disconcerting to you if the thoughts come bubbling close to the surface. What emerges may not seem rational or logical at the time, but a thread of meaning (that you can't see) connects them. It's not chaotic to the creative mind, but it appears that way to others. Usually these episodes are related to the perception and discovery phases of the creative process. In hindsight, once you see the finished product you will see how the chaos made sense all along.

> Julie: As the partner of a creative person who thinks differently, it would be easy to feel intimidated by their talent, the elasticity of their thinking and their ability to focus and achieve at a high level. That's why maintaining confidence in your cognitive ability is vital – not allowing their virtuosity of thinking to diminish you.

When fluid thought is combined with skinless sense, the overwhelming sensory information heightens the need for internal space. A wise partner recognizes what's going on and lets them have some time to explore. That same partner also knows that, eventually, they will need to draw the creative person into a still place that allows their thought processes to become less rapid.

> Jeff: My episodes of fluid thought make me go quiet. When I talk it's often composed of unfinished sentences or stuff that seems totally random to everybody else. Julie calls this my 'time bubble', as if I'm lost in my own separate reality with its own time frame. It is disconcerting to everyone else because she is right – I am operating on my own clock, and what is important to everybody else just doesn't seem important to me at the time. It only lasts a little while though.

Under some circumstances, a creative person may not be able to still the rapid thinking. When this becomes increasingly illogical and fantastical and is accompanied by an inability to sleep – a visit to the doctor may be warranted.

Sense

The dimension of sense, like that of ego, needs the strategy of affirmation, but combined with focus and energy. You will need to remind your partner about the basics: sleep, diet and exercise. When they are caught up with the sensory stimulation of sound, light, colour or the intense focus of their creative task – they won't think about their need for rest or a healthy diet. As we noted earlier, artists who have achieved longevity all speak about the importance of these basics. Paul McCartney became a strict vegetarian out of concern for his wellbeing. Vegetarian Paul is a far cry from his earlier lifestyle. This kind of story is not uncommon in artists who have survived to enjoy a long career.

Toolbox

You can break into the time bubble from a position of trust by asking the kind of questions that remind your partner that your priorities are important.

Revisit the previous chapter and the section entitled Protective Clothing. You can help your partner to get insulated when they have been skinless for too long.

Don't forget the power of being present. Your presence alone will provide safety for the creative mind particularly during episodes of heightened skinlessness.

Learn to judge the ebb and flow of these two dimensions, and provide some space for both low and high tides to take place.

SPACE, FOCUS AND ENERGY

When you've got a musician in the house ... that's loud noise... and then you've got somebody who's like writing ... directing ... editing, who needs quiet focus, who needs kinda zoom noise. We are trying to work that out ... [Belinda] will burst all day while I'm on a shoot, recording, singing, being silly ... whatever, and I'll come home and I'll be emotionally spent. But she'll want to show me everything and if

I don't have all of that to give her straightaway then it almost kills it instantly ... because she's like: "Hey, hey look what I've done," and I'm like: "I can't right now. I just need five minutes," because I've got all that white noise in my head.
- Anthony

External Space

Many relationships can be placed under pressure if there is no understanding of the need for creative space and its association with the creative process. Recognize the importance of creative space and the extent to which it mirrors their internal world.

Well when we first got married I would nag ... and then I realized that had a negative effect and made him push into it more. So I had to learn to respect how he was downloading and how he was using that zoom time, regardless of whether it was creative [or not] ... I had to learn to respect that ... so I stopped nagging, which was good because it would leave the decision to him. **- Charlotte**

Space is such a big deal for your creative partner. Messing with it is like messing with their head. Not having a creative space, or shutting it down, is like killing a part of them. These issues become pressure points in relationships when children are small, or when finances are limited, placing limitations not only on physical space but also on emotional and relational space, which are equally as important.

Internal Space – Focus

There is an inherent intensity around the world of the creative person. When they are intensely focusing on something, the rest of the world can disappear for them, and the rest of the world includes you. It's not that you're not important, it's that their attention is totally consumed.

I can spend a whole evening not speaking to anyone and once I'm drained, I can switch back on – so generally when I am in a creative mindset I'm switched off to people. **- JH**

I can become quite absorbed in the lead-up to final preparations and performance. **- TS**

Sometimes I disappear relationally when I am creating. **- AC**

I am only creative when my husband isn't at home, because I need to be alone.
- MD

I feel I really have to have space when I lock myself in my room and allow the
creativeness to fully flow. - PT

Manic Energy: Circadian Rhythm

The cyclical nature of the dimension of energy is not an easy quality to
live with.

How do you deal with the ups and downs of living creatively?

I think when we are both tired we compete as to who is going to be the one to fill
the gap ... I guess whoever is resting on the couch first wins ... You both feel it
and sense it with each other ... one of you has to have the higher ground ... it's a
choice. When you are single it's completely different. You can disappear from the
world for as long you need to heal and come back. But when you live with another
creative person there is no hiding at all. - Anthony

Julie: Jeff has always had two speeds: full on and dead stop. It is easy
for the creative person, because their energy is so intense ... to provide
the all-consuming impetus for creativity and self-motivation. For the
person living with this type of all-consuming intensity, it is like living
with someone in a hypomanic state.

It can feel like you are drawn into the gravitational pull of their world. Your daily
rhythms and your world become subsumed into their maelstrom of creativity.

Toolbox

You need to understand and manage your own body clock. Avoid allowing your
circadian rhythm to keep pace with your creative partner's. As we mentioned
in chapter two, a deregulated body clock can lead to health problems and
mood disorders. It's unlikely the creative mind's body clock will match yours.

If both of you have completely different 'time zones' in a romantic relationship
then your relationship will develop problems, even with the best of intentions.
Relationships don't survive without time together and good communication.
Imagine, for example, if you have a nine-to-five job. You leave home at seven
in the morning and you are in bed by ten at night. Imagine also that your

partner is a musician who leaves for work at five pm and gets home at two am. He is energized until three am. Additionally, weekends are your time off, but high-pressure work for him. The problem of body-clock mismatch will effectively reduce the amount of quality time you spend together.

Similarly, if your partner has a creative project that demands almost 24/7 time and focus for months on end, the same kind of mismatch will occur.

Work on finding connection points for your body clocks. This can take some adjusting and flexibility. Understand your own personal body clock and negotiate to maintain some level of your daily rhythms.

Julie: When we were first married I had a demanding eight-to-five job which meant that I had to leave home at seven in the morning. I was by nature an early riser and enjoyed getting up in the quiet of the morning. Jeff did his creative work of a night and as a musician had to be able to stay awake until early morning – quite natural for him. It was important to help him understand my need to maintain my rhythm. I couldn't shift to his daily rhythm – it wouldn't work for me. These were very important early aspects of our negotiations as a couple that proved vital when we had children. Later on, he was gigging six nights a week, I was working in an intense job and our baby was waking at five thirty in the morning. He would get home from the gig at two am. We had already established a pattern of understanding and respecting our different daily rhythms so that we were able to negotiate this very difficult period. I also recognized that for our long-term relationship I needed to have work that would give me flexibility, a job with set hours would not suit us as a couple in the long term. This was one of the impetuses for me continuing my study as a psychologist.

Jeff: Our solution was to negotiate a new way of sharing the responsibilities. Julie got up with our daughter, while I slept in until Sesame Street had finished. From a young age, our daughter was taught not to disturb me, although she did almost every day, albeit briefly. To catch up on sleep I would siesta whenever she took her nap. Our days off together were sacrosanct, and on days when Julie was not working I got better sleep.

Your emotional and energy comfort zones are going to be different from your creative partner's. Don't try and live at their energy levels, but find your own rhythm. In the end you will both have to make compromises – but that's what a relationship is.

When it comes to your creative partner needing a space that is chaotic, you should work out a satisfactory resolution early in the relationship. Both of you need to identify and define which spaces are okay for chaos and which ones are not. Your creative partner needs chaos, which can feel utterly unpredictable to you. Once you realize what is happening in this space it's not as confusing. The other side of this coin is that you both need to agree on a space that is defined as free from chaos.

Six weekly cycles for creative projects have been seen in workplace settings, suggesting that some people work best on intense six weekly cycles with time off in between. This pattern may be helpful for people in romantic relationships as well as for work colleagues. If your work cycle functions around periods of intense activity, then having a good break to restore, re-adjust and realign your body clocks is a necessary counterbalance. Spike Milligan apparently had a forty-day period of increasing productivity, followed by a plummet that included, not just the energy dimension, but that of ego as well.[5] Some of his colleagues adjusted to this rhythm, although it's not known how his family did.

As your partner goes through their cycle, learn to read the signs that indicate when you need to break into their world and bring them back to you. Energy and focus are dimensions that will benefit from you reminding your partner to look after sleep, diet and exercise.

LIVING WITH A RISK-TAKER

I tend to push or cross boundaries – or play with fire. I don't know why. I blame it on the fact I am creative and I need some sense of drama and adventure in my life. Sometimes I need to be careful with certain people in my life because they just don't understand why I am the way I am – why I am open to things. - AK

Julie: When we were only beginning our relationship, I had three defining experiences that let me know that this person did not play by the rules.

We were sitting flirting in the cafeteria at university where we were both students. Playing the 'I'm attracted to you game'. Suddenly Jeff stood up, threw a chair across the floor and stormed out saying: "No I'm not going to take my clothes off for you no matter how much money you pay me." There is nowhere that you can go with that, and, as a shy, quiet, very compliant person who preferred not to be noticed, this was excruciating for me. I can still remember that moment clearly. As I slunk away I realized that this person had no problem being the centre of attention and he stubbornly did not do what was socially acceptable. In fact the more conservative and inhibited the environment, the more socially unacceptable he became.

A few weeks later we were at a gig where he was playing and, during the performance, he grabbed a drum stick and stuck it up his nose. To this day I still don't know why – was it perhaps early performance art? I suspect it was a response to the headline band who were considered the best, most popular band at the time. Jeff looked up to them but they were quite arrogant in their dealings with people and with him. I think he and the drum stick were sending a message.

The third experience really gave me an indication of what I was to expect if I married him. We decided to go for a walk one sunny Sunday afternoon. He of course insisted on wearing a top hat and tails, as you do – anything to draw attention to himself and to confront social norms.

With every fibre of my conformist being I have to stop myself from using the influence of our relationship to force Jeff to conform. Needless to say there are plenty of others lining up for that job. I understand that he, along with other creative people, sees the world in new and unique ways. They are not meant to be monochrome, but are meant to bring richness of colour, texture, experience, risk and danger to the world. We should not expect them to see the world in the same way that we do.

How do you manage the creative person's need for risk-taking within a romantic relationship?

Isolate Risk

You need to define areas that are no-go zones for risk taking. They will be zones that together you have identified as potentially damaging to the relationship.

Everything that is not in the no-go zones is now subject to risk.

Substances

As we have already described, the creative person traditionally expresses their need for risk-taking by changing perception and changing context. This may occur in the form of taking mind altering drugs, alcohol abuse or anti-social behaviour. English poet Samuel Coleridge took opium, The Beatles used LSD and The Who had a reputation for wrecking hotel rooms. We have also mentioned the downside. Many famous artists have testified to the fact that drugs ended up destroying the very creativity they were trying to unlock. The drugs can also destroy personal relationships. Partners of alcohol- or drug-dependent artists pay a heavy price for continuing in the relationship.

Substances alter personality. When a partner starts using substances their personality changes. The warm, sensitive, vibrant, creative person becomes Mr Hyde – unpredictable, unreliable, deceptive, moody, and worse, often aggressive and belligerent. In a relationship you don't know whether you will be living with the original partner or the substance abuser. Many continue the relationship in the hope that Dr Jekyll will reappear or they are happy to live just for the occasional glimpses they get of the original. Others may decide to self-medicate and become numb to the confusion and pain – or they choose to leave. The toll on health, finances, and lifestyle is apparent and, all too frequently, the relationship ends abruptly, as one or the other pays the ultimate price of self-medication.

> *John [Lennon]'s long-term depression ... culminated in a series of weeklong LSD sessions during which he gobbled pills whenever he showed the slightest sign of coming down ... had he not met Yoko, there is strong evidence that John might have joined the ranks of acid casualties such as Pink Floyd's Syd Barrett and Fleetwood Mac's Peter Green ... shortly after they got together, John got strung out on heroin, which, although it killed the pain and probably did stabilize him mentally for a while, also gave him all the classic behaviour symptoms of a junkie: it made him devious, paranoid and manipulative.[6] - **Barry Miles***

We have touched on the subject here, but like the matter of libido, the causes of substance abuse and the mechanisms of addiction among creative people, are not explained solely by the dimension of risk. In many cases these kinds of behaviours can be thought of as self-medication for intense emotion, skinless sense or deflated ego. It is not our intention to lay the blame for self-medication solely at the feet of the nine dimensions either. Much research has been conducted into these matters, and we believe that dealing with it in depth is beyond the scope of this book.

Libido

Love is an action not a feeling. It is very difficult to continue to act in a loving way toward someone who is totally absorbed in their own world and creative processes – particularly when they are at that manic energy pole. The manic aspect of creativity is sometimes associated with promiscuity. There is nothing as attractive as someone in that heightened creative 'manic' state, oozing euphoria and ego. There is nothing that will raise insecurity in a partner more than being shut out of the creative person's world especially when they are in a fever of manic creativity with the unspoken risk of infidelity.

Sexuality is a huge area for creative people and issues of promiscuity and same sex attraction are really critical. One academic has observed that creative men tend to be more feminine and creative women more masculine,[7] although this is not our experience. Sexual exploration and promiscuity in creative communities are not only the stuff of anecdote; they are also well documented in research.

This issue is incredibly controversial, because it means touching on the matter of sexual morals and relational ethics – what is right and wrong. Readers of this book will hold varying beliefs. Some will believe that a sexual relationship is only appropriate in monogamous heterosexual matrimony, while at the other end of the spectrum, some will believe that having simultaneous, multiple sexual partners, both heterosexual and homosexual, is perfectly fine, as long is nobody is being hurt. Any debate about these mores inevitably creates a lot of heat and invariably fails to resolve the value differences that underlie every position across the spectrum. The discussion becomes even more complicated because marriages or committed romantic partnerships break down for many reasons, and even though sexual infidelity is high on the list, it is not the only causal factor. Consequently, we have decided not to tackle this complex area in substantial depth here. It warrants thorough and detailed discussion but, again, to do it justice it would require an entire book.

Nonetheless, we do have a few observations for the toolbox. We would prefer to describe the renowned sexual behaviour of creative artists as *sexual nonconformity,* given that the majority of people seem to aspire, at least, to eventually form committed monogamous partnerships. Despite the age of free 'love', infidelity is still the villain of the piece in the western zeitgeist. If popular culture is a guide to what people really think and value, then the 'he or she done me wrong' song or story-line is still at the top of the charts.

Toolbox

Sexual nonconformity may not be the issue in and of itself. It is likely to be the outworking of deeper concerns in the individual, or to be the manifestation of other relational problems. These will need to be identified and addressed, perhaps professionally, in order to prevent relational damage.

As in the case of substance abuse, negotiation may prove to be difficult with artists who have become sex addicts. If so, they need professional help. The key to negotiating in this area is to begin by talking openly about the partner's need for risk-taking and challenging social norms. It is also helpful to be open about the challenges that are inherent within the creative industry. In this way you can partner together to deal with sexual pressures. Try to find more positive ways for a creative person to take risks, rather than risking their relationship.

Sexual nonconformity can also be seen as the by-product of the tides – inflated ego, skinless sense, manic energy, risk action and intense emotion. Certainly risk action often manifests in nonconformity as the creative mind is flirting with danger to seek out new experiences. In fact we believe that with certain clusters of the dimensions, the outworking of the high tides is often to do with sex. We think inflated ego, manic energy and risk action together might well be manifested in this way. Conversely, the creative mind stuck in low tide might employ sexual exploration as a way of trying to shift out of that phase of the tides. If this is the case, then as a partner, your job is to recognize the tidal swings and channel that creative fuel into more productive endeavours. You must come to recognize when your partner, by virtue of their high tide, might be more likely to do harm to your relationship. This is the key to surrounding them with better choices and better opportunities than ones that will damage you.

Finally, the culture of the creative and performing arts is notoriously sexually nonconforming. If a monogamous committed partnership is what you believe in, then the promiscuous culture of the arts is problematic, because your partner's workplace is steeped in it. Ultimately, there is no choice but to build such a strong relationship that your partner won't want to harm it, no matter what other options are available. Here is what one of our focus group partners said about it:

> *Particularly, early in our marriage, Ethan was always worried about being unfaithful and it was an unspoken tension in our relationship. The late nights at the studio, where he wouldn't get home until four in the morning, the gigs where women would offer sex to the musician as a matter of course. We got into the habit of talking about these issues. I would always ask who he was attracted to, as something spoken about loses its power – illicit attraction is far more powerful when it is hidden. Particularly when I was pregnant and the children were young and I would feel as attractive as a toad – it was an opportunity for my insecurities to peak and his fear about infidelity to be a constant presence in our relationship. We had two rules; we always talked about it and I was always available for sex, particularly after gigs and creative highs and would not use sex as a manipulative weapon. - **Francesca***

TALKING EMOTION

Creative people experience intense, passionate and changing emotion. Your creative partner needs good self-management, but the relationship will need really good communication skills from you. Living with a creative mind involves much more additional time and effort in negotiation than with 'normal' people. You will both need to learn how to recognize, process and find language around emotion.

> *I think there is a danger when you are almost bipolar with your emotions, to try and not react when someone is down because you don't want them to bottle it up and not share how they are feeling. That's what we have been learning: 'teach me' or 'tell me' how you really are feeling because I can't guess and I want to*

*be there for you as much as I can ... but if you're holding it to yourself because you are worried it's going to bring me down then it's sort of a negative effect. It can go unnoticed for a while and then it comes out in horrible ways and can shock you. - **Charlotte***

Learning to communicate well without emotional intensity needs practice.

*I'm now trying to explain, trying to define in a language that I know my partner can understand, that I might need a couple of hours to listen to music or something that is going to recharge my creative battery ... I think people mix up their work sometimes. Yes, my work is creative, but it's not always fulfilling ... sometimes it's just mechanical, it's not my downtime. - **Anthony***

*Something I've had to learn ... that's part of growing up ... is to stop the emotional slagging off ... I feel like I'm only just learning to understand Anthony's language, as he was saying, when he needs downtime ... Now, when he says I just need some time in the cave, I'm like cool because he comes out better ... and that's him getting his energy back. - **Belinda***

*That trust you have in your marriage that regardless ... you have to get to a point where you don't feel judged by your wife because of how you feel ... even if it's something pretty out there ... because as soon as you talk about it, and get a release from it, the relationship is better. - **Dennis***

Emotional Subtypes of the Creative Mind

Researchers have found different responses in emotional stability and emotional expression among creative people. We believe that there are two subtypes of creative people as far as emotion is concerned. These two different groups, while both creative, have different ways of displaying emotion. Both are incredibly soft and sensitive – prone to skinlessness.[8]

The Creative Performer: is a volatile, passionate creative who tends to be found most often in performance disciplines, although novelists and painters have frequently displayed these qualities. This type is often overly dramatic and histrionic. They make things worse than they need to be and suffer from lack of attention. They tend to cycle more to the high end of the dimension of emotion and so need their partner to help them see reason and step back from the edge of the emotional cliff.

The Creative Geek: is superficially balanced emotionally. Sometimes they even have restricted emotional expression. They tend to work on their own a lot – in computer graphics, technical musical work, or something mathematical. They have an imaginative, rich inner world but rarely express it outside of their work. They can seem socially awkward and cut off emotionally, and need their partner to be able to see past the outward calm and draw them out of their internal focus into productive social situations.

We have observed that there is an emerging group of creative couples where one partner, usually the man, fits more into the creative geek category. These couples experience slightly different issues where the non-geek can feel emotionally cut off from their partner. When we look more closely we find that the geek can be very emotional and sensitive but does not show others this very deep part. This emotional shut down can lead the partner to believe that the creative geek is not present emotionally in the relationship.

In a very simplistic view, creativity is linked to the right hemisphere of the brain, although our emotions are more in the left hemisphere. We know that creativity connects emotions and that many creative people use their creativity, rather than words, to express their emotional world. This is great for their art but hopeless for their relationships. If you are mathematically creative – then working with your partner to find words to express what is inside of you is critical to the success of your relationship. Imagine that you have vast inner reserves of oil, but unless you can work out how to tap into them and bring them to the surface to lubricate your relationship, then the relationship can end up brittle and dry – relationally 'seized up'. Appropriate communication of emotions is the oil of a relationship and needs to be expressed to enable all the parts to run smoothly.

The Geek Toolbox

The creative geek or those with more male brain wiring (see note 4 at the end of this chapter) need more time and space to be able to express what is happening. Choose a place that is free from creative distraction. Allow time for them to dig deep and formulate words for their feelings.

Sometimes you can encourage them to start by playing music; writing; drawing; crafting; designing; painting what is inside and using that to begin a conversation about the inner world. Often we can use the words and emotions of others as a catalyst – like watching a movie; reading a book and simply saying to them: 'That's how I feel.'

The real issues may not even emerge in the first conversation. You may need to risk interrupting them in the geek space, but do so in order to draw them back into companionship.

The Performer Toolbox

Performers, as a subset of the creative mind, need to access their emotions in order to do their work. Great musicians relive emotional highs and lows in order to get the expression just right. Actors frequently find the truth of a character by accessing their own emotional memory banks in performance, night after night. Furthermore, emotional intensity is a natural outworking of the creative process – particularly during episodes of skinless sense. As we have also observed, this has an impact on relationships. Negative emotion, particularly anger, can be relationally destructive. Without emotional resilience, negative emotion can lead a partner to become numb and detached.

We now know that emotional intensity can lead to *flooding*. Flooding is the overwhelming injection of stress hormones that produce the fight/flight/freeze response. The problem may well be worse for men than women. During conflict men tend to experience more negative thoughts that maintain distress and contribute to flooding. Ultimately, one partner's negativity can be so overwhelming that it leaves both people emotionally stunned and shut down.[9]

The two diagrams on the following pages represent the anatomy of an emotional conflict.[10]

In one we see intense emotions, particularly anger, leading to a pattern of defensiveness then flooding, shutdown and a subsequent feeling of emotional abandonment and withdrawal by the partner.

As we described in the previous chapter, social support, venting and the processing of negative emotion is helpful, followed by trying to find more positive ways of interpreting why there was an emotional outburst in the first place. This will lead naturally to finding better ways of coping in the future.

In the other diagram we see good negotiation involving emotionally resilient responses.

ThE NEGATIVE EMOTIONAL CONFLICT CYCLE

Anger

Defensiveness

Flooding

Emotional Shutdown

Abandonment

Escalates Anger

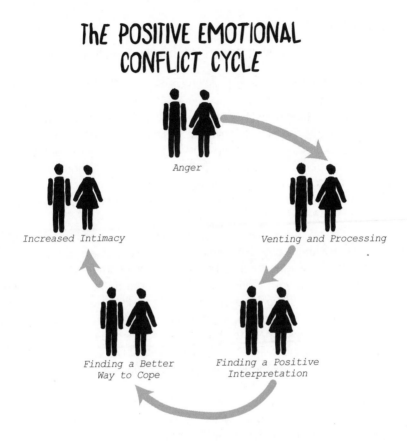

ThE POSITIVE EMOTIONAL CONFLICT CYCLE

Anger

Venting and Processing

Finding a Positive Interpretation

Finding a Better Way to Cope

Increased Intimacy

Partners need to help the creative mind redirect the powerful driver of intense emotion away from them and into their work. Avoid defensiveness. When we are on the defensive we are unable to take in new information.

Communication

Process why your emotions are building up before communicating. Discipline the verbal expression of your emotions so you can be heard clearly. Choose a place that is either free from distraction or is neutral ground. Be willing to confront and talk about something that is painful for you – denial offers only temporary relief.

Here are some opening lines to begin negotiating. Feel free to adapt them.

- Is this a good time to talk? There is something that I really need to discuss with you.
- I can understand how important it is for you to play the guitar until two or three in the morning. I know that you have said that it is the best time for you to practise and it's the time you feel most awake, but it actually stops me from falling asleep. I really need a full eight hours sleep to be able to function. So I would really appreciate it if we could talk about ways that enable you to get the practice you need and for me to get the sleep I need.
- I understand that it is important for you to work on your art/ideas for a movie without any distraction and I know that we agreed that for these three months I would be earning the income so that you could concentrate on your work. But when I come home and the house is a mess, the bed hasn't been made and the dishes are not done, I feel really overwhelmed and upset. I would really appreciate it if you could just do the basics – make the bed, do the dishes and tidy up a bit – before you start your work. This would help me feel like we were partners in this – rather than just feeling like I'm supporting you.

Learn to monitor a build up of emotion. Be aware of emotional triggers, including the normal hormonal cycles. Circumvent emotional explosions by escaping – keep a journal, debrief with a friend.[11]

ONWARD

The next two chapters describe how communities can empower the creative mind, and how best to collaborate with them. The dynamics that operate in the workplace and in the way groups function together, are different to the dynamics between couples in a relationship. It is to the dynamics of the workplace and the power of groups that we now turn our attention.

1   British rock icon Sting and his wife Trudi Styler were interviewed by Katie Couric in May 2010 for CBS News. Couric asked the couple what made their relationship successful. Available online at http://www.cbsnews.com/video/watch/?id=6481095n

2   Marney George was quoted by Kareen and Hagop Akiskal who cited Scwabacher's 1957 book *Arshile Gorky.*

3   These four negative communication tactics are identified by John Gottman as being predictors of a relationship that is headed for breakdown. For more on his work, visit www.gottman.com

4   It seems appropriate to provide a note on the brain and communication from the field of neuropsychology. At seven to ten weeks in utero, a foetus has an injection of testosterone that physically differentiates male and female on the basis of the X and Y chromosomes. The male brain develops in a different way to the female brain. The *corpus callosum*, separating the left and right hemispheres, is more developed in the female brain. This means that it is far easier for a person with a female brain to access and communicate emotion than it is for someone with a male brain. Note: a woman can have a very male type brain and a man can have a very female type brain. For more on this refer to the 1989 book *Brain Sex* by Anne Moir and David Jessel.

5   This observation of Milligan belongs to scriptwriter Neil Shand who is quoted by Norma Farnes in her 2010 book *Memories of Milligan.*

6   Barry Miles op. cit.

7   Csikszentmihalyi's 1997 observation that creative people tend to be androgynous has been previously noted in chapter four. His observation was based on a very small sample and we believe that this contention is open to question.

8   Unfortunately, research in the area of creative types and emotion is limited. Academic studies have tended to be restricted to small groups, which can severely skew results.

9   This assertion is made by Gottman and Silver in their 1999 book *The Seven Principles for Making Marriage Work.*

10   In the development of these two diagrams, we gratefully acknowledge the work of Moshe Zeidner, Gerald Matthews and Richard Roberts, whose detailed discussion of these issues can be found in *Emotional Intelligence in Everyday Life* (2006).

11   We have a friend who had a pattern of letting emotional buildup intensify to the point where she would 'fry' someone around her. She learnt to get regular debriefing from a professional that helped her to manage the emotion.

CHAPTER EIGHT
COMMUNITY

COMMUNITY

*WHAT IS THE PAYOFF IF YOU'RE A MEMBER OF A TRIBE?
NUMBER ONE YOU BELONG. YOU'RE PART OF A GROUP
THAT SURROUNDS YOU AND SUPPORTS YOU...*

*The second thing is that you know who you
are...you know who your friends are; you know
what is expected of you; you know what role
you have to play - you are absolutely secure in
your identity. You suffer none of the western ills
that we're all so aware of alienation, isolation
– loneliness. In a tribe your identity is solid
and grounded. You have significance - your
value and your world has meaning. This is a
tremendously powerful force that keeps people
in the tribe.* **- Steven Pressfield.**

No one is creative in isolation. The idea of the lone creative genius turns out to be a myth (as we mentioned in chapter three). The more closely we examine the lives of so-called great 'solo' geniuses, the more we realize that they had different kinds of people working with them as collaborators or facilitators. Some of these were directly responsible for bringing that person into the public eye. Others were patrons who ensured their financial survival – like Vincent Van Gogh's brother. Others collaborated in ways that facilitated the creative process, such as Jackson Pollock's wife, Lee Krasner. Without Krasner devoting her life to Pollock it is doubtful that he would have been able to produce the work that he did. The Beatles had a number of collaborators. The German girlfriend of original bassist, Stu Sutcliffe, designed the famous Beatle haircut. Manager Brian Epstein made all the commercial connections and got the band members to act and dress professionally. George Martin introduced them to Ringo Starr and was the crucial creative influence on the making of the groundbreaking Sgt. Pepper's album. On close examination, the lone genius doesn't exist -they rely on others for their success.

Great relationships make the creative life possible and broken relationships make it extremely challenging. We know now that a life where your sense of identity is based solely on your work is unsustainable. Much better to have a life whee your value comes from knowing and being known.

Therefore the creative mind needs to have communities of people who understand the passion and emotions that drive creativity, but who are trusted enough to drag them back from the edge if necessary.

Rejection and Spin

A community that understands the creative mind allows both high and low tide to work. This is why artists have traditionally and instinctively banded together in tribes of the like-minded – people who 'get' them. Because of the power of a group of people to positively influence each other, a community is one of the main mechanisms that prevents the creative mind from becoming fixed. This is particularly true for the undercurrents of rejection and spin. Acceptance and belonging in the tribe is the primary way the creative mind will cope with constant rejection in the marketplace.

I think community is crucial for artists – whether they realise it themselves or not. We spend all week pouring ourselves into the work. We care about how the work *is being perceived by the wider audience and how it fits into the current scene. We pretend it doesn't matter what anyone thinks, but when someone whose opinion we respect says something good about it - it gives us sustenance. At ParisCONCRET we have created a space for projects of a particular genre of art. The artists who gather there support one another. They discuss the work and go away with something indefinable but important. Our project is a non-profit initiative. One visitor could not understand why we spend so much time, money and energy doing this thing. Eventually after spending an entire evening at one of our openings she blurted out: "I know what you are! You are artist encouragers!" It all felt worthwhile to me at that moment.[1] - **Richard van der Aa**￼*

In our interview with Marina Prior, she beautifully and powerfully described the community of musical theatre and theatre performers:

Jeff: Can I ask you then, what are the unspoken codes? What are the rituals for the performance community?

Marina: *Well, there are just superficial rituals to start with. You do eight shows a week. You do Wednesday matinees – they're really hard. You do a physical warm-up; you put your make-up on at a certain call. You have silly, silly kind of in-jokes built around the life of the piece that really don't make any sense to anyone else but ...*

Jeff: *The script and the production process, the rehearsal process, the characters ...*

Marina: *Yes there's that, so actually, structurally, it creates this sort of culture ... there's a shared vulnerability and there's a shared understanding of when people need to be supported. At what point in the rehearsal people need to be told that they're really good and they're going to be great which is an intuitive thing ...*

Conversely, if an artist chooses to belong to a certain group, and it sends signals of rejection, then it is almost impossible for the creative mind to fight that undercurrent – it sweeps the artist away and they lose their ability to move between the high and low tides. The same is true for the undercurrent of spin. Artists need a community of trust and truth to be the countervailing influence. Without it, they begin to believe their own inflated ego, their own PR and lose their tidal nature. A group that doesn't place high value on authenticity and honest talk without judgment will have the same effect. You can't escape the current of spin by trying to find authenticity in a group that is enmeshed in its own spin.

Empowering communities subvert the undercurrents, and disempowering communities amplify them.

Most of us enjoy a range of different kinds of relationships, but creative people tend to find themselves living two distinct lives. Because creative minds exist at the extremes, they become isolated from the mainstream, and, at the same time, develop close circles of people who understand them. Without the latter, the creative mind cannot properly maintain elasticity.

GATEKEEPERS

Creativity [is a] process that results in an idea or product that is recognized and adopted by others.[2] - Mihaly Csikszentmihalyi

Somebody else decides whether or not some new thing is valuable in order for it to be considered creative.

People group together – we are social creatures and don't like to live isolated lives. Every group that comes together forms along certain lines, and develops its own ethos, patterns and ways of doing things. It also develops its own power structures.[3] Some people have more than their fair share of influence and others simply follow along. Some are outsiders, some are insiders, some are conformers and some are mavericks. Whether formally bestowed or not, people with influence lead the rest one way or another. It is amazing how small, but critical, groups of individuals cause new ideas to become widespread and eventually commonplace. Malcolm Gladwell identified three types of people who, when combined together, create social epidemics – *connectors* (people with extensive social networks), *mavens* (people who are 'in the know') and *salesmen* (people who are charismatic and persuasive).[4] On their own, each type is insufficient – the existence of a dynamic relationship is essential for widespread impact.

Whether in a small community or on a global scale, there are always people who determine what is valuable on behalf of the whole group. They act as guardians of value and become like oracles – their opinion is the one we look to. They are the gatekeepers of ideas, values and culture, and creative artists need to be able to network within their orbit, or face being disregarded. In large societies each creative specialty or community will have its own gatekeepers.

They may be Artists and Repertoire (A&R) managers for record companies, music critics, film critics, curators of art galleries and so on. Gatekeepers wield tremendous cultural power. In the film industry, the executive who is able to 'green light' a movie script is the one who truly decides what we all eventually see at the cinema. A tiny handful of people select film scripts from the thousands submitted, before they even get to the stage of being seen by the film studios. While audiences decide whether a work is popular, without the approval of a gatekeeper a work will only get limited distribution.[5]

Maintaining Strategic Relationships with Gatekeepers is a Fact of Life for Creative Artists.

Actors, directors, writers and producers tend to work together in cliques. Arts grants generally go to the usual suspects. Circles of associates like this can be formed simply by where and when you studied. Cambridge and Oxford are classic examples of how student associations can develop into creative communities that spawn prolific creative collaborations.[6] Once somebody achieves success, they open doors for their friends. The most successful member of that clique has become a gatekeeper. Similarly, music producers tend to work with a small group of artists and performers.

Sometimes these little circles become a means of survival in the face of rejection by the mainstream gatekeepers. This happened to a small school of French artists in the nineteenth century. The Paris art establishment initially treated Claude Monet and his friends, Renoir, Cézanne and Pissarro, with contempt. The prominent critic Louis Leroy coined a term that was intended as an insult. He described Monet's paintings as *impressions* because he considered them unworthy of being considered fully realized paintings. They responded by embracing the insult and began exhibiting together under the name: *Impressionists*. Gradually their painting style became widely accepted by the public. Today they are household names and Leroy is largely forgotten.

The success of the Impressionists demonstrates that the power of gatekeepers is not absolute. Gatekeepers have less control when public access to an art form is easy. YouTube and social networking websites have made public access so easy, that they have caused upheaval in the normal operations of critics and A&R managers. They publicly lament the loss of quality in music and film, while, behind the scenes, clever executives trawl through these sites looking for popular unsigned artists. Gatekeepers also monitor the web for changes at the cutting edge of culture. 'Modern', 'innovative' and 'cutting edge' are all ephemeral and unless gatekeepers are able to reinvent themselves and maintain credibility they suffer the same fate as artists as the culture changes.

Most creative people understand these kinds of relationships instinctively – and they learn to find the appropriate gatekeeper or patron, and network with them. Alternatively, they find new ways of getting to their public. At a professional level, successful creative people know how to foster, cultivate and protect good relationships. They also foster emotional resilience, which means they can predict and work with their own tides.

At the risk of stating the obvious, gaining a reputation for being offensive and difficult is a bad career move. The single most common social consequence of which is isolation. The isolated creative mind simply gets voted off the island.

THE POWER OF CULTURE

Neuroscience has discovered that our brain's very design makes it sociable, inexorably drawn into an intimate brain-to-brain linkup whenever we engage with another person.[7] *- Daniel Goleman*

In chapter four we talked about the negative impact of fear, rejection, insecurity and spin. The main kind of threat that most of us face these days is not about actual physical harm or survival. Much of our anxiety in modern societies relates to how we are perceived in our social settings. We suffer anxiety about our status in social or work groups and spend energy worrying about what other people think about us. We are hard-wired to be socially connected and, given what we now know about the four undercurrents, it's easy to understand why negative social experiences stand out in terms of their power to cause us distress.

We need our social groups to be positive, but we also need them to be authentic. Our social environment is so powerful it's like the climate. We pick up on behavioural and cultural signals and respond and adapt to them, like changes in the weather. Our social wiring picks up the 'tone' or 'vibe' of the group and responds with a similar 'tone' or 'vibe'. Clearly the opposite is also true. People who are socially inflexible or insensitive, who don't adjust and adapt to the group, are thought of as misfits rebels or outsiders.8 Expressions you might hear like: 'they are not us' or 'they are us', are just ways of describing the way people fit or don't fit within a group culture.

If someone really cares about being in a group then they will willingly make adjustments and adaptations to their attitudes and behaviour in order to maintain their sense of belonging. In fact, once it is established, group culture becomes a self-correcting force. Group members tend to think and behave in ways that reinforce the climate they like.

Death by Culture

The power of group culture to influence our attitudes and behaviour is so pervasive that we often don't count it as being a factor in contributing to our actions. The truth is actually extraordinary – we are so influenced by group culture that we will even die because of it. The culture on the flight deck of certain airlines was found to be the defining factor that led to a string of fatal accidents. Even though pilots were aware that their plane was in immediate danger, they could not be seen to question their captain. In some cases they knew they were about to die but would not allow themselves to overrule the group culture, even to save their own lives and those of their passengers.[9]

On 13 January 1982, Air Florida flight 90, a Boeing 737, crashed on takeoff into the Potomac River in Washington DC, killing 74 people aboard including the flight crew. The aircraft was attempting to take off in very cold conditions where ice was building up on the wings, constituting a safety hazard. Ice makes the plane heavier, can lock up the flight controls, but, more importantly, ice on the wing surfaces interrupts the aerodynamic shape of the wing, which is what makes a plane fly. Because the problem of ice build-up is well known in aviation, there are safety protocols in place that ensure safe operations in icy conditions. One of these is de-icing the plane shortly before takeoff.

On this occasion, Flight 90 was de-iced on the ground as per safety regulations, but then its departure was delayed long enough for the First Officer (FO) to become worried about ice building up again. Investigators would later conclude that he repeatedly tried to indicate his concerns about the build-up of ice to his captain. However, because of the culture in the cockpit, it was inappropriate for the FO to directly question the captain's command or his flying competence. So the warnings were given in a series of hints, suggestions and attempts to give advice disguised as jokes. The following exchange is edited from the full Cockpit Voice Recorder (CVR) transcript. It reveals the FO's attempts to warn his captain and the way the captain reinforces and asserts his command by resisting any suggestions that might call his judgment into question. Given the culture, the FO is unable to openly criticize his boss and tell him he is wrong.

As the plane nears take off, the hints become more direct, but each time are overruled by the captain, initially by the use of scorn, and finally by direct contradiction.

The FO first tried to warn his captain there was a problem some twenty minutes after the last attempt to de-ice the wings:

> *FO: Maybe we can taxi upside a some [727] sittin' there runnin' [and] blow off whatever [ice and snow has built up on the wings]*

The next attempt is several minutes later:

> *FO: It's been a while since we've been de-iced*

> *FO: See all those icicles on the back there and everything?*

And again, minutes later:

> *FO: Boy, this is a losing battle trying to de-ice those things. It [gives] you a false sense of security, that's all it does.*

> *CAPT: That, ah, satisfies the feds ...*

Then another attempt as the FO points out a nearby aircraft:

> *FO: This one's got about a quarter to half an inch [of ice] on it.*

The next warning from the FO comes immediately before they push back from the gate.

> *FO: Let's check those [wing] tops again, since we've been setting here awhile.*

> *CAPT: I think we get to go here in a minute.*

As they taxi out to the runway, the FO makes another oblique reference to his concerns.

FO: Slushy runway. Do you want me to do anything special for it or just go for it?

CAPT: Unless you got anything special you'd like to do, depending on how scared we are ...

The captain's remarks are couched in cultural terms to reinforce his superiority. They receive clearance for takeoff, and the FO expresses much more direct concerns about the safety of the plane from his reading of the instruments as they are rolling down the runway.

FO: God, look at that thing. That don't seem right, does it? Uh, that's not right.

CAPT: Yes, it is. There's 80 (referring to airspeed)

FO: Naw, I don't think that's right. Ah, maybe it is. I don't know.

CAPT: 120.

FO: I don't know

The captain announces that they are to commit to the takeoff.

CAPT: V1. Easy. V2.

Fifty-five seconds into the takeoff roll the wheels leave the ground and the 737 struggles to gain altitude. From this moment until impact the sound of the stall warning system can be heard as the plane warns the pilots that it is on the verge of losing its ability to fly (a stall). Twenty seconds later the 737 abruptly plummets out of the sky because of ice on the wings.

CAPT: Stalling, we're falling ...

FO: Larry, we're going down, Larry.

CAPT: I know it ...

At this point the CVR picks up the sound of crushing metal, as the 737 smashes into the 14th St. Bridge.10 For about twenty or so minutes, the FO knew they were in trouble but the culture in the cockpit did not permit him to do anything about it. For twenty minutes the captain used the same culture to reinforce his skill and status, even though he was wrong. The captain only conceded error as the Potomac River loomed in the windscreen in the last two seconds of his life.

As incredible as this story seems, if we think back over our own experience we can recognize similar situations. We can all point to moments where culture contributed to a metaphorical 'plane crash' or 'train wreck'. This kind of situation is referred to as *group think*. If a small community, pervaded by group think, can cause such a catastrophe, imagine how much more damaging it would be if it were also infected by spin. This is why truth and authenticity are crucial for fighting this undercurrent.

Group Think

We are like fish swimming in the ocean of our group culture. Although we are individuals with our own sense of identity, the way we are socially wired means that even our ways of thinking can be functionally impacted by the way the group thinks.

Group think is the term given to a phenomenon that effects decision-making and analysis of information inside a group – when the importance of maintaining group cohesion and group consensus overrides maintaining a reasonable balance and the seeking of alternative viewpoints or courses of action. Groups are vulnerable to group think where they involve highly charismatic directive leadership, experience pressure to make decisions quickly and where critical thinking is responded to with 'put-downs' or cultural humiliation.

The Eight Main Symptoms of Group Think"

1. **Invulnerable:** Members are overly optimistic and ignore negative data. They believe they are set apart and special in some way and the normal rules don't apply to them.

2. **Rationalize:** Members have a systematic way of discrediting and explaining away information that doesn't fit their worldview.

3. **Morality:** Members believe their decisions are morally correct, despite poor consequences.

4. **Stereotyping:** Members construct negative stereotypes of outsiders or rivals; developing an 'us and them' attitude.

5. **Conformity:** Members put pressure on each other to suppress dissenting thinking, viewing it as disloyalty.

6. **Censorship:** Group develops unspoken rules and methods that inhibit alternate points of view or any critical thought.

7. **Unanimity:** Members assume that everyone agrees with the group's decision.

8. **Mind guards:** Some members become protectors shielding others from adverse information that might threaten the group.

We can become so immersed in our own culture that we can't recognize when it's counterproductive. Add spin to this mix and it's a recipe for abuse and a recipe for the creative mind to lose elasticity. No group is perfect. The trick is being able to recognize how capable a community is of being self-critical about honesty and authenticity.

Creative communities are particularly susceptible to group think because of the creative person's manic-like qualities and inflated ego.[12] Creative people are often highly charismatic, charming others with their persuasive manner. Similarly, creative projects are often carried out with time pressures: due date; opening night; product launch. Therefore, if a culture of suppressing alternate or critical opinion exists, along with a pattern of overt, or covert ridicule or humiliation, then group think emerges.

Devotion

Although the story of Flight 90 is an incredibly negative example, it shows us just how powerful culture is in influencing our behaviour. Culture is a social force that also works positively, and, when it does, it is a dynamic influence that helps people self-correct their behaviour in amazing ways. At the positive end of the scale is the quality known as 'esprit de corps' or the common ethos that drives devotion for the group and the desire for that group to succeed and achieve honour.

But once you got it there you was proud to be ... we was proud of our boots, we was proud of our shoulder patch, and we was proud to be paratroopers. And we was proud to be working with the guys we was working with.[13] - **J. B. Stokes**

You know these people that you are in service with – you know those people better than you will know anybody in your life, I mean you know them right down to the final thing you know.[14] - **Darrell C. 'Shifty' Powers**

Esprit de corps is the kind of culture sought after by military units. The physical, mental and emotional demands of armed conflict are so great that something special is required to keep people in the battle. Those who have experienced battle report that the fear is so great, that it is only the thought of letting your mates down that keeps you there. US historian Stephen Ambrose has documented perhaps one of the best-known examples of this.[15] Survivors from the battlefields speak of the devotion of soldiers to their team-mates, even when they had been wounded, as in this testimony from the commanding officer of Easy Company – 506th PIR, 101st Airborne Division – US Army.

> *He's behind the enemy lines on D-Day. Does he holler "Help"? No. He hollers "I'm sorry Lieutenant, I'm sorry, I goofed." My God ... when you think of a guy who is that dedicated to his Company, to his buddies, that he apologizes for getting hit ...[16] -* ***Richard Winters***

The group culture of these soldiers was so great that men who were hospitalized went AWOL and rejoined their mates on the front line despite the near certainty of further injury or even death.

We referred to these two different examples because they are startling and powerful illustrations of how we rely heavily on external verification of our performance, identity and emotional state. The limbic system of the brain encompasses a number of structures that are critical to emotion, behaviour and long-term memory. It functions as an open loop system, in that it relies on external sources of information to maintain itself. We pick up on our environment all the time with our five senses, but the limbic system is particularly tuned to the social environment. We therefore depend on our social network to determine our mood. If everyone is upset, it's hard for us to stay happy. If everyone is laughing we tend to laugh with them.[17]

The very same forces that shaped these two different situations are at work in places where creative people gather together. So, in exactly the same way as with Flight 90 or Easy Company, a community has the power to empower or disempower the people in it. If the creative mind belongs to a great community, then the power of that culture will help the creative mind stay healthy and elastic. An unhealthy group will do just the opposite, forcing an artist to stay fixed in either high or low tide longer than they should.

Finally, belonging to a well respected creative community is highly sought after. Belonging to a renowned group confers a reputation of prominence on the individual, and reinforces personal identity – we are a member of this famous group as opposed to that other lesser known group.

It's critical that the creative mind becomes a part of a community that will empower them and their creativity as opposed to disempowering them.

EMPOWERING CULTURE

What kind of group empowers a creative mind? Here are some answers from our surveys:

"An open work environment, which is not 'boxed in'. I feel squished if the leadership puts too many limitations on me. I want leaders to trust me and my creativity. And to encourage me ..."

"A working environment where you can share your ideas and projects, not to have them rejected, but to be worked on and investigated as to whether it is a good project ..."

"... who tells me what they want then steps back and lets me create it."

"An open, trustworthy leader who is not dominant but is as open with me as they expect me to be with them, and a supportive and caring working environment ..."

"I need someone to lead by example, to make it a more positive atmosphere ..."

"I need the freedom to be myself to have good ideas ..."

"The best leadership loves and earns respect ..."

"I find it's all about encouragement and order for me. If order is not kept I struggle to keep motivated. I love a comfortable and caring atmosphere ..."

"... would have to be wisdom, respect, but fun also, and changes. I'm big on if something's not working, let's try something new ..."

"I love being under a leader who trusts me to do a good job, not somebody who is always scrutinizing. I also love to be able to laugh with my team – it's therapy."

"I can't be put in a box ..."

"One that believes in me and accepts me ... One that has a structure that I believe will work and not put me in a box ..."

"An open, easy flow, loose – as in not rigid structure – or time constricting leader ... One who understands the 'development' stage and the 'construction' of it ..." [18]

Creative people look for places where there are other creative people and for places that value high quality creative output. They are looking for environments that encourage and embrace diversity and difference. Most creative people feel like they are already 'outsiders' to some degree, so a place that welcomes mavericks and individualists looks great to them. Such an environment guarantees that they will be able to absorb different stimuli, and come into contact with new ideas and new experiences – the kind that fill up the memory banks.

[Creative people are looking for] a place to have low entry barriers for people ... where newcomers are accepted quickly into all sorts of social and economic arrangements ... these are places where people can find opportunity, build support structures, be themselves, and not get stuck in any one identity.[19] - **Richard Florida**

It is easy to see the recurring themes. It seems that transformational leadership and natural, relaxed and unrestrained environments, among other things, promote the creative process.[20]

Culture Making

- Transforming leadership that is non-authoritarian.
- Encouraging and visionary leadership and culture. Risks can be taken without fear of punishment for failure.
- Tolerant – understanding and inclusive of differences.
- Recognizing and valuing uniqueness and skill – meritocracy.
- Structure that is highly flexible.
- Rewards collegiate or collaborative work styles.
- Empathetic – sensitive to emotional state of others. Facilitates dealing with personal issues.
- Open to exploration, improvisation and new experiences.

- A climate of innovation and problem solving.
- Accepting and non-judgmental – lets members find their strengths.
- A community built on trust and fun – makes room for play.
- An appreciation of mystery.

Groups that possess these qualities inherently create a climate where they make room for the creative tides. Strong messages of acceptance, belonging, affirmation and freedom to explore, are required to overcome the hard-wired bias to see things negatively.

> *[It was] an encouraging culture – so you felt like, if you were going to fall down, someone else would help pick you up, and there was like, not so much an expectation, but an expectancy that you would succeed, and failure wasn't really an option, but that no matter what you did there would be people on the sidelines cheering you on and believing that you could come out the best person you could possibly come out ...- MP*

Non-authoritarian leaders intuitively understand the power of encouragement. A positive climate impacts on the open loop of the limbic system to change the way people feel about belonging. Artists who stay in such communities are able to resist the undercurrents.

Creative people are looking for authenticity because this helps them resist spin. Once a place or a community is identified and recognized as authentic, artists are attracted to it. Authenticity comes about by a collision of intangibles. There are unique cultural markers that make up authenticity. It can be a location, an artistic genre or the presence of a unique ideology or creative form. Often key creative people are already there. A group or a place can be known as the centre for a particular movement. Artists will flock to such a group or place if it promises real access to the new experiences.

Misunderstood?

Because the creative mind functions in ways that are unconventional, conventional people can misunderstand them and mistake their behaviour for unreliability, inconsistency, disobedience and rebellion. In fact, they are just exploring, imagining and avoiding boredom. Frequently the gulf of misunderstanding can become too wide to cross. The artist then picks up on the frustration of others. They interpret this frustration as a message that they are only being tolerated, not accepted. Ultimately, this cycle of thinking leads them to believe that they aren't valued and that they don't belong.

Most people we have worked with who desperately want creative people in their teams are unaware of the way their culture will need to change in order to make room for the way the creative mind functions. What is meant as a reward might well appear to be manipulative; what is meant as humour might be interpreted as humiliation.

DISEMPOWERING CULTURE

The following story is a classic example of what not to do with your creative colleagues.

Sally[21] had studied for three years to complete her major performance piece. She became determined to deliver the best recital that anyone had ever seen. She had seen other recitals by previous students and she developed some strong ideas about how she would do things differently. Most of the students talked with each other about their frustrations, which mostly involved how to get the rest of the team to practise and attend rehearsals. The recital process demanded that a student not only perform a 45-minute series of works, but a great deal of emphasis was placed on gathering and leading the team that made the performance possible – not just the execution of the music.

Sally decided that what was needed was a strict set of expectations and standards that would end all problems of commitment. She found her team quickly because she was talented, and other students were keen to get into her recital. At the first meeting, she was incredibly organized and gave out a set of charts, a recording of the songs, an outline of the performance theme and the dates and times of her extensive rehearsal schedule. She outlined the standards she expected from the team and set a vision for the performance. Everyone was on board.

As the weeks went by, other last-minute, high-priority tasks, like assignments, and unforeseen circumstances started to impact on her rehearsals – like every other student before her. Finally, Sally called a team meeting. She made it clear that some members of the team were letting the others down. One of the band members was highly talented and was called on frequently to play or rehearse in other bands. He was the worst offender, and so, after his next non-attendance, Sally decided to make an example of him so that her standards wouldn't slip. She fired him.

Following the shock firing there was a crisis. Other students had study commitments that were slowing down their practice time. Targets and timelines were slipping. Sally got more and more tense at rehearsals and then one night rebuked the team for not meeting their commitments. Gradually over the next few days, two of them dropped out, saying that they couldn't afford the new clothes Sally wanted them to buy for the show. Then three other players realized that the quality musicians had left and they found excuses to go. Only a matter of days after her rebuke, Sally's band had left her.

Sally had created a task-driven group culture that was dominated by rules. It was inflexible and had a top-down authoritarian approach. A faculty member took de facto leadership and created a culture where the band could contribute ideas. The group modified the recital outcomes to suit the shorter time frame. Many of the original players returned and the band agreed to a rehearsal schedule that was more realistic. The recital went well and was well received. Sally was unhappy because her dream to set the bar higher than anyone else had been shattered.

Unknowingly, Sally had sent all the wrong cultural messages to her little community. She implied that they were not good enough, even though she herself had only ever received affirmation from the college staff. Sally's need for control and her driven-ness were symptoms – she had become fixed, and lost her ability to move with the creative tides.

IT SEEMED LIKE A GOOD IDEA AT THE TIME

... when you ask people about love, they tell you about heartbreak. When you ask people about belonging, they'll tell you their most excruciating experiences of

being excluded. And when you ask people about connection, the stories they told me were about disconnection.[22] *- **Brené Brown***

When a community culture works like Sally's did, it feels like a fundamental betrayal for the group members. Most leaders don't intend to cause harm to their people, but few who lead creative people appreciate that their job is akin to herding cats. Conventional structures unwittingly serve to stifle the creative process, because they function to limit ambiguity and increase certainty. Therefore the creative artist feels like they are in a straightjacket.

Groups that function in a more restrictive way actually achieve early success. In fact, the more that this kind of culture is reinforced by fear, the more successful it will appear to be in the short term. Unfortunately, using fear as a motivating force undermines natural creative flow. Such groups, at best, pay no attention to the undercurrents, and at worst create climates of fear, rejection and insecurity. You cannot fight an undercurrent that is embedded in the culture. Following a short brilliant trajectory, things will begin to gradually disintegrate with a steady trickle of departing artists traumatized or cauterized by the environment. Imagine how being in this group impacts on a skinless creative mind! It feels completely alien to them, although it is the norm in most workplaces.

Creative people don't fit into groups that possess a rigid culture. Their need for ambiguity, flexibility and recognition of their uniqueness is in direct conflict with fundamentalist mindsets. Such cultures cause them to either shut down or lose natural creative flow and elasticity that is essential to the creative process. Unfortunately it is precisely that attribute of the creative mind that reinforces the prevailing mindsets of rigid cultures. The story rarely ends well.

All in all, such groups are the worst kind of environments for the creative mind to try to maintain a tidal nature. While the written rules never say it, the unwritten message for the creative mind is: *conform or leave.*

It happened in my first year of jazz studies at the Con.[23] *On a Wednesday, when we were all together in Jazz History, the lecturer asked which of us had played in pop or rock bands over the weekend. A whole bunch of us stood up. He went on to ream us out, and said 'There is nothing creative about pop music. Jazz harmony is the epitome of music. If you want to be into jazz you've got to be into it totally, totally ... totally!' I was one of the people standing so I asked him, 'What have you got against rock players. ' He replied, 'All of the musicianship is in the volume knob.' It was really humiliating and he was asking us to choose whether we were going to be hip but earn no money, or going to have a broad appreciation of all music – in its entirety. For those who wanted to feel a sense of acceptance you had to conform. Concert practice on Wednesday afternoons was an exercise in public character assassination. The teachers basically got to defame you in front of everyone else. It was very dangerous for a young guy just out of high school. Everybody wants acceptance and support. So they had you by the balls. In my final assessment they asked me, 'So what's the jazz course taught you?' I answered, 'It's taught me I don't want to be a jazz musician.' There was definitely a stigma about rock music. Most of the graduates went on to play in pop and rock bands on the weekends just to earn a living. The graduates who really did well went on to do it all.*[24] - **RS**

When I was doing the acting in the city I was in a culture where my first day there I was told I needed Botox on my creased brow ... I was continually pulled down and basically stripped of who I was as a creative person ... You had your people there who would encourage you and believe in you but then ... the majority of people would just stab you in the back the minute they got the opportunity ... It didn't make it creative, it made it restricting, and it made it feel like everyone was in a race[25] *...-* **ST**

Creative People Go where They Are Wanted

Most people leave groups because they feel unwanted. They migrate to other groups where they feel wanted. If you want creative people in your community, you must be willing to create an environment that makes them feel at home. They feel at home when they are free to be themselves without sensing their non-conventional life patterns are being judged.

Creative People Need to Belong

Everybody needs to belong somewhere – significance and identity are frequently worked out through the social context. The truth is nobody likes to be alone. Belonging is not just a quality of location or convenience – it's the recognition of 'likeness' or 'fit'. At an unspoken level people recognize when they are like this group – they fit. They also sense when they're not like them – they don't feel comfortable. Creative people are tribal. They want to be in a good tribe. When they feel they're where they belong they will respect and respond to other members of the tribe, and the needs of the tribe.

Creative People Need to Be Productive

Creative people are usually not satisfied being spectators. Although they need down time like anybody else, they normally see a group or a community through the lens of: 'How can I make this better?' Sitting on the sidelines for a while is okay but it quickly becomes boredom – and boredom, as we know, is bad. Artists want to be practising their art. A creative mind will want to leave a group that makes them unproductive and will be attracted to groups that empower them to be productive. The maxim: *use them or lose them* is true, as long as using them does not mean exploitation or abuse.

Creative People Need Space

Communities that make room for the creative process and unconventional ways of living and doing will attract creative people. The properties of metaphor, ambiguity and exploration require different ways of structuring space and time. The culture and work style of innovative Internet company Google is a landmark example of structuring for creativity.

> *It's a very relaxed atmosphere, there's flexibility in time...there's a notion of twenty percent time where twenty percent of my time I am free to choose what I want to work on, and that freedom has actually led to some really great projects.*[26] *- **Corey Anderson (Google software engineer)***

The chapter that follows develops these themes further and looks at why some work practices are good for creativity and ultimately good for business.

A WORST CASE SCENARIO

If love, trust and understanding fail, try manipulation, control and intimidation. As we mentioned earlier, you will get almost instantaneous results, particularly if you have the luxury of a ready supply of young hopefuls who want to get 'in'. However, this is a recipe for disaster for building a longstanding and productive creative community. Over the long term, the creative people will escape – looking for tribes that will help them thrive.

Sadly, there are groups and cultures that are toxic. Leaders can set whatever culture they want when the available places are few. What emerges in these circumstances will depend on the character of those at the top. Unfortunately, a lack of moral compass can make these groups quite ruthless. Successful artists who have emerged from these environments will often reflect on how they were willing to kill or be killed as a temporary means of achieving success. The collateral damage from these groups, however, is immense.

Such cultures are so damaging that creative people become fixated and shut down for periods long after they have left. Here is an extract from an interview we conducted with a survivor:[27]

Question: What was that turning point when you were aware of the fear and intimidation?

Michael: At a moment where I was very vulnerable, he criticized me and ridiculed me. It was so sharp-tongued, the spirit behind it was so nasty ... it felt like judgment. So out of fear ... I completely conformed to his way, from that moment onwards.

Question: So there's words that are said, and then there's ulterior communication. What was that?

Michael: I would have said it was 'conform to my way, or the highway – either do it my way, or I'll get rid of you'. The only thing that made me stay was that I felt committed to do what I was doing ... I was prepared to do whatever it took. That was the thing that kept me there.

Question: What internal changes did you make to conform?

Michael: Adjust. Just adjust. Just adapt. For the sake of survival, for the sake of my wife, for the sake of the kids, for the sake of peace.

Question: Is that 'I had to be who he wanted me to be'?

Michael: Exactly. Completely. I never really felt that I had the freedom to be myself. Certainly in some things I could have ... but not to play music the way I wanted to play it; not to dress the way I wanted to dress; or socialize with people I wanted to socialize with, or how I spent my time. It actually felt like I was ... in the dungeon cell ... and I only realized that after I came out of it. It was like: 'You're not going home now, you're going to do this' – the constant phone calls – it actually felt like I was held hostage.

Question: So if you were trying to put into words the things that were shut down ...

Michael: Confidence, definitely ... I felt like he exposed my weaknesses early on, so the result of that was my confidence was rattled. Confidence to write songs the way I wanted ... which I don't think I've been able to recover. It was definitely the songwriting, definitely the way I played guitar, definitely those two. The irony of it is ... that I'd wanted to sing for years, and he was the trigger point that got me into doing that ... Even though it was incredibly dysfunctional, there was some good that came out of it. All those little bits of good, were always making me question the bad – like, can it all be really that bad? It was a constant state of confusion.

Question: How was it maintained?

Michael: He was very charming, very flattering, wasn't afraid of silence. Very good at embarrassing people. When it was fun, it was really fun, and when it was going off, it was really going off. But it was always coupled with extreme bad. So there was never a real balance, it was either really really good or really really bad. And the really really good stuff was enough of a hook to keep you in, but the really really bad stuff was so nasty and punishing ... It was the fact that he created opportunities for people to be used, and for their talents – he'd always put people on the edge, to a point where their heart was racing, their palms were going clammy, or that they were forced to come up with stuff on the spot ... he would then expose people's weaknesses and use that against them publicly ... it was always this charming, seductive, fairytale dream, like a Disneyland, but... it never felt right. It was abusive.

Question: So you are saying that ... he nailed your weaknesses ... then he would publicly expose your weaknesses?

Michael: Yes, absolutely ... because he made you feel that even though he was publicly shaming you, that you were big enough to take it. 'You gotta understand you're my best, you gotta understand you're a cut above the rest ... others can't take it, but you can and that's why I do it.' ... I think the biggest thing was, what was reasonable and what was right, went completely out the door, even to the point of [my] fighting for him when people would privately challenge what he was doing, and you knew that what they were saying was right, but you still made excuses ... Fear completely and utterly altered my perception of what was reality.

Question: How did this type of personality affect a creative team?

Michael: He would tell every leader that they were his go-to person and he would *ask them to keep tabs on everyone else and get back to him. So I think he wanted to create more and more confusion so the truth was completely lost in the mix.*

Question: Did that experience affect their ongoing ability to be creative?

Michael: *Those that left early are still creative but many are not creative in the way they originally were. All their creative flair has been sabotaged.*

WHO MAKES GROUP CULTURE?

The culture of a group is determined by the people who are the key influencers. Every group has at its core a number of people who influence everyone else in that group. In groups with formal leadership structures, hopefully, the formal leaders are also the key influencers. Leaders are social architects; they set culture, they model it. In fact, a culture that a leader does not model will be unstable because of the innate hypocrisy. Leaders also create culture by the kinds of stories they tell to the community. Every group has its *myths* – its underlying narratives that inform the group members where they came from, what's important, and therefore where they are going.[28] Leaders reinforce culture through what they reward and encourage and how they behave – because behaviour never lies.

> Jeff: Once I realized the power of culture I set about consciously creating it. I spent time articulating what I thought our culture was, and I met with my key leaders and got their input too. I wrote it down in a cogent form and presented it to my staff and key leaders as our culture. I did this for three years without ever mentioning it to the student body. I did my best to live it and I positively reinforced staff who modelled it and corrected staff who didn't. I kept presenting our culture statement at all our staff-training events. After three years, on enrolment day with a whole bunch of new students, I surprised everyone by asking the second and third year students to tell the newbies what it was like to be at the college. I asked for volunteers and I didn't prompt them or prime them in any way. As each of them talked about life in the college I was able to literally tick off every item on my culture statement. I knew then it was working. My people could articulate our culture without my ever having told them what it was.

Finally, culture is developed and reinforced by shared experiences – *weren't you there when* ... Whenever a community comes together, culture is either forming or being reinforced. Even if no one is intentionally setting culture, it is happening anyway. Nature abhors a vacuum.

The power of culture lies in the fact that it is a constant, and once established it creates a self-adjusting social mechanism. We pick up the unspoken signals and adjust to them, or react against them.

DO CREATIVE PEOPLE GET A FREE RIDE?

No.

A culture is the way a group of people agree to conduct a working or social life together. So there are implied responsibilities that the group has to the individual and also, in return, responsibilities the individual has to the group. There is no free ride for anybody.

We have kept returning to the matter of affirmation throughout these last few chapters, because it has extraordinary power to help creative people fight fear, rejection and insecurity. Affirmation has to be based on real behaviour otherwise it is valueless. In fact, affirmation needs to be dependent on the accomplishment.

When people feel more a part of something they move from *belonging* to *contributing* and then finally to *influencing*. A person's sense of belonging increases as their sense of acceptance increases. As they feel more affirmed at a personal level, their commitment becomes deeper until their belonging becomes a desire to contribute.

Your primary creative relationships may not be within a community or group, rather within a collaborative or working relationship. Lets move on to understanding how to make a collaborative relationship work in the long term, as well as all the things you wish you could tell your boss, your CEO, the financial controller, about how to work with creative people.

1   Richard van der Aa is the director of ParisCONCRET project space (in Paris), www.parisconcret.org. This communication with the authors came via email.

2   For more on this, see Csikszentmihalyi's 1999 contribution to *Handbook of Creativity*, 'Implications of a Systems Perspective for the Study of Creativity'.

3   It is beyond the scope of this book to discuss the theories of group dynamics. For further detail on the way groups form and function see the following authors among others in this field: Kurt Lewin, William Schutz and Bruce W. Tuckman.

4   For more detail on this see Gladwell's book *The Tipping Point* (2000).

5   See also the dimension of attitude in chapter three.

6   Stephen Fry's account of the Cambridge theatre scene is a particularly good example. We have cited his autobiography in previous chapters.

7   Daniel Goleman is one of the leading thinkers in the field of Emotional Intelligence. This quote is from his 2002 book *Primal Leadership: The Hidden Driver of Great Performance* co-authored with Richard Boyatzis and Annie McKee.

8   ibid.

9   For more on the power of culture in aviation safety, see Chapter 7 'The Ethnic Theory of Plane Crashes' in Gladwell's 2008 book *Outliers: The Story of Success*.

10 This edited version of events has been put together primarily from Chris Kilroy's 1982 TIME magazine article published a month after the accident: as well as from online aviation safety website www.airdisaster.com (including part of the cockpit voice recorder transcript in addition to Gladwell's account in *Outliers* and the NTSB accident report. Full citations, including web links, are listed in the bibliography.

11 Irving Janis is a leading researcher into group think. This list is derived from his (co-authored) 1977 book *Decision making: A psychological analysis of conflict, choice, and commitment*. The list was found online but may no longer be available: http://www.cedu.niu.edu/~fulmer/groupthink.htm (accessed 29/01/10).

12 See chapter two.

13 From the 2006 HBO documentary *We Stand Alone Together: The Men of Easy Company*

14 ibid.

15 Ambrose's 2001 book *Band Of Brothers* was also made into a miniseries by HBO.

16 Cowen (2006) op. cit.

17 This claim is made by Goleman et al in the book we cited earlier in this chapter.

18 All of these excerpts were extracted from our survey of creative and performing artists.

19 Richard Florida wrote an article reporting on his research in 2002 for *The Washington Monthly*.

20 Hsen-Hsing Ma conducted a survey of creative research in 2009.

21 Sally is not her real name, and although this story is an amalgam of a number of different people and events, it is in essence true.

22 This excerpt is from Brown's presentation to the 2010 TED Conference.

23 The Sydney Conservatorium of Music.

24 This extract is from a personal interview with the authors. The story is memorable for the use of manipulation to try and enforce an unrealistic set of values.

25 This extract is from a personal interview with the authors.

26 Although what we know about the work environment at Google is disseminated by the company as part of its

recruitment program, its relaxed workplace is notoriously different to normal corporate practice. Some more of the 'home videos' produced by Google staff can be found at http://www.youtube.com/lifeatgoogle#p/c/AA877111339682D8/0/dhR_EYJcbZo and http://www.youtube.com/lifeatgoogle#p/c/AA877111339682D8/1/Aeve9N5-CWc (accessed 29/4/11).

27 This extract is from a personal interview with the authors. Michael is not his real name.

28 The term myth is often misunderstood. A cultural myth is a story that tells us who we are – like the story of the Boston Tea Party, or the Eureka Stockade, or the Storming of the Bastille. A lot of cultural myths are in fact true.

CHAPTER NINE

COLLABORATION

COLLABORATION

*CREATIVE PEOPLE NEED THIS SORT OF DUALITY - OF
FEELING VERY SECURE IN SOME DEEP SENSE, ENOUGH
SO THAT THEY CAN BE VERY RISKY AND PUT THEMSELVES
INTO THE WORK. WHAT I TRY TO DO IS FOCUS ON THE
ENVIRONMENT IN WHICH PEOPLE WORK… AND LET THEM
RELAX AND BE THEMSELVES AND BE ADVENTURESOME.*[1]
- DAN WIEDEN

There is an increasing demand for the
kind of people who can make new things
– people who dream, imagine, invent,
design, compose, produce and form. The
digital and online revolutions mean that
we have so many more ways of accessing
music, movies and books. This in turn is
putting pressure on content providers to
come up with more content. Even book
publishers are only just beginning to
come to terms with what this means for
one of the most traditional of all creative
industries.

If we think more broadly than just the creative and performing arts, and include those with professional level skills in a creative field, *Pro C* creatives, then the increase in the proportion of creatives as part of the general workforce is massive. Author Richard Florida estimated that in 2001, thirty percent of the US workforce was engaged in creative occupations, compared to ten percent in 1901 and around twenty percent in 1980.[2]

So what?

We need to understand how to work with them, how to collaborate with them and how to lead them. The twenty-first century economy will be characterized by global connectedness and marked by rapid technological change. Creative minds will be the drivers – the in-demand workers of the new age. In fact, Florida identifies a new class of workers. He calls them the *creative class*. They are already causing economic and social revolution.[3]

WHAT DO WE KNOW?

The 1982 cult sci-fi thriller *Blade Runner* is considered one of the greatest movies ever made.[4] Its writing and production were notoriously difficult and yet the final result has stood the test of time. What follows is the dialogue from its pinnacle moment. The deadly dangerous Roy Batty (played by Rutger Hauer) is a cloned human, whose genetically built-in four-year life span is about to come to a close. Rick Deckard (played by Harrison Ford) has been hunting him for most of the film, because Batty and his friends have broken the law. Although Deckard is Batty's nemesis, at the crucial moment Batty saves his life. Then Batty sits down in front of the exhausted and terrified Deckard, who is slumped against a wall. As the rain pours down out of the early dawn sky he speaks.

```
                  BATTY

        I've seen things … you people
        wouldn't    believe.    Attack
        ships on fire off the shoulder
        of Orion.  I  watched  c-beams
        glitter  in  the  dark  near  the
```

```
Tanhauser Gate. (pause) All
those moments … will be lost …
in time like … tears in rain
… (pauses and smiles) Time to
die.
```

Batty's head slowly slumps forward as life ebbs from his body, leaving Deckard speechless.

Getting to this amazing and visually stunning moment involved a lot of people, including director Ridley Scott, original writer Hampton Fancher, and subsequent co-writer David Peoples. The script was reworked by Peoples to rescue the project without Fancher's prior knowledge because he was not able to deliver what Scott needed to begin shooting. Here, in their own words, is what each had to say about this difficult and painful process.

Hampton Fancher: *I remember arguing with Ridley … I was angry and I walked out by the pool and I was standing there and [assistant producer] Ivor … came out and he tried to tell me … and it hurt somehow … he didn't come right out and say it … he said … 'I know me man, he'll do what he wants to do.'*

Ridley Scott: *We got it up the point where Hampton was just getting exhausted …*

Hampton Fancher: *I was at a Christmas dinner … and [producer Michael] Deeley put this script on my plate … then I looked at a couple of pages … because I recognized the idea … and I looked at him and … I said, 'What's this?' He says, 'This is the new script.' I said, 'What new script?' and he told me. 'David Peoples is …' and I said, 'Who's he?' I couldn't hear anything … I stood up … because I was going to cry, my whole world fell apart … I remember beseeching him – 'No this is wrong … whoever this guy is who is writing this stuff …'*

Ridley Scott: *Peoples, I think … and I mean this in the best possible way … was simpler. Hampton is more cerebral … and I thought bringing in Peoples would create some fresh air in the corridors to make it move … my danger as a director is I tend to get very cerebral …*

David Peoples: *I know some of those speeches … was me, except for the fact that in the first read around … Rutger [Hauer] read that speech and then went on with a couple of lines about 'memories in the rain' and then he looked at me like a naughty little boy … I didn't let on that I was upset, but at the time I was – and I was* *a little threatened by it. Later, seeing the movie, that was a brilliant contribution of Rutger's – that line about the rain and tears … It's absolutely beautiful.*

Hampton Fancher: *They had the good fortune to get David Peoples … and I see that movie afterwards and I think, 'Oh yeah … and I would not have done that, and David knew how to do this and David worked well with Ridley'… I was completely wrong and Ridley was totally right and Peoples definitely totally right … If that hadn't have happened there would be no Blade Runner.*[5]

Their story reminds us that we do not have all the parts of the final product. We need others to fill in the gaps to bring a creative project into reality. The ability to collaborate, to let go, to let others in to help create your baby is part of the price of making something good become something great. One of the most collaborative art forms these days is the motion picture. Like musical theatre, it brings together a diverse group of creative and conventional professionals with the aim of realizing a single product. Creative collaboration is an attempt to marry different imaginations, different worldviews, and different ideas about how everything should look, sound and feel. It is in this melting pot that uniqueness emerges.

The problem with the melting pot is that it can be a struggle. Sometimes the collaborators don't even know what it is they are looking for on their own, let alone with each other. Great art is created in an environment of conflict. Neither writer had the complete ingredients for *Blade Runner,* although much later they came to realize that the script was stronger for all the different inputs. During the filming there were conflicts between Scott and his crew; between Scott and lead actor, Harrison Ford, who was looking for more direction and attention from Scott; and between Ford and the relatively inexperienced female lead, Sean Young. Yet these tensions became part of the magic of this creative collaboration. Ford carries an on-camera tension and broodiness. Young portrays exquisite beauty, yet an underdeveloped emotional expression that was perfect for her role as an artificial human. Scott's unswerving focus on creating the rich visual world of the movie with absolute attention to detail led to tension with the film's financiers who even tried to dismiss him from the project.[6] However, twenty-five years later *Blade Runner* is considered a masterpiece. Ford was lauded for his performance, but he referred to the experience as 'a bitch … not the most pleasant shoot'. He later conceded that he was fortunate to have been cast in *Blade Runner* (amongst other films) – but that he doesn't have 'a particular appetite' for the genre[7] He still refers to his relationship with Scott in very guarded terms.

In the same way that the creative mind experiences tidal flows, and operates within them to produce great art, so a creative collaboration will rarely be free of disagreement. Imagine a whole group of people with the same dynamic. It's rare to find overwhelming unity of ideas and approach. There will always be a wrestling of creative ideas, time pressure, and eruptions of emotion.

U2 have been frank in describing the intense conflict that is part of their working history. However, early in their career they established a foundation for their working relationship, based on a fierce commitment to each other. There is a clear understanding that their collaborative process is far from tension free, but they have all developed an incredible respect for what each member brings to the band. Not many successful bands manage to stay together for as long as U2. Few bands that are still playing after twenty-five years still have all of the original members.

If conflict is a necessary aspect of creative collaboration, then developing skills to manage it is important.

This chapter will attempt to help you with three questions:

- How do you collaborate with creative people?
- How do you lead a team of creative people?
- Why do creative types keep leaving ?

MIXING IT UP

The band was in the studio, the clock was ticking, the budget was tight, and whatever opportunity the players had to work out what to do had passed. This was the moment of truth. The atmosphere was tense. The recording engineer pressed the record button and the tape was rolling. He pressed the talkback from the control room and leaned towards the microphone.

We're making a chicken sandwich.[8] *- **Hugh Wilson***

The band all started laughing. The tension evaporated because they all knew what he meant – they were putting the ingredients together. That take was brilliant.

The currency of creative collaboration is **trust**. You can't expect people to bare their souls if they're not sure how their soul will be treated once they have opened up. The starting point is being able to feel secure with your colleagues. At the core of collaboration must be a willingness to take risks with how people regard you and your ideas. Without trust there can be no real collaboration. Trust is like money in the bank – we can invest in it and bank on it. If you haven't deposited enough of the things that build trust, it won't be there when you need it. Insecurity makes trust impossible, and therefore collaboration is impossible.

Not every idea is a good idea, but one thing will often be the start of something, that leads to something else and finally finishes up being something entirely different. You have to be prepared to let go of the initial idea, even if it was yours and even if you thought it was a good idea. Without trust and a secure identity you will not be able to escape the fear that perhaps you are being sidelined. Without trust and a secure identity you can never unlock and share your experience or feelings.

The end product of collaboration is always bigger than any one individual involved. Collaborators are at their best when they are unselfish. Getting the best result should be so much more important than any consideration of individual credit or adulation. Finally there must be an agreement and respect for the way the creative process plays out between all of you.

CONFLICT IS YOUR FRIEND

The films that I've worked on that have been filled with angst, trepidation, pain – those seem to be the films that seem to be successful ...[9] *- **Lawrence G Paull***

So much has been written about resolving conflict that it is unnecessary for us to go over old ground. However, we will outline some principles that are important to keep in mind.

When you're collaborating with somebody, it should be because you want to. This dynamic heightens the chances of the creative product being better.

Always approach disagreement with all the outcomes in mind. Rather than getting what you want in the moment, ask yourself what it is you really want in the big picture. Ultimately, if the creative partnership is valuable, what you really want is to keep it together. Therefore, you need to learn how to negotiate with your colleague so that both of you are heard, feel valued, and can work together to get the best result.

What Do You Value?

Negotiating comes down to the interplay of two main factors: how much you value the other person and how much you value what you are fighting for. In fact, these two - the person and the outcome, underlie every interpersonal negotiation we undertake. If you see the outcome you want as critical, and you don't place a high value on your colleague, you will play hardball.

Every time you negotiate with somebody you are unwittingly revealing your real opinion of them, and also the value you place on what it is you're fighting for. At the same time, the other person is weighing up whether your values line up with theirs. If they sense that what you want is very important to you, and they don't think much of you, then they're likely to extract a higher price. Conversely, if they lean towards helping you, it's a sign that they value working with you.

If you are fighting your colleague for something, and they don't think it's worth very much, they will naturally conclude that you don't really value them. This will impact on your working relationship. So any time you are in situation where you are negotiating, remember you are not just trying to get what you want, you are actually reinforcing or redefining your relationships.

There is always going to be disagreement about what colour it should be, or what instrument goes where, or which camera angle to use, or whatever. It is the way you communicate your position that leaves the lasting impression. People may forget what you say to them, but they will never forget how you made them feel.

Arguing about such matters is fine; in fact, you don't really have collaboration unless there are different perspectives. If you agree on everything then obviously you're going over the same old comfortable ground and not getting out and discovering new things. Conflict is beneficial. It's through argument that new things emerge. It's through disagreement that new possibilities arise. In a conflict our ideas collide, and from that collision new things come into being.

Argue about Choices

The right kind of conflict is about creative choices. Relish in it when it's happening because it means the juices are flowing. Disengaged colleagues don't argue about things because they couldn't care less. People who care argue about the details. Expect disagreement, and come to enjoy it, because you know that when it's going on good things are happening.

Therefore, all the argument needs to be directed at the project, and at the toolkit of techniques. Any comment about aesthetics is permissible, but comments that denigrate your colleagues will undermine their confidence and trust. You may think that you can do this in the context of your group culture without undermining the process, but you are fooling yourself. We met a group of musicians who said it was their culture to show contempt for each other. The leader told us that everyone understood that the insults weren't serious. What the other group members really understood was that you were not permitted to take offence, but in actuality it was a power play. Although denigration was delivered in the guise of a joke - it was still real, allowing powerful members of the group to get away with humiliating others. Although initially successful, this group disintegrated spectacularly after only two projects together. You can't undermine people's trust and personal security and get away with it.

Big problems arise when there is conflict about the way you do things. When you are fighting about your joint processes, you are disagreeing about the foundations before anything can be built. Effective partnerships place great importance on how they have learnt to find their creative groove together. Arguments about method are a sign of a collaborative partnership with only a short-term life span. On a project-by-project basis, like a film shoot, you can still produce amazing work with this kind of conflict. The Blade Runner experience shows that greatness can emerge from the most intense disagreement about everything, although those involved can be so scarred by the experience that they never want to work with you again. On the Blade Runner set, only a few of the key people understood Scott's process and adjusted their style to work with him.

Creative people are intensely passionate about their work, which generates a level of conviction that adds extra heat to any disagreement. So there has to be something bigger that binds a partnership together. People stay in collaborative partnerships that are heavily conflicted for lots of reasons: if they feel you have something that they only get from you; if there is someone famous working on the project or if it looks like the project might make them famous; if the project already has a great reputation; if the money's good, or if there is no other work around; or if they like the genre or the style. However, as soon as any of these factors change, they will leave.

The best possible situation is where the collaborative partners are committed to a shared ideal, and also committed to each other. Such partnerships enjoy longevity and productivity.

Have a Prenup

Have clear rules from the outset. Everybody comes into collaboration with hopes and expectations. Often these are never talked about – and this is where some partnerships come unstuck. Not all expectations are realistic, but if all the issues are on the table, at least everyone's ideas about what will come out of the project can be dealt with up front.

There is no such thing as equality in a creative partnership, because there is no real way of quantifying the value of what each collaborator brings. Is the vocal tone of the singer worth more to the band than the groove of the drummer, or the textural knowledge of the keyboard player, or the technical mastery of the guitarist? At least, when you sit down together and develop rules about things like who gets what credit or how fees are divided, you can, hopefully, take the pain out of unmet expectations.

> Jeff: Everybody has a different idea of how to handle collaboration, but in projects I've been involved in, all the contributors received an equal share of credit and financial reward, regardless of their talent or their level of contribution to the process. I've always thought that relational interaction is often undervalued in creative collaborations. Someone always says just one thing at a crucial moment that changes everything. Someone always plays one note that changes everything. They may do nothing else except make everyone else feel great. I believe that if someone is invited to be a part of a creative partnership they should be treated with equality.

In some industries it's much easier to quantify. Have you noticed how, in stories about movie stars and film directors, the box office take from their projects is always mentioned? Director A has made fifteen movies with a total box office of $105 billion, Actor B has starred in seven movies with a total box office of $600 million, and so on. The same is true of songwriters and musicians. Such and such a producer has written twenty number one songs; this band member was in such and such a band that sold 20 million albums. A creative artist's worth is quantifiable in these terms. So if you're a new director and you are collaborating with Steven Spielberg, I don't think you can reasonably expect to get the same fee he does – his commercial value is far greater than yours.

What you need in a creative collaboration is a kind of prenuptial agreement that specifies things like credit and payment as well as time commitment and expectations. While no one is making any money, or fame and reputation are not at stake, everybody will be pretty easygoing about it. As soon as a creative project becomes financially successful or critically acclaimed, it is much more difficult for everybody to maintain an altruistic frame of mind.

RESPECT THE ROLES

In the field of rock music, the singer is normally the famous one. After the singer it's the guitar player. The musicians themselves do not impose this value system, but the machinery of the music industry does. It needs personalities to promote. Then the public adopts the same values. When we think of U2, we immediately think of Bono and The Edge, but U2 would not be who they are without Adam Clayton and Larry Mullen Jr. Even though Bono gets 90 per cent of the media and public attention, within the band itself, all four members are equal partners.

In creative collaboration we must understand that people take on different roles and perform different functions in order to get something realized. Long-term productive collaborations value those members of the group who may not get the same share of public acclaim.

There are many different kinds of roles that people play in the collaborative process, and not every one of them shows up in every project. In creative collaborations, participants can actually play a number of roles, sometimes simultaneously, sometimes one after another. In many ways these roles allow either the high or low tides of the dimensions to function in complementary ways. Some participants can be at low tide as a counterweight to others who are at high tide.

In the time we have been researching creative people we have observed certain roles emerge repeatedly in collaborative groups.

The Technician

A problem-solver. Always says no at first, then thinks about how it can be done and provides the method and the details. Takes pride in the achievement of the impossible. May be frustrating to work with – they cannot be hurried. They work at their own pace.

> *Schematic thought, insulated sense, zoom focus, order space and safety action.*

The Blue Sky Thinker

Thinks of things no one else thinks of. A lot of suggestions and ideas will be totally impractical, impossible and unrelated but perhaps one in every five or six is brilliant. You just need to be patient and not come down too heavily on the awful ideas.

> *Confronting attitude, fluid thought, wide angle focus, chaos space and risk action.*

The Glue

This person is the one who feels the pain of others and tries to empower everyone in the group. A peacemaker, a negotiator and the one who reminds everybody that they are better off stuck together than falling apart. Keeps everyone on track and sometimes may contribute nothing more than this. May not even see themselves as creative – but they are essential to the creative process.

> *Deflated ego, conforming attitude, skinless sense, order space and safety action.*

The Devil's Advocate

Always asks the questions no one wants to hear. Identifies where the group is going wrong and is fearless enough to put it out there. May appear difficult to please. Doesn't necessarily have the answers – just the questions.

Inflated ego, confronting attitude, schematic thought, order space and safety action.

The Terrorist

Throws in a bomb. Blows up everything and changes the game. Destructive to old mindsets and habits. In the aftermath we discover how creatively potent this kind of person can be.

Inflated ego, confronting attitude, wide angle focus, chaos space, risk action and intense emotion.

The Child

Everything is a game. The whole thing is just like a little kid playing in the garden, full of fun and frivolity. May frustrate others in the group. Willing to try anything. Can easily revert to childlike states of distress.

Fluid thought, skinless sense, wide angle focus, chaos space and intense emotion.

The Face

The visible personification of success – a spokesman, a persona, someone the public and the media can identify. May have no other role.

Inflated ego and risk action.

The Visionary

Can see the big picture. Capable of getting a huge idea – but may have absolutely no idea of how to realize it.

Inflated ego, fluid thought, wide angle focus, manic energy and risk action.

The Joker

This person is always the naughty one; the comedian or the troublemaker. Says the things the rest of the group think privately but are too afraid to say out loud. Constantly breaches social conventions.

Inflated ego, confronting attitude, fluid thought, wide angle focus, risk action and intense emotion.

The Purist

Is always standing up for ideological or artistic integrity. When others are willing to try anything, this person will always resist ideas that take the group away from what have been the core values.

Inflated ego, conforming attitude, schematic thought, zoom focus, order space and safety action.

The Interpreter

Is able to communicate effectively with colleagues outside the creative group and speak on behalf of it. Acts as an intermediary, particularly with business heads and financiers.

Deflated ego, conforming attitude, schematic thought, insulated sense, wide angle focus, safety action and calm emotion.

ROLE PLAY

At some point, each of those in the group is going to frustrate the others and yet each role will contribute something positive to the process. It is the responsibility of every member of a successful group to remember that they didn't accomplish success on their own. This trap catches many artists, particularly as they cycle through the ego dimension and if their insecurity is strong.

It's easy, in hindsight, for us to convince ourselves that we were the ones who really made it happen. Time and time again we have seen the most extraordinary collaborations fall to pieces because of selective memory.

What is crucial to success is the creative power of each of the roles interacting with the others. On our own we are never as good or as successful, we simply move from one group context to the next carrying our baggage with us.

Each role challenges what we think and believe, this is what creates tension. Our default position is not to question our beliefs – surely what *we* think and believe must be right! Effective collaboration is not possible without accepting that we may not be right, and that we don't need to be right all the time. The undercurrent of insecurity makes the creative mind unable to give up being right, and torpedoes collaboration.

Not all of these roles are necessary for a successful creative collaboration. A person may play more than one role – alternating as the process unfolds.

LEADING

In the previous chapter we identified the optimum culture for creativity to flourish. Creating the right culture is the primary way to lead creative people. The second way we lead them is by recognising the challenges they face in moving with the creative tides.

ELASTICITY

Creative people live by a separate set of rules, not because they're being rebellious or difficult, but because what they do is difficult. Therefore, if you want to lead creative people, you have to build flexible environments that facilitate the different ways they need to do things in order to be productive.

This insight comes from understanding the science behind the way creative people think and process information. It is like a high-performance car that is designed to run on premium petrol. Premium petrol minimizes the wear and tear on your car's engine over the long term – the car performs better and lasts longer. You can put standard petrol in the car and it will still run. It's cheaper in the short term, but there's more friction, the engine parts wear out faster and the car eventually makes funny noises. Less flexible workplaces are to the creative mind what standard petrol is to your high performance car. You'll still get results, but there will be more friction; they will make funny noises and wear out faster – or leave faster. Telling them to perform better is like trying to make a Porsche perform at a premium level without premium fuel – impossible.

The key to unlocking premium productivity is to build elastic management structures. Remember, outcomes are sacred but methods are disposable. Small teams or workplaces find this elasticity easier to achieve because they naturally tend to be more ad hoc and flexible. The larger an organization becomes, the more inflexible it becomes. This phenomenon is an unintended consequence of organizational growth. Large organizations require a bureaucracy to function. Bureaucracies attract bureaucrats. Bureaucrats and creative people are nearly exact opposites in terms of work styles, preferences and structures. The more bureaucracy it requires, the more inflexible an organization becomes and the less able it is to allow for the creative mind.[10]

Author and software writer Paul Graham has coined the terms *manager's schedule* and *maker's schedule* as a way of describing how creative people operate on a different way of scheduling time from everyone else. What he is really identifying is the need for ordered space in which to create.[11] Graham describes how 'managers' subdivide their working day into hour or half-hour time units, moving from meeting to meeting or appointment to appointment in those kinds of time frames, because their work can be broken down into discrete or separate tasks. He also describes how 'makers', such as software writers, cannot undertake their work in the same kind of time units.

Makers tend to subdivide their working day into half-day units, or set aside whole-day time divisions because as Graham says, *you can't write or program well in units of an hour ... [it is] barely enough time to get started.* There are inherent conflicts in trying to merge the two kinds of approaches to scheduling time. A 'quick half-hour meeting' in the middle of a day actually has the effect of destroying the creative process for someone in the midst of creating something. When the creative mind is at work on a project, uninterrupted time is necessary for productivity. The more a project is testing the abilities or limits of a creative person's ability or capacity, then the bigger the time slice – big things take a longer time.

Large organizations with extensive bureaucracies are inherently uncreative – unless they allow for pockets or centres of creative space. Such creative centres allow creative people to work to different patterns. Their work cultures are different compared to the organization as a whole. They have different protocols and different management methods.

The leadership challenge then becomes communication and the synchronising of differing organizational cultures. This can be achieved primarily through intelligent project management, which focuses on coordinating various deadlines and deliverables.

Creative minds meet deadlines but through different methods, whereas bureaucrats structure for uniformity in order to achieve ease of management on a large scale. In many ways they view organizations from an industrial manufacturing model. That is why they don't comprehend maker's time, nor understand why, for a creative mind to function productively; about twenty percent of their time should be for non-deadline or non-core activity.[12]

Such ways of operating are unthinkable for those whose training makes them devoted to efficiency and risk minimization. However, as we have already mentioned, if you are managing creative people, you are in the cat herding business.

HERDING CATS

An elastic leadership structure looks more like a trampoline. Creative people respond well to flexible approaches, as they will jump up and down emotionally, ideologically and in terms of energy. In the same way that the creative mind swings in the nine dimensions, anyone who leads creative people has to be able to give and flex like a trampoline. In the pursuit of this flexible approach there seem to be eight golden rules for leading creative people.

Methodology Is Elastic

Outcomes are sacred and methods are just ways of getting to what is sacred. This means that you should not be precious about your own ideas of how to do things.

Don't Fake It till You Make It

Don't try and speak a language you don't understand. If you don't know anything about music, then don't try and talk to a musician as if you know their secret language. If you don't know anything about acting, don't display the little knowledge that you got watching 'The Making of ...' on your DVD extras menu, in the vain hope you can impress your actors. They will spot you are not one of them in a heartbeat.

When you communicate with an artist about what you want, give them reference points based on the work of other creative artists whose work you like, and then let them find their own way. Be honest about what you like and don't like. Always refer to how the work in progress makes you feel, and what kind of emotional notes you want them to hit or the kind of feeling you want them to achieve.

Respect Maker's Time

Enough said.

Be There

If you want to make a contribution to a creative project then get engaged with it from the earliest stages of its production and stay engaged. Coming in right at the end and expecting massive changes to a project that has taken sixteen weeks is counter-productive. It causes deep frustration for the artist, and any changes you make can only be superficial. It is too late at the end of a project to make major structural changes.

Be committed to the process all the way through. Spend time negotiating and getting involved, particularly in the formative stages.

Influence.

Leadership equals influence. In the creative world influence is everything and position is nothing. Creative people will only respond to you if you have earned their respect. You can't force people to respect you. You don't have to be an artist to gain their respect, because they will recognize and respect you and your accomplishments in your field of expertise.

In the creative world, the entry point for influence is your technical skill. After that, an artist will make judgments about how creatively you use your skill, and adjust their level of respect for you accordingly. After that it's down to things like fame, record sales, sheer originality or having been part of the business for a long time. A reputation is built over a lifetime of work. A leader of creative people must either have creative credibility, or have what it takes to earn respect by other means. Character, integrity and good judgment are always in vogue.

If trust is the currency of collaboration, then influence is the currency of leadership. Every time you do something as a leader you are either depositing into your influence bank or making a withdrawal – either building respect or undermining it.

Every time you exert your influence in order to get someone to do something they don't want to do, you are making a massive withdrawal from your influence bank. It's okay to spend your influence this way, but make sure you're spending it on something really worthwhile.

Success.

Nobody likes the feeling of failure and nowhere is this truer than in the creative arts. Creative people live and die by their reputation. Remember: they are only as good as their last gig. If their last gig was with you and it was bad then you will have lost influence as a leader just as it has impacted their reputation. If their last gig with you was great they will come back to you again and again.

What you promise you must deliver.

> *The best work that's happened for me recently has been when I have worked with this one chap from Melbourne, (name omitted). I've done three plays with him and every play's been successful. He puts together casts that all get on well, that are nice; he doesn't like tension in the rehearsal room; everything's got to come out of the text, and everything must all tie together. I hate it when there's tension in the rehearsal room, it's totally unnecessary. You don't need to get nasty to get your own way. - Garry McDonald*

Know Them.

You must understand the creative mind and their world well enough to know that positive reinforcement and accurate affirmation are the most powerful means of getting creative people to do something. You just can't go up to them and say, 'Great job! Well done!' thinking that will do the trick. This kind of affirmation means little unless it's from a colleague, who holds an informed opinion. So get into their world, find out something about what they do and what it's like for them. Then when you say, 'Well done,' you can point to some aspect of the work that you think is good and say why.

Like culture, relationships develop depth through shared experience. That's why creative people form tribes so easily. All the dancers understand each other's world because they share the experience of dance. If you are leading creative people but are not a creative person yourself, then you have to find ways of creating shared experiences upon which the bridges of relationship can be built. In the short term you can build relationship by getting them to be a part of things that you like – but in the long term, you will have to try something that they like. You will come to learn and appreciate what things are important to them. The best relationships are a two-way street.

> **Marina Prior:** *Relationships are very complicated with creative people. And it is very tribal – because there's a ritual and things that are particular to what you do. Nobody really gets it other than the people that all do It ...*

> **Jeff:** *They identify you, don't they?*

> **Marina Prior:** *Yes ... recently we lost a really close friend, [actor and singer] Rob Guest, who was very close to me. I spoke at the funeral, and I talked about us, we got this real sense that we all came together – all these crazy sort of artist people came together, and there was this real sense that ... this is our people. This is our tribe.*

Inclusion.

You may have to cope with answering a lot of questions that other people might not ask. Accept that not every part of the process is going to be emotion free. There will be tensions and, in some cases, you may feel like every assumption you have is being questioned. That's because the creative mind sees things others don't.

If you have creative people who feel underutilized or ignored, they are probably already looking for somewhere else to go – somewhere their work is accepted and recognized. Involve them, bring them into the decision-making process. The more they know about you and your deepest motives and intentions, the better they will be able to produce for you.

We also know now that creative people have a unique and sophisticated problem-solving ability. By engaging and including them in ways that allow their creativity to flourish, you can access their cognitive creative ability.

THERE ARE TWO SIDES TO EVERY STORY

Often there's some indignation when managers and leaders discuss changing their leadership methods in ways that empower the creative mind.

"It's my way or the highway."

"These creatives are no different to anyone else; they just have to get with the program."

"Why can't they just do what they're told for once?"

"I solve problems too. Why should they get special treatment?"[13]

It's not special treatment, but it is an adaptive response to the mechanisms of the creative mind and the creative process. We now know these are quite different from conventional thinking and deductive reasoning. Secure leaders are able to recognize the questioning, and the to and fro, as normal aspects of the creative mind at work and don't feel threatened by it. Conversely insecurity makes us uncomfortable when people don't immediately fall into line.

Good For Business

Most corporate or structured work environments stem from the standard management practices that have been promoted by MBA programs worldwide for the last fifty years. In that time there have been massive shifts in the nature of work, business, corporations and the global economy. We now know that standard workplace practice negatively correlates with creativity. The kind of workplace envisioned by standard business management models actually inhibits it.[14] If you want to maximize the productivity and innovation of your creative employees the following list of workplace qualities is the 'what-not-to-do' list.

IDENTIFYING A DISEMPOWERING CREATIVE ENVIRONMENT

WORKPLACE CULTURAL FEATURES	IMPACT AND UNDERCURRENTS
Autocratic, authoritarian leadership – top down flow of information and ideas.	Limits exploration – limits creative problem solving. *Fear and spin*.
Goal-oriented behaviour is positively reinforced – behaviour that seems not to be goal oriented is frowned upon.	Limits perception in the creative process – inhibits play. *Rejection and insecurity*.
Defined set of behavioural standards – required and reinforced	Limits the discovery phase of the creative process. *Insecurity*.
Requires compliance – rewards compliance over being competent	Increases boredom – will promote confrontational and acting-out behaviour. *Insecurity*.
Inflexible structures or procedures	Antithesis to the tidal nature of the creative person; inhibits exploration and play. *Rejection*.
Competitive behaviour is rewarded among the group members	Prevents trust and therefore true collaboration. *Fear and Insecurity*.
Emotional issues are considered inappropriate or are not given consideration	Denies the tidal nature of emotions. *Rejection and insecurity*.
Risk averse: 'If it's not broken don't fix it.' 'Failure is not an option.'	Inhibits openness to experience and risk-taking. *Fear*.
Directive and commanding culture – group members asking questions is not encouraged	Inhibits cognitive exploration – fluid thinking. *Rejection*.
Laissez-faire development and training: 'Throw them in at the deep end.'	Promotes anxiety. *Fear and insecurity*.
An environment built on the seriousness of its purpose	No play, no humour, no exploration, no fluid thinking. *Fear and spin*.
Methods can't be questioned – they are unshakable because they achieve the outcome	Increases boredom. *Rejection and spin*.

Those who claim that creative people can be successfully led without paying any heed to these principles are those who offer the promise of fame and wealth as an inducement. It's a fact – if you are offering enough money or fame, you can lead creatives any way you want. But if the money or the fame is withheld, or is not forthcoming, then creative people gradually drift away and look for a better environment. Leaders who disregard cultural and relational dynamics also experience high turnover levels in their creative teams. There is a consequent long-term loss of productivity and corporate identity.

Even when offered generous financial and personal inducements, the creative mind is still looking for an empowering environment. Creatives tend to leave boring or constricting environments sooner or later. The more negative the environment the sooner they will leave. It doesn't matter how much money is on offer, many will still leave a stifling environment because no amount of money can compensate them for the loss of their creativity.

The Other Side of the Coin

It would be a mistake to regard this section as being one-sided – slanted in favour of the creative artist. The scales are more balanced than they appear. The creative mind has to produce. If creative artists don't come up with the goods, they will be overlooked next time. The arts, media and entertainment worlds don't provide easy career pathways. Make a successful feature film, perform an intense dance routine, paint a captivating canvas or write a hit song – it sounds simple but the dedication needed to gain the skills is huge, the obstacles to achievement are great and the possibility of financial security is slim. The reward of having successful creative artists in your community is that they make it a worthwhile place to be. The price is taking the trouble to engage in the give and take necessary to attract, lead and motivate them.

WHY DO THEY LEAVE?

In our discussions with people in creative management positions, a key question is often: 'Why is it that creative people keep leaving?'

They will run from a rigid and inflexible environment. They assess the situation, work out exactly how much creativity is permissible and make their decision. If the culture only pays lip service to diversity and there is a lack of authenticity, they will move on.

Creative people keep leaving because managers keep making the same mistakes. If you are leading a team of creative people ask yourself the following questions – or, if you are brave enough, ask your creative team:

- Are methods considered too important to be subject to question? Is the underlying cultural message: 'Follow my instructions to the letter?'
- Do managers try to communicate to the creative team in the language of the craft? Have they learnt the idiom or do they only know a few phrases? Is there frequent communication breakdown? Who gets the blame?
- Are there too many meetings, too many interruptions, too little maker's time?
- Do managers constantly request major changes to large-scale projects at the last minute? Are the changes they seek always possible? If things go wrong, who gets the blame?
- Do managers lead by virtue of position or authority rather than lead by relationship and influence? Do they use intimidation or manipulation to achieve short-term success?
- Do managers initially promise influence, position, accolades, creative freedom and a positive work environment in order to engage the creative team but then fail to deliver?
- Do managers put creative people in the too-hard basket and leave them on the shelf rather than investing in their personal and professional development?

SURVIVING IN A COMMERCIAL WORLD

We've written extensively about the importance of authenticity to a creative person. Feeling the truth of something is vital to the working process of a creative person, because they need it to reach deep inside themselves and use their skills to hit the right emotional note, or to tell the right story.

Of course the average commercial client doesn't care about such things. Ultimately, the CEO just wants the ad to work - measured by increased sales

– that's all that really matters. However, the creative artist who makes the ad needs to find those truths or the ad will be terrible. This is where an interpreter is important, standing between the artist and the CEO, to help them work towards finding the truth in their process.

Jeff: In my first introduction to making commercial music I was in a session and found myself feeling totally cynical about the music and the product – I couldn't play anything worthwhile. I was working with an experienced older colleague. His name was Roger Hanlon. He was a bass player and recording engineer. He stopped the tape and turned to me and I will never forget what he said.

"You've got to find something in it that you love, even if you don't love the thing itself. I've played a lot of music in my life, a lot of it I didn't like, but if you're making a living from it, nobody really cares whether you like it or not – they care whether they like it or not. My secret was I would try and find something in the music that I loved, that I could love, even if it was just the sound of my instrument. Then I would let the love that I had for that one thing fill the rest of the music, and I could play like I loved the whole thing. Just find something in it that you can believe in, something you can love, even if it's only one or two notes."

I was speechless. He turned around and pressed record. I found something in my part that I loved and the next take was a winner. It was as if Roger had taken a blindfold off me.

You can't really make something good without there being a little bit of love and truth in it somewhere. However, never forget that creative people are motivated by practicalities as well as ideas and ideals. They know the job has to be done, they know there is a deadline, they know there is a budget – but at the same time they want to be doing work that satisfies them, not just pays the bills. No matter how commercial the project, the best of them will try to find something in the work that they can believe in.

The world of the creative artist is the world of the imagination. If you mess that world up, you handicap them. That's why creative people hate a hidden agenda. As we have already described in chapter four, they hate it when they feel like they are being manipulated; it doesn't just make them feel used – it undermines their ability to know the truth.

Creative people like to be working – actively deployed, engaged in a project, or commissioned to do something. Musicians love to play; dancers love to dance; actors love performing for an audience. Using an artist is not the problem. The problem is when a leader abuses the willingness of a performer to engage their skills, life and talents in the service of a plan they were not aware of.

Be honest with them and let them know what's going on. As long as they can see good reasons for doing something, they will be on board. When they feel that they have been misled in some way – you will lose them. You mess with their imagination and their sense of the truth at your peril. Once a creative person loses trust in your truthfulness and authenticity, it is very difficult for to you to regain it.

KEY PLAYER

Creative people are also attracted to a key person. There are a number of business situations where negotiators will insist on what's called a *key man clause* being inserted into a contract. Such a clause states that they are only willing to do business with that company as long as the specified key individual remains in their position. The clause recognizes the value of that individual to the conduct of the business and its aim is to prevent a company from signing a contract and then sacking the key player.

As in business a key person in the creative arts is someone on whom the success of the enterprise depends. It is normally somebody who has a good reputation, or is highly successful – a name other creative people will want to be associated with. Young hopefuls will hope to ride to success on their coat-tails. There is a halo effect around any organization that possesses a significant key person.[15] It's as if that individual's aura of success is imparted to the organization. Others will be keen to come on board in the hope that the halo is more than an effect and that they will become successful too. If they do, it lends added weight to the attractiveness of the key player – and the organization.[16]

All influential creative communities have someone who is, at the very least, highly regarded in the creative world and influential among other creative artists. Creative people leave when they leave, and they go where they go. Creative people are attracted to projects and organizations that have a key player, and are not attracted to those that don't. Key team members are valuable in terms of hanging on to an existing creative team and attracting new talent.

MENTORS

The other reason creative people are attracted to a key player, is the possibility of being mentored by them. Almost all learning in the creative fields comes through somebody showing how to do something – the passing on of trade secrets.

The great tradition of learning to become a creative or performing artist is that of apprenticeship. The move to place creative training into dedicated institutions like the Julliard School, the Royal Academy of Dramatic Art or Frankfurt's Hoch Conservatory, is comparatively recent. Only in the last one or two hundred years have the academies, conservatories and specialist tertiary colleges really become influential. Prior to this time, performers and artists always learnt by being apprenticed to masters. Michelangelo had many apprentices – they actually did much of the less significant painting work in the Sistine Chapel.

In music and acting, young apprentices would become *journeymen,* travelling with their master on the road and learning, not only every aspect of their craft, but also every aspect of the career first-hand.

Despite the best institutional training in the world, artists and performers still value the importance of the one-to-one relationship. Mentors help us become what we wish to be. It is crucial that younger artists find wise and knowledgeable mentors. It is also crucial that experienced artists pass on their hard-won secrets eventually.

The mentor relationship is a vital aspect of collaboration. Creating an environment where mentoring can take place in the creative arts is a vital component of organizational culture.

You can't lead someone somewhere you've never been yourself. No one can show someone something that they don't know themselves. It is the role of the mentor to accomplish these tasks – particularly as the job of the creative mind is to learn how to explore new territory and find new ways of seeing and hearing.

It is at this point in our journey that we turn to the third and final strategy for moving with the creative tides.

1   Dan Wieden is a partner in US advertising agency Wieden + Kennedy. This remark was made in Doug Pray's (2009) documentary on the advertising industry.

2   Florida's assertions were published in the May 2002 issue of *Washington Monthly*.

3   For more on Richard Florida's observations go to http://www.creativeclass.com

4   *TIME* magazine lists *Blade Runner* in its 'All Time 100 Movies' as selected by critics Richard Corliss and Richard Schickel.

5   These remarks are excerpts from the 2007 documentary *Dangerous Days – Making Blade Runner*.

6   Executive producers Bud Yorkin and Jerry Perenchio were so concerned about budget over runs that they were on set when the *Tears In Rain* scene was shot, waiting to 'pull the plug'. The sequence was filmed on the open air set as dawn was approaching, with cast and crew aware that time was running out. This added pressure contributed something to the moment. The blue pre-dawn light lends an ethereal quality to Batty's final words. The crew had been shooting all night, trying to beat the deadline. No doubt this contributes to the palpable sense of exhaustion visible in Harrison Ford's performance.

7   ibid.

8   Singer, songwriter, recording engineer, producer Hugh Wilson made this remark during the *Prayerworks* recording sessions in 1998. Owing to unusually severe budget pressure, the entire album was recorded in only a day and a half. For more on these recordings see Crabtree (2008).

9   Lawrence G Paull is an art director and production designer, and was nominated for an Academy Award for Best Art Direction for *Blade Runner*.

10 British academic Joseph Needham has documented the history of Chinese innovation. China developed many original and unique versions of 'Western' technology long before any European culture. Why then did China not emerge to dominate the globe before the European nations? One explanation may be that the Chinese bureaucratic class – known as the mandarins – who became entrenched in Chinese society in the second millennium AD, stifled innovation and creative development in favour of traditional forms.

11 Paul Graham is the author of *Hackers and Painters* and writes regularly about issues that arise from the digital age. His 2009 essay 'Maker's Schedule, Manager's Schedule' can be found online at www.paulgraham.com/makersschedule. html (accessed 29/1/11).

12 See previous chapter. The twenty percent non-core principle for creative workers is not only applied at Google, but is also used at the offices of Facebook which employs a large percentage of designers and innovators (TIME magazine, December 15, 2010).

13 Some of these remarks have been excerpted from actual conversations with the authors. The first two remarks are so prevalent that we think they are now are part of the zeitgeist of management philosophy.

14 For more on this see The Effect Size of Variables Associated with Creativity: A Meta Analysis Hsen-Hsing Ma (2009).

15 This effect is not limited to creative people – it is a universal human quality.

16 In reality there are too many variables that account for success – including, dare we say it, the factor of chance – that make predicting or ensuring success much less simple than we would like to think.

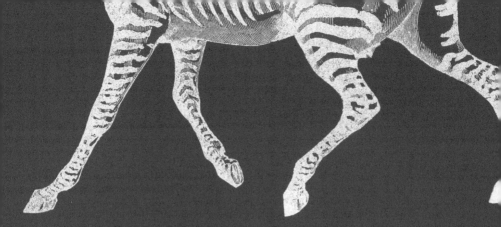

CHAPTER TEN
SPIRITUALITY

SPIRITUALITY

*CREATIVITY IS AN EXPERIENCE ... A SPIRITUAL
EXPERIENCE. IT DOES NOT MATTER WHICH WAY YOU
THINK OF IT: CREATIVITY LEADING TO SPIRITUALITY OR
SPIRITUALITY LEADING TO CREATIVITY. IN FACT, I DO NOT
MAKE A DISTINCTION BETWEEN THE TWO. IN THE FACE OF
SUCH EXPERIENCE, THE WHOLE QUESTION OF BELIEF IS
RENDERED OBSOLETE.*
- JULIA CAMERON

It is sunset, and after a day's sailing among tropical islands it's time to drop anchor for the night. We find a lee shore and calm water and slow the boat by pointing it up into the evening breeze. Once we have no headway the anchor is dropped straight overboard and the cable is payed out from the foredeck as she drifts slowly off the mark. We watch carefully to make sure the boat can swing freely; not too close to others lying at anchor, not in water that will be too shallow at low tide. When we've payed out enough rope, we secure it on the cleat, then sit back and enjoy the silence as dusk descends, watching for a while to make sure our anchor is set and doesn't drag.

An anchor is security. It keeps you in your place while still allowing you to swing freely. It keeps you from coming to harm. It is the one immovable thing that allows you to have peace of mind. If an anchor moves there is a serious problem because you can no longer rely on it for safety. Spirituality is anchor for your soul. The tides can flow, the wind can blow, but if your spiritual anchor is firmly set then all will be well.

> *We are not human beings having a spiritual experience. We are spiritual beings having a human experience.[1]* **- Pierre Teilhard de Chardin**

Renowned psychologists Chris Peterson and Martin Seligman, in their groundbreaking work *Character Strengths and Virtues*[2], refer to spirituality as something that 'allows individuals to forge connections to the larger universe and thereby provide meaning to their lives'. They specifically define it as 'beliefs and practices that are grounded in the conviction that there is a transcendent (non-physical) aspect to life. These beliefs are persuasive, pervasive and stable. They inform the kinds of attributions that people make, the meanings they construct, and the ways they conduct relationships'.

We feel compelled to include spirituality as our third strategy for moving with the creative tides, because so many creative people have spoken about its importance to their creativity. Peterson and Seligman assert that spirituality is universal and that every culture has 'a concept of an ultimate, transcendent, sacred and divine force'. They also note that the content of spirituality varies from culture to culture – indeed from person to person.

> *The aboriginals understand that ... it's about the spiritual dimension. Aboriginals believe ... [that] we're all connected - we're connected to the land. In fact we all return to the land, to the dirt. The concept is that the land is the recorder of man's passing, of people passing, the stories of man's journeys in the land and it's all about the Holy Spirit – He's all across the land, He's here, His presence is all throughout...The indigenous people understand that more than anything. When I was up in the Kimberleys, I had to go and find caves with this old fella, and he would say to me, "Little bit long way..." and after a couple of days, "One jump up, maybe two..." which is a hill. We'd walked for days and still hadn't found this thing and walked over lots of hills, and I said finally, "You've got to be kidding. I've been asking you and you keep saying 'little bit long way, one jump up, maybe two' and it's not here! Come on! What's going on?" Because that was me. And he said, "Shouldn't the journey be just as important as the destination? It's the journey that*

gives significance to whatever discovery you make." And I said, "Good point." And he said, "You must settle down and just feel the land, and you find the cave." And I'm thinking, 'I'm in the middle of nowhere, how can I find the cave? I'm in the Kimberleys, I'm going to get lost.' So he just lets me find it. And I said, "How am I going to find it?" And he said, "Just listen to the good and bad. Just feel good is this way – say, 'God, is it this way?'" I thought, 'This is insanity!' But you know what? It actually worked, it took me a little while to get into it, but I found the cave. It's a very strange thing but it's the reality. **- Ken Duncan**

We are always confronting the inexplicable and it seems this is never more so than with the experience of creativity. When artists talk about their experiences, it's surprising how many of them, even those who prefer to be considered non-religious, refer to the influence of spirituality in their work. Most of them talk about the creative process as something that defies the rational. From our own experience and from our investigations among the 'broad church' of creative artists, these inexplicable and mysterious moments are best described as spiritual.

If I knew where the good songs come from, I'd go there more often. It's a mysterious condition. It's much like the life of a Catholic nun. You're married to a mystery.[3] **- Leonard Cohen**

So many artists, like Cohen and Duncan, say that in their experience, you can't understand creativity without embracing spirituality.

This capacity to focus intensely, to dissociate and to realize an apparently remote and transcendent "place" is one of the hallmarks of the creative personality... **- Nancy Andreasen.**

This association has been supported in a study by Professor James Averill from the University of Massachusetts. He found that there is a correlation between creativity, mystical experience, and a belief in the mystical.

There are so many shared experiences among artists and creative practitioners that we will refer to the impact and influence of these experiences in the terms used by artists themselves, such as *God, creator* or *source* or the terms used by researchers: *spiritual, numinous, mystical, spirituality* and *transcendence*. These terms are universal enough to help you navigate through your own journey of living with a creative mind.

Music is God speaking to us and letting us know that he's there.[4] **- Chrissie Hynde.**

SPIRITUALITY AND CREATIVITY

Straightaway the ideas flow in upon me, directly from God.[5] - **Johannes Brahms**

I think that when you get real inspirations you are tapping something outside, beyond your normal consciousness. - **David Byrne**

Well that just seems like God to me. I mean so you could say you are assimilating things all the time, and if you just listened, you could find you have a wise point of view about things in your life. But I more enjoy thinking that I'm just listening to somebody else's ideas and then just write them down. It's probably a little of both. I like to think that spirit speaks through all of us. - **Rickie Lee Jones**.

I know a lot of people in Nashville make their living doing that. That's not my style. My stuff has to come from the Creator. It has to come from an inspirational source. - **Dan Fogelberg**.

...You're responding to a world that you're subject to. It's transcendental. It's beyond possession, it really is.[6] - **Van Dyke Parks.**

We are writing here about things that are experienced but not well understood. How do you really distinguish between a thought that has been generated from your own inner resources, or from something that is transcendent? Even those artists who are able to articulate their experiences often find it difficult to know where one thing ends and the other begins. In reality, every moment of encounter with the divine, and every moment of new perception is unique, so the distinction is probably too elusive to nail down. The moment of perception seems to come like a flash of insight from somewhere. In practice, no artist really stops to analyse whether the flash has come from within or without, they just get busy creating.

So whether these flashes of insight are transcendence, or a sudden upsurge of emotions and memory, or a combination of both, it's absolutely clear that they are so vital for initiating the creative process or progressing it when it has stalled – that the creative mind is instinctively hungry for them. Therefore, it is crucial that we do nothing to hinder such moments, and do everything we can to encourage and nurture them – or at least the ability to have them.

Perception is probably not just the product of direct thinking or direct observation. It's more likely a moment of something deeper – a mysterious interaction of direct observation, of thought and memory, and the spiritual. In fact, because of the elusive nature of these moments, a lot of creative people deliberately avoid directly thinking about their work because they believe it interferes with the mystery.

> *Usually I sit down and I go until I'm trying to think. As soon as I start thinking, I quit ... I mean that I start consciously trying to think of what I'm going to do next. Then I quit. Then when I have an idea out of nowhere, I start up again. When that idea stops, I stop. I don't force it. If it's not there, it's not there and there's nothing you can do about it.*[7] *- Neil Young*

At the perception and discovery phases of the creative process, the creative mind is reliant to a large degree on things that are not within conscious control. The part of the creative process that sets things in motion cannot be forced into occurring. An artist or performer can only wait until the moment of perception strikes. They may go searching for it, but until they find that first spark, the work they are planning to produce will stay unmade. They cannot know when or where the perception will come, or indeed, if it will come at all. Without an understanding of the transcendent, the only conclusion that the artist can reach is that their professional existence is at the whim of chance.

> *The frightening and most difficult thing about being what somebody calls a creative person is that you have absolutely no idea where any of your thoughts come from really, and especially you don't have any idea about where they're going to come from tomorrow.*[8] *- Hal Riney*

It takes a well-centred individual to live significant episodes of their professional life in a state of not knowing – a state of uncertainty – especially when it is coupled with the knowledge that they absolutely must produce something valuable in order to be able to pay the bills. It takes a strongly centred person to live as a performer, when there are periods of downtime between shows, or movies or concert tours. Sometimes there seems to be absolutely no work on the horizon and stress about finances can be crippling.

Imagine if your job was like that – working at a factory and not knowing whether anything would come down the production line, or, if it did, whether the machines would work today. It is unusually stressful not knowing from one day to the next if you will have a job or whether you will actually be able to do your job, or if all your competence and skill will suddenly and mysteriously disappear when you need them the most, only to reappear some time later when it doesn't matter.

> *[Because of my fears] I've gotten to the point where I really can't sing anymore. I'm going to have to go through some very serious physiotherapy and recovery ... to be able to sing again ... I realised that just too much suppression from the very beginning of my life ... manifested itself and closed off my voice.*[9] **- Shania Twain**

Even if you can do your job well, management might suddenly decide they don't like you and replace you with a factory worker who they think looks better, is younger or will work for less money.

> ***Hugh Laurie:*** *You know the way these things are, we could just ... any day they could just go, 'No we've had enough of this – you can go home.'*

> ***Ellen DeGeneres:*** *It's funny how you live like that, like it's a huge success. Everybody is talking about how brilliant you are and yet you're still, like, you never know ...*

> ***Laurie:*** *I'm convinced I could be fired any day, any day – yeah absolutely.*

> ***DeGeneres:*** *Well I think anybody in this business feels like that.*

> ***Laurie:*** *Probably yeah, yeah ...*

> ***DeGeneres:*** *... Cause you just never know ... all of a sudden people change their minds ...*

> ***Laurie:*** *Yeah, yeah ...*

> ***DeGeneres:*** *... All of a sudden people change their minds...*

> ***Laurie:*** *Yeah.*[10]

Constant job insecurity and the fear of imminent rejection over whim or the trends of fashion is not what most people generally thrive in. In most countries replacing a worker because there is someone younger or better looking is actually illegal. In times of economic uncertainty, however, a climate of sudden job losses recreates, for normal workers, the kind of profound stress that creative artists experience as a matter of course. Such stress and insecurity is the normal environment of the creative mind. Because fear, rejection and insecurity act to prevent the creative mind being tidal, their very working environment is one that can be inherently dangerous to their wellbeing.

A PECULIAR STRESS

In most normal occupations you can have a bad day without losing a career, and, when you have been asked to produce something on a limited budget, people will modify their expectations accordingly. Not so in the creative world. For the creative mind - work, reputation and livelihood are all dependent upon how well they performed or created the last time they did something. Audiences don't factor in budget restrictions when they listen to an album – they just hear the music and either like it or not. Career and reputation are on the line every time. Add to that the uncertainty of not knowing where or when your next good idea will come and the fact that nobody in the real world really understands you. This combination places unusual stress on any individual, let alone one possessing a mind that is a cluster of opposites. Little wonder that creative people experience such difficulty in their personal world if they fail to manage themselves well.

> *I ... have had work or ideas come through me from a source that I honestly cannot identify ... What is that thing and how are we to relate to it in a way that will not make us lose our minds, but in fact might actually keep us sane?[11]*
> **- Elizabeth Gilbert**

The high incidence of mental health problems among the creative community is not just evidence of the creative mind and the creative process being poorly understood. It is evidence that, ultimately, the artist needs the metaphysical – the existence of a spiritual reality that can help anchor identity and make meaning of the world.

Attempting a life of creative productivity without being able to fill the well from somewhere transcendent can lead to a kind of metaphysical torment. Perhaps the high rates of depression and bipolar disorder that have been documented among creative people are evidence of this.[12] Without a lifeline to a larger reality - a larger meaning than just flesh and blood existence or skill and technique, a creative life can be filled with torment. Psychiatrist Viktor Frankl developed an entire therapy on this assumption, based on his experiences in a WWII concentration camp. He observed that those who had a meaning to their lives – something to live for – were more likely to survive the camps than those who didn't.[13] A recent study showed that if you are a successful professional musician in the contemporary pop and rock music genres, you are nearly twice as likely to die prematurely compared to the population as a whole. What we have dismissed as the 'rock and roll lifestyle' is really a symptom of a deeper malaise. The writers of that study concluded that pop stars suffer high levels of stress and this, combined with risk-taking behaviour and the availability of drugs and alcohol, was causing high mortality rates.[14] How can anyone establish how much of the behaviour we label 'artistic temperament' is, in fact, a search for meaning and significance beyond material and financial gain? Although impossible to quantify, a common thread among those who 'have it all' is that, once they get there, they find themselves still unfulfilled at the deepest level of their soul.

I think there was a little bit of emptiness in our souls, a lack of spiritual fulfilment.[15]
- Paul McCartney

The pressure of fame is an unusual pressure. Novelist Elizabeth Gilbert described how her success as a writer created unusual psychological pressure on her that exposed her to high levels of anxiety. She too advocates that creative people need to embrace the existence of the spiritual as an antidote to these stresses and to avoid a descent into mental ill health. Dealing with significant acclaim is something that the human mind does not seem to cope with well.

I have to create some sort of protective psychological construct ... find some sort of way to have a safe distance between me as I am writing and my very natural anxiety about what the reaction to that writing is going to be from now on.
- Elizabeth Gilbert

For hundreds of years, the accepted view of creativity was that it had a spiritual component; the gods revealed things to the artists who then brought them into being. Artists had a disembodied spirit called a 'genius' that would gift them with ideas. It was during the Renaissance that some major shifts in thinking occurred in Western Europe. One of these was a change in how we saw the place of individual human beings in the cosmos. Instead of being a small part of the universe, the individual came to be regarded as the centre of things. Instead of humanity being the jewel of creation, God the creator was relegated to the sidelines and the individual elevated to a position that was formerly the province of the divine. This philosophical leap had the side effect of shifting the sole responsibility of the creative process onto the human frame. Rather than being a channel for something universal, the artist was the progenitor. Rather than being influenced by a 'genius', the artist became the genius. This fundamental shift is nowhere better illustrated than in the way the meaning of the word 'genius' came to be attached to a person rather than the divine.

As this new world view took hold throughout Western civilization, so too did mental and emotional distress among creative artists. The concept of 'artistic temperament' once recognized, gradually became more commonplace until eventually it was expected behaviour for an artist. During and after the Renaissance, art and artists were elevated to a valued place in society. In hindsight, the additional burden of such social prominence posed unusual stresses on the already complex creative mind. The demands of always having to produce another successful performance (or work) and the pressure of acclaim had massive impact on people who were already skinless, and suffered from wild swings of self-esteem. As a consequence of these unfamiliar stresses, egos became warped and distorted trying to cope. So the artistic temperament became acceptable behaviour, even a sign of greatness, in our collective thinking. In any other group such eccentric or outrageous behaviour would have been socially and professionally unacceptable.

Living the creative life without a spiritual dimension is too great a responsibility to place on the human mind. As a result, creative people experience unusual stress. We believe that the solution to this problem of living with a creative mind is to embrace the spiritual dimension. The creative mind has to realize that there are elements of their work that do not strictly depend on them, but on a bigger, transcendent reality – what some people call God. We described previously how essential it is for an artist to draw their identity from something other than their work. A belief in the spiritual undermines the power of insecurity, because identity is no longer drawn from the material but from the mystical. If the creative mind must run with the tides, it needs an anchor – something that will allow movement but prevent it drifting away totally or running aground. Spirituality is that anchor, because it is universal and pervasive. A spiritual reality is greater than any single problem, issue or concern about identity. It is the way an artist can find meaning in their life and work when assailed by the 'slings and arrows of outrageous fortune'.[16]

Spirituality anchors against the undercurrents.

ANCHORING THE CREATIVE MIND

I can't take credit for this stuff. I've been successful too long. I'm only human and these things are the makings of God ... I'd be stupid to say that there is no other force than my own that is guiding me through this ... It's possible to connect with the creative source by thinking right and being right ... And you'll tap into all these positive forces.[17] **- Lamont Dozier**

It's easy to see how and why a creative person runs aground. Not letting one tide of any single dimension become dominant is a challenge. In the face of pressure to perform, it is easier to gravitate to inflated ego to avoid the confidence sapping state of being deflated. In the face of the pressure of coming up with new ideas, and finding the flash of insight, it is easier to gravitate to risk action and to skinless sense, rather than potentially affect perception. Similarly, the pressure to produce makes it easier for the artist to stay as long as possible at manic energy rather than suffer a possible loss of productivity by spending too much time at still.

If you never happened to believe in the first place that the most extraordinary aspects of your being came from you, but maybe if you just believed that they were on loan to you, from some unimaginable source for some exquisite portion of your life to be passed along ... if we think about it this way, it starts to change everything. **- Elizabeth Gilbert.**

When the creative mind becomes anchored in a transcendent reality, he or she is no longer dependent solely on their own resources to continue being creative. This reduces performance stress. It means that fear and rejection lose much of their power because they become transitory experiences rather than defining ones. A spiritual reality means that something greater than other people's opinions define us. Negative opinions, worries and social threats can then be held at a distance. It brings a realisation that the creative work can have a meaning and purpose beyond personal motivations. Spirituality is also the perfect context for entering the last stage of the journey to creative maturity.[18]

The belief that we are a part of something more significant than the physical world anchors the creative mind by forging 'connections to the larger universe'.[19] Every life event, either positive or catastrophic can be understood from a framework that helps us find purpose and value in the ordinary and the extraordinary. It impacts how and why we relate to others. Even the power of spin is diminished by a spiritual connection – a larger view of the universe enables us to discern the fine line between truth and artifice.

WHAT SPIRITUALITY DOES: OF TIDES AND ANCHORS

The Spiritual And Identity

There is an indescribable relief in knowing that it is not *all about you* and *not all up to you*. This can only come from a belief in something or someone bigger. It comes when creativity is not solely entwined with identity. It means that the artist's inflated ego has a place to rest, where they don't have to perform, or be 'on': the centre of attention, or be noticed. It allows for the acknowledgement that we are not the centre of the universe.

The anchor of spirituality makes fear of failure far less incapacitating, and prevents the creative person from being pulled into the black pit of depression and self-condemnation. In fact, the deflated ego can become attractive, because of the change in perspective it brings and the possibilities for different perception. It is refreshing working with other artists who don't react by always swinging defensively into their inflated egos. It makes collaboration nowhere near as difficult.

The creative artist is then free to confront society out of a place of principle and idea rather than a personal sense of injustice or self-aggrandisement. The art becomes less cathartic, less of an exercise in self-therapy and becomes more about challenging the established and the accepted. In a healthy way, it can push everyone else's world into seeing and sensing differently. It gives freedom for the artist to be who and what they were meant to be.

Spirituality And Risk

Risk can often be satisfied in a spiritual encounter as opposed to exploring other potentially more harmful avenues. Paul McCartney's biographer cited George Harrison's discovery that a spiritual life replaced the need for drug taking.20 However, Harrison is only one of many who have found that faith is an important key that unlocks a way of managing their creative lives. Some have even written entire books about it, the most notable being Elizabeth Gilbert's memoir *Eat, Pray, Love* – but she is far from being alone. Writers such as Julia Cameron, Steven Pressfield and Kenny Werner all describe how mystical encounters are a way of opening up new experiences that lead to new discoveries. It may seem counterintuitive, but the stillness of a meditation or a prayer might well be the high-risk option when faced with a looming deadline and nothing but a blank canvas, blank tape or empty page in front of you.

> *The whole idea of spiritual practice is to teach you how to be right there in the moment. The more you can be there in the moment the more your problems seem to dissipate – your problems aren't as great.* **- Garry McDonald**

On Being Brave

> *I have a spiritual life, therefore [performing] actually doesn't define me. That's why I can be brave with it ... everything doesn't hang on it ... therefore I can be kind of careless and brave at the same time.* **- Marina Prior**

An identity anchored in spirituality, rather than in success or accolade can lead to work that is brave and full of innovation. What follows is from our interview with songwriter, performer, author and speaker Chris Falson.

> *I like the way Paolo Coelho... talks about how the universe conspires for you to find your destiny... I really identify with that, the sense of the universe leading me on a journey – I grew up in a musical family my parents were both busy... but having a guitar... learning to sit there and play two chords... just dreaming. Years later...[a spiritual mentor] he saw me play somewhere... in his own language he was saying – that was a spiritual moment... – and I thought "Wow I was doing that when I was 13..." and I didn't really feel spiritual but I felt like it really helped me dream and imagine.*

My mother equates my whole life as...”You jump out of airplanes with no parachute and you expect to land in a haystack.” I realize I do that. I was playing in Switzerland... to a crowd of people that I kind of know...and it’s a sold out show and all of a sudden I have this incredible nervousness... and so I go away to a quiet place and just be still for a moment...and so I’m going to go out there and make up a song on the spot...I don’t know what I did but...I’m making it up...and after that it was good...

Without the possibility of failing, I think for me, the joy of doing a thing is gone

Spirituality eases the pressure for acceptance, and the pressure to be constantly responsible for innovation. The emotional weight of these things is no longer solely on the shoulders of the individual.

SPIRITUALITY IN THE CREATIVE PROCESS

Spirituality feeds the creative process.

A transcendent encounter creates perception, changes discovery and alters production because heightened awareness and unique shifts in perspective are a part of an engagement with the spiritual.[21] Some spiritual encounters involve deep experiences of peace, or feelings of being lifted up or removed from the physical world. Some encounters involve visions and dreams and the impression of having been in communion with a higher plane of existence. We once asked Jon Lord, keyboardist for seminal heavy rock band Deep Purple about this.[22]

Jeff: *Where does the music come from?*

Jon Lord: *Oh! My God! Oh! (Looks around uncomfortably, shifts in his seat, looks up, looks back, laughs, shakes his head) Ah ... from up there? From somewhere, I don’t know, I don’t really know, but it comes from somewhere, and when it comes through me I’m really glad that it does. ...*

When the unique make-up of the creative mind encounters the transcendent, the result is often a perception. Sometimes the circumstances cause the creative process to progress fluidly and rapidly.

Jeff: In one instance I remember playing in a piano bar in the early

1990s. While I was performing one song, I could simultaneously hear (in my imagination) snatches of another entirely original song, which I remembered enough of to be able to write completely later on. During the writing phase for the first Doctor Bob live recording[23], I remember, some months from the deadline and with only a third of the songs written, that I wasn't worried about writing all the songs for the album, because I could 'see' the songs lined up, as it were, like planes in the night sky lining up for their final approach to an airport. I felt no pressure because it seemed to me that I just had to get in the right spiritual zone to bring the songs in to land one after the other, like aeroplanes.

So powerful is this experience of composing that we know many musicians who actively seek the same kind of spiritual zone from which to compose. Not knowing everything about a song or a piece of music can be a powerful aspect of its writing. The recording sessions from the work of a band called *Prayerworks*[24] deliberately sought to create an environment of spiritual engagement. All the participants in the recording considered that aspect of the process to be crucial to the success of the music.

> *... we prayed, we played – and in a day and a half it was on tape. We didn't set out to create a functional thing out of this music; it was more an expression of the connection of the soul and the spirit ...*[25]

> *At midday on Thursday 21 August 2003 this music didn't exist. By 10 pm four days later it did. Miracles happen ... we partner with each other as musicians and we partner with the Divine ...*[26]

The musicians all felt that the spiritual environment and the improvisational approach to the recording process meant that they were in touch with something bigger than just them. At the conclusion of the third, and ultimately final, take on one of the tracks from the *Breathe* album, the guitarist was observed to be weeping. He later explained that during that take he had 'heard music' but was unable to play it.[27] On most of the sessions from the first two albums at least, the takes were selected partly on the basis of a somewhat indefinable quality that was talked about by the players later - saying that they had 'gone somewhere' during a particular take.[28] It is hard to articulate a spiritual encounter without resorting to this kind of language. Moments like these are highly prized though.

Visual artist and music producer Brian Eno, who was intimately involved in the making of the 2009 U2 album *No Line on the Horizon,* used similar language to describe the inexplicable in the recording sessions. Eno reports that the song *Moment of Surrender* began only with a loop of his making, which he was trying to fix up because, to his mind, it was flawed. Drummer Larry Mullens Jr. then started playing something that immediately put the loop in sudden focus, and 'made it right somehow'. The rest of the band picked up their instruments and spontaneously began to add to what was being played. There followed a brief discussion about a few technical details, and then they started playing the song – literally from out of nowhere. The finished track was recorded in that moment and on the first take. Eno considers the song his favourite on the album, and describes it as 'the most magical experience [he has] ever had in a studio'.[29] Eno describes himself as an atheist, and someone who believes that there is no higher power in the universe.[30] He is an extraordinarily intelligent and articulate person yet, in the interview that was posted on the U2 website, he struggled to accurately describe this experience. Strangely, he found himself using language that is common when trying to describe the feeling of being a part of something bigger - something beyond present material reality.

> *So we're all playing ... and completely in the spell of this piece of music. I've never played like that in my life ... I'm a terrible keyboard player, but when I listen to that I think, 'God, was that me?' I'm really proud of it ... how did I know to do all that without any prior agreement?*
>
> *It finished and there was just complete silence, nobody said a thing. Cause it was so ... (sighs) dear where have we just been? It was really like one had been on an emotional adventure of one kind. I remember Bono said, 'I usually think we go into the studio to find music ... I felt this time it found us,' and it really was like that.*
>
> *Do you know this thing they talk about: channelling ... well that's actually what it felt like. It didn't feel like me sitting there, playing, making decisions. I wasn't making any decisions really ... my fingers happened to be part of it ... it seemed to be separate from my will somehow.* **- Brian Eno**

Despite his scepticism about 'channelling', Eno accepted that what had happened was something out of his normal experience. His choice of words, and the sort of experience he describes are hauntingly similar to the Prayerworks' experience of making music by embracing the transcendent.

Writer's Block

Embracing the spiritual dimension also helps with creative blockages too. The awful terrors of writer's block (or stage fright) can be diminished when the artist or performer feels that they are not relying solely on themselves for successful performance or for a creative source.

> Jeff: One morning I heard a short melodic phrase, which I immediately realized was a signature motif for a song that was as yet unwritten. I made some quick notes about it so the idea wouldn't be lost, but I didn't have time to work on it that day. For the next three years I tried in vain to write the rest of the song. Each attempt was met with frustration. I knew that the song was waiting for me to write it, but no music I was writing was actually living up to what I felt the song should be. I was in the studio one afternoon having tried again to write something and, in my frustration, I sat on the floor and prayed. It was no special prayer, more like a long sustained complaint to God that I couldn't write this song. I immediately had a sense of knowing deep within me that I had not yet been through what I needed to go through to write the song. I gave up trying to write it and shelved all my notes and scratch tracks. Fast forward – two years later I was producing music for another project, and in the midst of it I felt a sudden urge to write the song that I had given up on. More than that, I felt a sense of release – I was now ready. The intervening period had been extremely challenging for me on a personal level, and so, in hindsight, I understood that I needed to have lived through those hard years in order to write *Perpetual Motion*.[31]

Normally artists are frightened by creative blockages. However, the spiritual dimension allows the writer or performer to see blockages or anxieties in terms of the transcendent. Therefore a blockage is not necessarily a blockage – it may well become leverage for an alternative perception. Instead of the frustration and fear of feeling blocked they can engage the spiritual dimension through prayer or meditation. In a similar vein to the story of *Perpetual Motion*, songwriter and recording artist Tom Waits actually talks to his creative source. He 'prays', for want of a better word, particularly when he gets a sudden new perception at an inconvenient moment, such as when he is stuck in traffic on the freeway. He has even asked his 'source' to hold on until he gets home.[32]

Such experiences seem incomprehensible to rational thinking, and yet they occur. Some artists believe that these moments are a glimpse of God or a glimpse of the transcendent.

Stage Fright

For actors, dancers, musicians and vocalists, stage fright or performance anxiety is a crippling phenomenon. The fight/flight/freeze reaction pumps them with adrenaline. All performers report that this is important in preparation for a performance. The adrenaline speeds up their senses and sharpens physical responses. Somehow the performer has to achieve a curious balance between having the adrenaline rush – and yet retaining a calmness that comes from being what most performers describe as *centred*. However, many performers suffer from far more than the initial 'fight' response and its adrenaline rush. They experience such a level of fear that it is disabling, pushing them into the freeze response. When the fear of performance is very pronounced, the chemical inrush can be so overwhelming it prevents any hope of calm. British actor Laurence Olivier suffered from stage fright in the latter part of his career and asked other actors not to make eye contact for fear it might make him forget his lines.[33] For vocalists, performance fear can have a debilitating effect on the entire musculature needed for vocal articulation, from the abdominal muscles through to the vocal chords, causing an inability to breathe properly and accurately control tone and pitch, even though, in rehearsal, they experience no difficulties. Accessing the spiritual dimension prior to performance is a way of managing performance anxiety.

A more experienced performer really helped me with my stage fright. He taught me to breathe and pray and to think about my performance as a contribution to music that is bigger than just myself. Just before I go on stage I look for my God space and just pray. I go into a corner and start to pray and I speak out the things I want to come out of the performance – I get such a peace from that. Then when I go out on stage it gets very surreal; I sort of become another person and get a kind of numb feeling that takes away the insecurity – so that I can perform with emotion and no fear. When I get that feeling I know it is a good performance. - MV

Skinlessness and the Spiritual

Spirituality is critical for the highly skinless. It forms a part of the protective clothing that the creative mind can put on for insulation. Our stories from skinless artists reflect how important spirituality has been in helping them manage the dimension of sense.

> *I also know that I can't afford to live a sloppy lifestyle. I need healthy food, nine hours of good sleep, and exercise. Being a spiritual person I need to spend alone time with God, which seems to just strengthen my protective layers around me. I know when I get that empty/disconnected awareness inside that I have to withdraw and rest.[34]*

The need for sensory protection following a skinless episode can be met in a spiritual place, a practice or community. A spiritual retreat is just such a method. It is like taking time out to repair from being skinless and to help the shift to being insulated. Mature artists understand the need for taking this kind of time out.

> *It's the thing of resting I think is so important... In the middle of the busy time it's the quietness. Learning to be quiet - I live in a very noisy part of the world... Hollywood Hills East ... but its so noisy and so loud, that – where is quietness? Part of me escapes. I go to Santa Barbara with some friends and I can hide in their little orchard ... and it's a wonderful escape, or I go walk in the woods. But it's a learning thing about finding quietness in the noise. So ... I got rid of television and I don't listen to radio too much and I don't read the papers too much and so there is that lack of noise, or voices in my head, but also its that inner quietness and just being still. So on a spiritual level that's like being still and waiting on God-* **Chris Falson.**[35]

SPIRITUAL DISCIPLINES THAT ANCHOR

The problem with the transcendent is that, for most people, a spiritual encounter is a wonderful but fleeting thing. The phrase a 'glimpse of God' is not uncommon and, for many, the idea of even having one such encounter seems beyond the realms of possibility. Many creative people who acknowledge its importance in their lives still regard it as fragile and transient – although amazing. However, there are personal disciplines that can strengthen spiritual consciousness, even without the experience of a numinous encounter.

We are not going to present any startling new method for building a spiritual life. Humankind has known for a long time how to be spiritual.

- Prayer and/or meditation.
- Acts of devotion – worship, pilgrimage or reverence.
- Reading sacred literature.
- Communion with like-minded others. Meeting together in a corporate context.
- A periodic retreat from everyday life.
- Acts of selflessness – giving or helping others in need.

Practices such as prayer and meditation can help protect the creative mind mentally, by anchoring fluid thinking. Rapid, fluid thinking – particularly when it is fuelled by any anxiety, can be like an out of control train ready to plunge over an abyss into obsession, worry, fear, panic and anxiety.

For many creative people their often and unspoken prayer is "Dear God, please don't let me screw up!"

Ultimately we all need to find our own, personal way to communicate with the divine, but to start you on your journey, here is a way to begin.

A MEDITATION FOR LIVING WITH A CREATIVE MIND

PRAY	MEDITATE
To the divine through a personal relationship	On God – a creator bigger than you
For divine purposes to come to pass	Accept that we are never actually in control
For creative perception to come	On letting go of being the source of your creativity
For forgiveness for yourself - for others	Release intense emotions - forgive others
To be kept from harm	On letting go of fear and rejection
Thankfulness	On being authentic, and truthful

The Artist's Prayer

Creator God,

Let it be Your way not mine.

Be my source,

Let me be open.

Let me see, feel and dream,

And not take credit for your creative breath.

Forgive me and release me.

Help me forgive others and release them.

Preserve and protect me,

And surround me with love.

Thank you*

*For the gift of...(dance, writing, music, film – whatever)

Growth means change and change involves risk, stepping from the known to the unknown. [36]
- Anonymous.

1   The Phenomenon of Man (1955).

2   *Character Strengths and Virtues* is intended to be a handbook and classification of positive human qualities in the same way that the *Diagnostic Statistical Manual IV* is a handbook and classification of abnormal and pathological behaviour for mental health workers. Peterson and Seligman say that their book 'focuses on what is right about people and specifically about the strengths of character that make the good life possible'.

3   Leonard Cohen is a Canadian-born poet, novelist and singer/songwriter with a creative output that spans 50 years. He wrote some of the most influential songs in the singer/songwriter era of the 60s and 70s and is still writing and producing collaboratively.

4   Hynde made this remark in her interview with Andrew Zuckerman in his 2010 book *Music*.

5   This quote from Brahms is cited by Julia Cameron in *The Artist's Way*

6   Parks, Fogelberg, Jones and Byrne were originally interviewed by Paul Zollo in *Songwriters On Songwriting*.

7   Neil Young's solo career as a songwriter extends from the 1960s to the present. He was also a member of Crosby, Stills, Nash and Young.

8   Hal Riney was the founder of Publicis & Hal Riney an advertising agency in San Francisco.

9   Shania Twain attributes the loss of her ability to sing to the trauma of her divorce. She made this claim during an interview broadcast in 2011 on CTV.

10 This extract is from an interview with Hugh Laurie broadcast on the *Ellen DeGeneres Show* at an undetermined date. The interview segment was uploaded to the web on 13 March 2007.

11 This quote is from Elizabeth Gilbert's address on nurturing creativity to the TED conference in 2009.

12 This claim is supported in detail by the writing of Schildkraut, Hirshfeld, & Murphy, J. in their 1996 chapter entitled 'Depressive Disorders, Spirituality and Early Deaths in the Abstract Expressionist Artists of the New York School.'

13 Viktor Frankl's account of his Holocaust survival and his subsequent observations can be found in the book *Man's Search for Meaning*.

14 This study was conducted by Mark Bellis et. al and was published in the *Journal of Epidemiology and Community Health*.

15 Biographer Barry Miles quotes McCartney as referring to the time just prior to manager Brian Epstein's death when The Beatles were at the pinnacle of their success. *Sgt. Pepper's Lonely Hearts Club Band* had just been released to critical acclaim.

16 From the 'To be or not to be' soliloquy in *Hamlet* Act III Scene 1.

17 Lamont Dozier is an American songwriter and record producer, best known for his work in crafting the hit music of Motown Records in the 1960s. The full version of this interview can be found in *Songwriters on Songwriting*.

18 See the chapter entitled *Living It*.

19 Petersen, C. & Seligman, M. (2004) *Character Strengths and Virtues*.

20 For more on this see Barry Miles's book *Paul McCartney: Many Years from Now*.

21 This idea is widely attested to in numerous books and in diverse religious contexts.

22 This exchange occurred during a public forum at the Sydney Opera House when Jon Lord was in Sydney in 2003 for a live performance of musical works released on the album entitled *Pictured Within*.

23 *The Doctor Is In, Doctor Bob And The Amazing Disciples of Groove* (Token Resistance Music, 1995)

24 Four albums have been made under this soubriquet: *Prayerworks* (1998), *Breathe* (2000), *Flight* (2001) and *True* (2003). For more on these recordings see Crabtree (2008).

25 This quote is from the liner notes of *Prayerworks* by Prayerworks.

26 This quote is an extract from the liner notes from *True* by Prayerworks.

27 This remark was made by a band member during personal communication with the authors.

28 This remark was made during personal communication with the authors.

29 The full interview with Eno is entitled *Brian Eno's Moment of Surrender* and was posted on U2.com on February 17, 2009.

30 For more on Eno's beliefs see *An unpublished Brian Eno interview* online at http://music.hyperreal.org/artists/brian_eno.

31 *Perpetual Motion* was released in 2002 on the second Doctor Bob live album, *Therapy*.

32 This account of Tom Waits was related by Elizabeth Gilbert in her TED conference address.

33 This is mentioned in the Internet Movie Database biography of Olivier http://www.imdb.com/name/nm0000059/bio (accessed 3/3/11)

34 A respondent in our surveys made this remark. This person is a visual artist and wishes to remain anonymous.

35 This is an excerpt from an exclusive interview granted to the authors by songwriter Chris Falson.

36 This quote was cited by William Young in his 2007 book *The Shack*.

WHAT NOW?

We believe that human creativity is one of the primary ways we will prosper in the twenty-first century. If we look back only thirty years, the social, political scientific and technological differences are enormous –the rate of change has been dramatic. No one in 1980 could have predicted the way the world is today: the global connectedness of the internet; the shift in armed conflicts away from huge armies towards small bands of insurgents who can paralyse governments; the disappearance of nations and the birth of others; and the moral dilemmas posed by genetic engineering – to name but a few. No one could have dreamt that an entire CD collection could be stored on a device not much bigger than a credit card. In the face of all this change, one thing is certain – no one has any idea what the world will be like thirty years from now. It is only the extraordinary power of creativity to dream up new ways of doing things that will enable us to adapt to the coming changes.

Strangely, we don't really teach creativity in our schools, although it may well be the one human quality that is most valuable in terms of future-proofing us against our own mistakes. It seems to us that some of the greatest creative developments of recent times have been made by those who rebel against the system, rather than submitting to it: these rebels are proof of the importance of ideas that challenge and confront.

What we recognize as a creative profession has also changed over recent times. The concept of a creative artist, which used to denote a small, elite group of painters, musicians, actors and dancers, now includes many practitioners of what were once thought of as the technical professions. We have witnessed the rise of geek creativity. In the digital age software engineers, filmmakers, choreographers and musicians often find themselves working together due to the convergence of technologies. The Carpenters 1970 hit song *We've Only Just Begun* was originally composed as part of a television advertising campaign for a bank. It went on to become one of *Rolling Stone* magazine's 500 greatest songs of all time. Who knows where convergence will take us next, but don't dismiss the quiet guy or girl with glasses and no social life sitting alone at the front of your classroom – they could well turn out to be the saviour of the new economy.

Whatever problems we all have to face in the future, the solution lies buried deep inside someone's creativity. Maybe that someone is you. Our hope for you all is that you will be not just produce, and produce over a long life, but that you will be profoundly satisfied with the journey.

Living With A Creative Mind – What's Next In This Series?

Living With A Creative Child

The Creative Process

We will update Julie's research online across all of our websites (see page 304).

The Zebra Collective

We wrote over 180,000 words for this book in its first version – and we knew that we wanted to print something much shorter than that! So we culled and cut back on a lot of our stories, as well as some of our big ideas. Instead we are making that content available online. The Zebra Collective is our solution to the many enquiries we have received for this material and for additional content about creativity, being more creative – and surviving it! Please visit www.zebracollective.com to find out how to subscribe to our daily emails and weekly posting of new content.

Zebra Collective is more than just a place for you to hear about our ideas and future publications. We are extending to anyone who joins the collective the opportunity to not just hear the latest material we are working on. We are sourcing the insights of creative professionals worldwide, which we are interviewing exclusively for the Zebra. Eventually members will be able to contribute to the ongoing discussion about living creatively. Eventually you will be able to upload your own videos, leave comments and tell us your stories.

We anticipate running Zebra collective gatherings in various locations around the world – but for that you will need to be on our site, or on our Facebook pages.

Zebra Psychology

We run offer a range of therapeutically based services for creative people including 6-week programs on applications of Living With A Creative Mind. The first of these: Living With A Creative Mind - Building Mental Resilience is now available. Check website for details: www.zebrapsychology.com

FINALLY...

This book has been written out of a love for creative people. There is deep satisfaction in seeing parents of creative children suddenly 'get it', and creative artists sigh with relief. The realization that they belong among a not so normal community of like-minded creative types is a huge relief.

Our desire is for a shift in society's attitudes towards creative artists and performers that leads to a change in behaviour. In particular we are concerned about how they have become viewed as an expendable commodity.

Dancers, actors and musicians are frequently seen as disposable. All too often imaginative and enthusiastic graphic designers are driven to crippling depression and performance managed out. We believe there is a better way. We believe that managing the creative mind well is not just more ethically sound, but also more commercially sensible.

If you are a creative mind or find yourself living or working with one as a partner or colleague, look after that creative mind – nurture it, nourish it and see what emerges from the garden of that unique imagination.

www.zebracollective.com

www.livingwithacreativemind.com

www.zebrapsychology.com

www.facebook.com/zebracollective

www.facebook.com/livingwithacreativemind

GLOSSARY

Action (the dimension of) – our willingness to pursue new experiences, and the lengths we are prepared to go to in order to have them.

Amygdala – the part of the brain associated with strong emotions also processes our memory of strong emotional reactions. Part of the Limbic System.

Anxiety – fear, worry, uneasiness and dread that occur in the absence of any immediate threat.

Attitude (the dimension of) – the way we orient ourselves towards our social groupings. How important is that group to us? How do we feel about what the group is like?

Behaviour – the way we act because of what we think and believe - what everyone else sees when they see us.

Big C Creativity – eminent level creativity.

Bipolar Disorder – Manic-depressive disorder is also called bipolar disorder. It is a condition that can be characterised by extreme highs and extreme lows.

Calm (Emotion) – the state of being free from agitation.

CBT – Cognitive Behavioural Therapy

Chaos (Space) – an apparent lack of structure, system, reason or order.

Cognition – the process of knowing and thinking.

Cognitive Behavioural Therapy – is a therapeutic approach that aims to solve a range of dysfunctional conditions using amongst other methods, a systematic reframing of the way we interpret events, and also a systematic reprogramming of our responses.

Conforming (Attitude) – the belief that we need to adjust and adapt our behaviour to become part of a group.

Confronting (Attitude) – the belief that we should openly address flaws and faults in a group, in the hope of bringing change.

Creative Process – the way we are creative. Creativity is not a magical thing, it is an active and dynamic process that we can engage in or disengage from. It has three parts: *perception, discovery* and *production.*

Creative Tides – the natural cycle that occurs in a creative person between the more manic-like poles of a dimension, and the more depressive-like poles. The cycle of highs and lows.

Deflated (Ego) – a diminished sense of self confidence and self worth.

Depression – is a condition in which someone's mood, thoughts and behaviour are consistently and abnormally low or negative. It can include feelings of hopelessness, worthlessness and the belief that nothing will ever be good again.

Dimension – a way of describing a specific human quality that avoids dealing with absolutes. We exhibit varying amounts or levels of a particular aspect. A dimension is a continuum that goes from one extreme to its polar opposite of a particular quality.

Discovery – that part of the creative process that has been previously thought of as incubation of an idea. It's the mulling around on the inside of a perception. It is where ideas are referenced, memory banks trawled through, beliefs consulted, experiences are weighed up. Formulations are developed and rearranged.

Driven – obsessed by the need to complete a task, or accomplish a goal in the belief that doing so will remove the fear or anxiety felt by the individual.

Ego (the dimension of) – our sense of self, self image, self esteem and importance to the world around us.

Emotion (the dimension of) – our immediate display of feelings.

Energy (the dimension of) – the amount of physical, emotional and mental resources we have to apply to life at any given time.

Fixated – to be unable to shift from a pole.

Fixed – to become stuck at a pole. To lose the willingness or ability to go with the creative tides.

Flow – a state of complete and highly motivated focus on a task - where someone is totally immersed in and energized by something. To achieve flow one must be challenged by the task (but not so much as to cause fear) and yet have sufficient depth of skill to meet the challenge (but not so much as it to appear too easy). Flow is an idea proposed by psychologist Mihaly Csikszentmihalyi.

Fluid (Thought) – the rapid flight of ideas that creates new links between concepts and things.

Focus (the dimension of) – our field of perception or our field of awareness. We are incapable of being fully conscious of every single event that is happening around us, so we selectively tune our awareness, or our attention to focus on things.

High Tide (Pole) – the end point of a dimension that is more typically associated with manic-like qualities.

Identity – our idea of who we really are. What we believe about ourselves.

Inflated (Ego) – a disproportionately high sense of self worth, bordering on narcissism – but not narcissism.

Insulated (Sense) –A state of self protection from overwhelming sensory input.

Intense (Emotion) – the experience of feeling passionate emotions.

Low Tide (Pole) – the end point of a dimension that is more typically associated with depressive-like qualities.

Limbic System – a set of parts in the brain that are thought to work together to process emotion, behaviour, long term memory, smell and social awareness. Includes parts of the brain that control blood pressure, heart rate, hunger, thirst, sexual arousal, the sleep/wake cycle and the way we selectively pay attention to our external world.

Little C Creativity – the more everyday kind of creativity.

Mania – abnormally high levels of mood, energy and thought processes.

Manic (Energy) – Unusually high and sustained levels of physical, emotional and mental activity.

Mood – our underlying emotional state or our longer lasting emotional state.

Narcissism – a pathological self-absorption marked by vanity, egotism and an inability to have normal care and regard for others.

Numbness – the state of not feeling anything, in circumstances when it is normal to feel something. Linked to sensory shutdown.

Obsessive Behaviour – repetitive ways of behaving that are not rationally based. When people act from inner compulsions in an attempt to reduce fear and anxiety.

Order (Space) – a high level of structure, system and planning.

Perception – that part of the *creative process* that has been previously thought of as the moment of inspiration or flash of insight. While it can be these things, it is more correctly thought of as a new way of seeing or feeling something. It can be a new realization. It often occurs unexpectedly.

Poles – the opposite and end points in a dimension, e.g. hot and cold, smooth and rough, cool and uncool and so on.

Production – that part of the *creative process* where the creative work materializes. Something is getting produced. When the paint goes on the canvas, when the red light is on in the recording studio, when the performers start to rehearse, and when they go on stage.

Resilience – the ability to recover readily from intense emotional pressure.

Risk (Action) – the willingness to explore and push boundaries to the extent that they may pose a threat and lead to negative consequences.

Safety (Action) – the need to make choices which preserve physical and relational health and well being, to minimise threat and optimise positive consequences.

Schematic (Thought) – convergent, conceptual, reasoned, literal, asserting, rational and planned thinking.

Sense (the dimension of) – how deeply we feel and experience the sensations of life.

Sensory Shutdown – the loss of sensitivity or the loss of the ability to feel or see.

Skinless (Sense) – a state of high sensitivity or high vulnerability to external sensory or empathic input.

Skinlessness – being incredibly sensitive, or vulnerable to external input (see above). Can be specific, for example one can be skinless to the emotions of others, or to colours and form, or to music.

Space (the dimension of) – how we manage being in the space around us, and how we like to organize and relate to it. Space is not necessarily physical, but can be social. Time can be thought of as a space – because it is something we manage, organize and relate to.

Still (Energy) – unusual state of calm, marked by measured and considered application of physical, mental and emotional resources.

Thought (the dimension of) – the way our thinking works, whether it falls into certain patterns, or not. More technically thought of as cognitive processes.

Well (The) – the inner reservoir of memories of all kinds, not just facts, but emotions. We fill up the well by constantly being awake to new things, and new experiences.

Wide Angle (Focus) – a wide field of perception or awareness with the ability to grasp the big picture but not necessarily the detail.

Zoom (Focus) - an intensely narrowed field of perception or awareness with the ability to see the minute details at the cost of the big picture.

APPENDIX

SOME MORE DETAIL ON THE RESEARCH

In chapter two, we outlined how the wider research community has begun to focus on the issues of creative people, particularly over the last forty years. Knowing the detail of all the work that has been done is not necessary for most readers, so we left it out of the main body of the book, but thought it better to include some of it as an appendix for those who are interested.

The following table summarizes some of this research we referred to early in chapter two. The full citations can be found in the bibliography.

YEAR	AUTHOR	SUMMARY
1987	Andreason	Study of 30 creative writers from University of Iowa Writers Workshop: 80% had experienced one episode of major depression (control group: 30% depression); 43% history of hypomania or mania.
1989	Jamison	Study of 47 distinguished writers and visual artists, selected for their creativity based on professional accolades: 38% previously treated for mood disorder of those 75% required medication or hospitalisation, or both. Poets in particular were the most highly represented group.
1988	Akiskal et al.	Twenty award-winning European artists, poets, sculptors:75% exhibited depressive/manic symptoms and 50% major depression. Similar to blues musicians studied in collaboration with Dr David Evans.
1992	Ludwig	Biographical survey of 1005 famous twentieth century artists, writers and other professionals. He found that artists and writers experienced two to three times the rate of psychosis, mood disorders, suicide attempts and substance abuse compared to those who were successful in business and other forms of academic and public life.
2005	Nowakowska et al.	The temperament of highly creative students similar to the temperament of those with bipolar disorder (in remission) and with either mania or depression, when compared to a 'normal' population
2008	Rybakowski et al.	The neurobiology (the brain mechanisms of how we think and feel) of those with bipolar disorder and creative individuals found to be similar. Also some similarity with the ' magical thinking' and openness to experience found in those with schizotypy. (Schizotypy is a term used to describe individuals who are socially withdrawn and exhibiting eccentric and unusual thinking and behaviour.) It is primarily in the area of their unique thinking that those with schizotypy show some similarity with creative people.

A Summary of the Kay Jameson study

Jameson explored the similarities highly creative people share with those experiencing bipolar disorder.

Virtually all creative writers and artists (89 per cent) said they had experienced intense, highly productive, and creative episodes ...These intensely creative episodes were characterized by pronounced increases in enthusiasm, energy, self-confidence, speed of mental association, fluency of thoughts and elevated mood, and a strong sense of wellbeing.

At least 50 per cent of the respondents described increases in: enthusiasm, energy, self-confidence, speed of mental association, fluency of thoughts, mood, euphoria, ability to concentrate, emotional intensity, sense of wellbeing, rapid thinking, expansiveness (ideas/feelings), and a decreased need for sleep. Many of these changes mirror the changes that occur as people move into a manic state.

Cognitive and mood changes shared far more overlap than behavioural ones, indicating that the milder forms of hypomania may represent the more productive phases of affective illness. The affective continuum that ranges from normal states through hypomania and then mania is very important, but poorly understood.

Mania and the Creative Process

Simply put, the perception phase is when we perceive something in a new way. So let's look at this through the lens of our understanding of mania. There are a number of qualities that define mania:

- Unflagging energy
- Rapid thinking
- Speed of association of ideas
- Impulsive behaviour
- Euphoria
- Grandiose self-belief (ego)
- Personality and the Creative Process

There have been many attempts to research and characterize the creative personality or creative identity. As we have just outlined, researchers have looked mostly at temperament and described aspects of what it means to be bipolar, particularly manic, such as the ability to be open to new experiences. Often the results have been contradictory. Hsen-Hsing Ma (2009) cites research that supports creative people showing both high and low neuroticism (or emotional instability). However the low scores were mostly associated with 'scientific' creative people rather than artistic – therefore the idea that artists are more prone to emotional instability still holds. However, most studies confirm that creative people show higher levels of emotional instability – again referring to the highs and lows we have outlined previously.

Psychologists have defined a five-factor model to describe the structure of personality traits. These personality traits are:

- **Neuroticism** – vulnerable, emotionally unstable and temperamental
- **Extraversion** – fun-loving, talkative, passionate

- **Openness to experience** – imaginative, curious, preferring variety
- **Agreeableness** – soft-hearted, trusting, generous
- **Conscientiousness** – hardworking, well-organized, punctual

Nowakowska et. al. assert that creative people consistently demonstrate higher scores on openness to experience, higher scores on neuroticism and lower scores on conscientiousness. This was based on a study conducted in 2005 among 49 patients with bipolar disorder; 25 patients with either depression or mania; 32 students of creative arts and 47 controls.

One of the key areas where a creative person demonstrates this is in the area of their ego. The ego is the 'I' or 'self' of any person: a person as thinking, willing and distinguishing itself from the selves of others. Also can refer to feelings of self-image or self-esteem and can include ideas of conceit or self-importance.

Flight of Ideas, Divergent Thinking and the Creative Process

Psychologists often refer to the phenomenon of divergent thinking. The highly respected US neuropsychiatrist Nancy Andreasen described it this way in 1996:

> … fluency, rapidity and flexibility of thought on the one hand and the ability to combine ideas or categories of thought in order to form new and original connections on the other. The importance of rapid, fluid and divergent thought in the creative process has been described by most psychologists and writers who have studied human imagination.

Researchers talk about the similarity between how a creative person thinks and how a manic person thinks – the so-called 'flight of ideas'. While there are similarities between mania and creative thinking – one does not equate with the other. As Andreasen also noted:

> Both writers and manics tend to sort in large groups, change dimensions while in the process of sorting, arbitrarily change starting points, or use vague distantly related concepts as categorising principles.

> Writers and manics differed primarily in the degree of control they were able to exert over their patterns of thought, with the writers able to carry out controlled flights of fancy during the process of sorting, while the manics tended to sort many objects for bizarre or personalized reasons.

Living with Creative Thinking and the Flight of Ideas

There are two common mistakes by partners of a creative person.

The first is to not understand the importance of the creative spark or imprint and to try to get in the way or to interrupt this process. On the one hand a relationship needs attention and investment for it to continue to flourish. Therefore, time together, listening and relating to each other are essential building blocks of a relationship. However, trying to demand relationship time or energy and investment while the creative person is immersed in that spark of creativity is to invite frustration, rejection and relationship tension.

The second is to listen to the 'hypomania' of the creative person while they are in the passion of creativity and then sublimate their own needs to the other's creative process. This creates an unequal relationship and one that is ultimately not satisfying for the partner. This is how relationships fragment.

Julie: I was listening to a wonderful, warm and insightful woman in her late forties. She had been married to a very successful artist and film maker. They had four highly creative children. She started describing how she expends herself supporting the creativity of her family and has been doing so for many years, and how that has left her feeling frustrated and agitated. Her level of resentment towards her husband and family is increasing and that concerns her. She described how she feels that she has lost herself over the years and that she has had little opportunity to develop her own expression of her creativity. This is not an unusual sentiment from people who have lived and worked around creative people and highlights the pressures of living with this type of consuming creative mind.

Music, Memory and the Creative Mind

Daniel Levitin in his 2006 book *This Is Your Brain on Music: The Science of Human Obsession,* makes the following claims about music and memory and how musicians categorize memory. These observations can be applied to other creative artists:

1. The strength of a memory is dependent on how many times it is experienced. Levitin asserts that gaining mastery of a creative talent requires 10,000 hours of practice.

2. Emotion, (either positive or negative) encodes a memory as more important. Dopamine, the neurotransmitter associated with emotional regulation, alertness and mood is released and the dopaminergic system aids in the encoding of the memory trace. Emotion, memory and creativity are intrinsically linked.

3. Musicians develop a memory that allows them to learn new information in chunks. We believe that this is the same for actors and dancers as well. Successful creative people have to have good memories within the area of their expertise. They rely on a structure for their memory and fit a few musical pieces within that structure (referred to as 'chunking').

4. Musicians develop an ability to identify musical (or performance) sequences. This identification memory is found in the *planum temporale,* which is also associated with perfect pitch.

Bink and Marsh in their 1999 article *Cognitive Regularities in Creative Activity,* attempted to explore creative thinking from a cognitive process and memory perspective. Rather than our creative process model of perception, processing and production, some researchers have used the terms generation and exploration. Bink and Marsh adopted these concepts and described the processes involved in generation. They believe that generation involves the use of mental constructs called pre-inventive structures. This concept similar to that of an initial spark or imprint – what we call perception.

In what Bink and Marsh call the generative phase, they suggest that the hallmark of creativity is how widely the memory is searched. Creative people access a broad range of memory from within them, and synthesize it to form new ways of seeing things. Part of the skill of this process is selecting what is relevant and what is not relevant to the process. This may be what Andreason identified as one of the primary differences between the manic and the highly creative person, in that manic thinking cannot filter out what is irrelevant.

Bink and Marsh highlight the factors that distinguish highly creative processes as:

1. Working memory capacity,
2. Speed of retrieval,
3. Perceptual fluency,
4. Activation of relevant concepts and inhibition of irrelevant ones,
5. Recollective ability,
6. Inspection of memories and a host of other processes used in everyday cognition.

Similarities in Bipolar and Creative People

Both bipolar and creative students when compared with 'non-creative people' recorded similarly high scores in the following as reported by Nowakowska et. al. in 2005:

- Cyclothymia: a mood disorder that causes hypomanic (high, elevated mood) and mild depressive episodes.
- Dysthymia: a chronic mood disorder and means that someone can be mildly depressed, flat and low over a one-to-two year period.
- Irritability

Exploring Skinlessness

Researchers in more recent years have looked at the association between creativity and what is called schizotypy. They are seeing an overlap between both bipolar qualities and the qualities usually associated with schizotypy. Researchers now use these words to describe the presence of particular qualities. They are not necessarily trying to label creative people in a certain way. The qualities that they have associated with creativity are:

- Openness to experience – (which we have described previously)
- Low latent inhibition – which translated means that highly creative people may see and feel things that others do not
- Eccentricity, magical thinking and unusual experiences.

This openness to experience, along with the ability to see and feel things that others do not, is what has colloquially been called skinlessness. Here are some further thoughts about skinlessness.

Skinlessness and Attention

Andreasen (1996) suggested that creative individuals have a different quality of quantity of attentional mechanisms. This means that creative people are less able to filter out sensory material.

This is what is currently being described as low latent inhibition, or the inability to shut out sensory information – present in both those with schizotypy-like qualities and highly creative people. In fact, prominent Polish psychiatrist Janus Rybakowski has suggested that it is high intelligence combined with low latent inhibition that leads to creative achievement. Or, as has also been suggested, low filtering mechanisms along with fast memory recall and developed problem-solving ability.

This is why it is thought that low latent inhibition only leads to increased creativity when it's paired with a willingness to analyse our excess of thoughts, to constantly search for the signal amid the noise. We need to let more information in, but we also need to be ruthless about throwing out the 'useless' stuff.

Skinlessness and Emotional Memory

Performance involves both technique and connection with the emotional. Daniel Levitin (2006) suggests that musicians who are incredible performers are those who can connect to the memory they had when they were writing the song when they perform it.

> *As we have seen, remembering music involves setting the neurons that were originally active in the perception of a piece of music back to the original state – reactivating their particular pattern of connectivity and getting the firing rates as close as possible to their original levels.*

A performance musician, says Levitin, *needs his brain state to match the emotional state he is trying to express.* This means that emotion; memory and creativity are intrinsically linked.

Background to Emotions and Emotional Memory

Let's imagine that you are a songwriter, and at age four your parents separated and ultimately divorced. The moment when your father left the family home created a strong and painful memory with overwhelming feelings of abandonment, rejection and anguish as you saw your father, whom you adored, pack his bags and leave home. You store that memory as the smell of his sweat and aftershave as he hugged you, the feel of his slightly unshaven chin against your hair, along with the overwhelming, confusing ache – the impression that your world had just shattered.

Fast forward to your twenties. A relationship you have been in for several years is beginning to disintegrate. As you hug your boyfriend, the smell of sweat and aftershave triggers this overwhelming ache within you. It is the ache associated with abandonment, separation, and sudden shattering change and, as a creative person, the rapid interconnection of memory, emotion and new associations emerges and a poignant lyric idea forms.

This is the beginning of the creative process we have called perception.

We believe that it is not only great performers that need access to emotional memory. Our work with artists from other disciplines informs us that, like musicians and actors, the need to access emotional memory applies to visual artists, writers and songwriters as well. We have already described a little of how emotions work. What follows sheds more light on the nature of emotional memory, and how it is triggered. It turns out memories are not always like little movie excerpts from our past. We can relive the emotion of the past without necessarily remembering the actual events.

Memory and the emotions associated with it are stored in two different ways:

1. Hot memory, also called implicit or *amygdaloid* memory, is stored in the *amygdala*.
2. Cold memory, also called explicit or *hippocampal* memory is stored in the *hippocampus*.

Let's look at hot or implicit (amygdaloid) memory first as the amygdala is the centre in the brain for strong emotion and it is this memory that shapes our emotional experiences, self-image and relationships.

Amygdaloid memory is usually stored in a different way than we would imagine. It is not stored as a narrative but as a fragment – a sensory experience. It may be a sound, a smell, a touch or something visual. In the story described above, the songwriter's memory was stored as the smell of aftershave, the unique feel of skin against skin, along with the ache of abandonment.

Amygdaloid memory cannot be recalled, it can only be triggered, and when it is triggered we don't understand it as a memory. It's just a sensory experience attached to a strong feeling – fear, love, shame, anger, guilt or yearning. This emotion has a belief attached to it; not usually a belief we can put words to, although we act out of this belief, particularly in relationships. These beliefs, founded in emotion, become a part of our implicit relational schema as we have already described in the case of Adrian the actor. So, going back to our songwriter, she may respond to her boyfriend leaving from the belief that "if men get close they will abandon me" which is a hot memory of her father leaving her. Out of such pain comes great songwriting. When hot memory is accessed on stage great performances are given.

Of course this may mean that a creative person, especially a performer, continually has their painful memories accessed like a person walking on a bruised heel. It may also imply that creative people have entrenched painful memories – a rut in the road that gets deeper with use.

If this is something of the process a creative person engages in, then learning how to manage their emotions is paramount to long-term health and productivity personally and in relationships.

Cold or explicit (hippocampal) memory is an entirely different story. The *hippocampus* is the area of our brain primarily associated with conscious learning and our later memory. This is the area of our brain that develops as we begin to store narrative memory. We usually don't have many clear sequential cold memories prior to about age four and that is because our *hippocampus* is just developing and creating connections within our cortex – the thinking part of our brains. This is the part of the brain that remembers how to play an instrument, learn dialogue or remember how to repair a car.

WHAT WE DIDN'T COVER
Addiction, Obsession and Sex

How could we write about creative people without really covering addiction, obsession and sex – either separately or in any combination? Except for a few brief mentions here and there, we thought that diving into these areas was a recipe for how to instantly double the size of the book. These are issues that are known to plague the creative mind at their worst moments. However, rather than concentrating on the behavioural manifestations, we preferred to unpack the underlying constructs – the things that make creative people the way they are.

The other factor involved the mountain of research that has already been conducted into these three areas. To give each of these topics due attention would have taken us away from our central purpose. You might think this strange if you or your colleague or partner struggle with addictions or obsessions. The truth is that these behaviours are incredibly complex, and we cannot hope to do justice to them in one book. It is also true that researchers and behavioural specialists have conducted very helpful studies into these behaviours and proposed successful treatment approaches.

However, without dealing with addiction, obsession and sex in great depth, or engaging with the existing research in these areas, it is still possible to comment on some possible links with the nine dimensions of the creative mind.

Addiction can be thought of as a reaction to intense emotion, an ego that erratically oscillates between an inflated and deflated ego and skinless sense, which desperately needs any form of pain killers. In such cases, the creative mind becomes addicted as a means of avoiding insecurity and pain respectively. Alternatively, it can be seen as a way of reproducing manic energy, fluid thought and wide angle zoom if an artist feels that they have lost the ability to experience perception all on their own. Addiction may also be a manifestation of risk action in response to the same fear of losing perception or in response to sheer boredom.

Obsession could well be a manifestation of becoming stuck at low tide in many dimensions. A creative mind that is both fluid thinking but highly anxious can conceivably shift to rumination and obsessional thinking and behaviour. This can be seen as a consequence of lack of tidal flow at one, or a combination of, schematic thought, protected sense, zoom focus, order space and safety action. When the creative mind becomes driven in these dimensions it can look a lot like obsessive behaviour in these cases. We can imagine the creative mind in the grip of fear or anxiety acting obsessively in order to try to manage or control the circumstances, and thus minimize the negative feelings.

Sexual nonconformity (as we have termed it) could well be a by-product of remaining too long at high tide in a number of dimensions. Inflated ego, confronting attitude, manic energy and risk action could singularly provoke differing sexual behaviour and we can see how, clustered together, they could make the creative mind become unusually sexually adventurous. Alternatively, a creative mind that has run aground at cold emotion and deflated ego might attempt some experimentation in order to try to become unstuck. Clearly the dimensions of identity are crucial to sexual choices. What is also true is that a moral framework or ethos is equally crucial in terms of determining how sexual behaviour manifests.

Our final warning is that nothing we have written here should substitute for a diagnosis from a qualified health practitioner. When there is any doubt, consult a skilled professional in the appropriate field. When writing a book, some generalizations are inevitable but every individual needs to be seen as an individual, not as an example drawn from these pages.

A Final Word on Talent

We have touched on the subject of talent only briefly in this book. It deserves one final moment of our attention, but in a holistic sense. Talent is what you are born with, so it's a gift. The term is often used very widely to include notions of accomplishment as well as giftedness, but we restrict it here to meaning the innate giftedness of an individual. We all enter this world with a range of potential in every area of human endeavour. Not all of us are going to have the kind of singing voice that is considered popular or aesthetically pleasing. Not all of us are going to have the body shape considered best for the Royal Ballet. Not all of us are going to have the long fingers usually thought of as ideal for a concert pianist. We are all born different. Some are blessed with a physique or a certain mental acuity that makes the techniques of music or dance come much more easily. If you have been blessed with prodigious talent, then you must realize that it had nothing to do with you. Spend the rest of your life being thankful because technical accomplishment will be quicker and easier for you to achieve than for others. If you are somewhat less than brilliantly talented, then you should be thankful for what you have been given. Don't waste time wishing for something that will never happen. Instead you must get to work building on what you have been given and work hard to attain technical excellence. Remember, talent is only a part of the equation.

Actually, prodigious talent is quite rare. Most people who appear talented have actually worked hard developing whatever talent they have been given. There are famous and successful painters who are colourblind, actors who are deaf or blind, successful dancers who are too short, too tall or too bulky. There are successful piano players with short fingers and successful singers who seem unable to hold accurate pitch. The key is to become an apprentice in your craft and to work on reinforcing the strengths and overcoming the weaknesses in your start-up pack of talent. Finally, you must work out where you best fit. There is a place for you and your unique spectrum of gifts, but you have to find it.

Supremely talented people have an undeniably easier pathway to technical excellence, but they also face the danger of taking their giftedness for granted. There is a nobility to be found in gifted people who are able to maintain an attitude of gratitude for their talent. Those with the alternative outlook are a lot more difficult to work with.

Moderately talented people have to work much harder to achieve technical excellence, and generally they do not treat their accomplishments lightly. However, they face the danger of taking inordinate credit for their success, which they feel is due to their intense effort. There is a graciousness that becomes those who have worked hard for success. It results from never forgetting the nature of the gift that allowed them a head start on their journey of discipline and hard work.

ACKNOWLEDGEMENTS

WhERE?

We wrote this book in lots of places. Our best work it seems was produced when we had time to get away from everything else.

In Australia: Ilaroo Rd, Lake Cathie NSW. Macquarie Waters Hotel, Mantra Quayside Hotel and Starbucks - Port Macquarie NSW. Pacific Marina Apartments Coffs Harbour NSW. Utopia Café, Bangalow NSW. The fabulous house in Kulburra, NSW (thanks to Rob and Terese Cheadle). Das Kaffeehaus, Ground Zero, Hemingway's, Hugo's, Manly Interpolitan Café, Organicus Kitchen and Pantry, The Bower Restaurant and Three Beans Café, Manly NSW. Maisie's Café, Neutral Bay NSW. Pablo and Rusty's, Gordon NSW. Cotton Beach Resort and Santai Resort, Kingscliff, NSW. Duke St and Fratellinis Café, Sunshine Beach, QLD.

In Canada: Banff Springs Hotel, Banff, AB.

In England: Trains from London to Bath and back again.

In France: Trains from Paris to Amsterdam

In Greece: Nostos Apartments, Oia, Santorini

Plus: various Qantas, British Airways and Cathay Pacific Aircraft.

WhO?

A huge and gracious thank you to all the following:

To our two daughters – Jess and Maddie. Even though we dedicated the book to them they were heartily sick of it by the end. They called it our other child with more than a hint of jealousy. Thanks also to Jason our son in law, for enduring our last rewrites right up until the day before the wedding.

To those who gave us exclusive interviews on the record: Marina Prior, Chris Falson, Ken Duncan and Garry McDonald. Thanks also to those who gave us exclusive interviews off the record. We know who you are!

To our faithful band of interview transcribers: Amy Kings, Aya Saito, Emma Schuberg and Emily Rawson.

To those who read our first draft and gave us such sage advice: Stephen Thomas, Mick Martin and Simon Ray.

To all of our creative friends and all of our students who completed the surveys. To all of our friends who came to our focus groups. Thanks to you all for allowing us a glimpse into your creative minds. Thank you too Robi.

To our photographer Melinda Di Mauro, thanks for your patience, generosity and beautiful eye for composition.

To our designers led by Simon Ray and Brad Goosen from Imperial Metric. Thanks for adding the visual magic.

To all those who gave freely of their time to help and encourage us, particularly Wendy and Geoff Simpson, Simon and Jen Le Couteur, Paul and Sally-Ann Haddow, Chris and Veronica Munoz and George and Kesty Munoz - who all believed in us so passionately before ever seeing a printed version.

To all of those brave souls who lets us experiment and try out our ideas in their communities: Mark and Gail Smallcombe, Stephen and Melissa Hickson, Amanda and Charl Vivier, Mark and Penny Webb, Phil and Heather Baker, Andrew and Betsy de Thierry, Phil and Julie Oldfield, Thierry and Marianne Moehr, Lorne and Kelly Tebbutt.

To all of our partners in creative enterprises – Greg and Linda, Leo and Suzanne, Gav and Nat, Paul and Sally-Anne, Chris and Karyn, Mark and Vicky, Stephen, Liz, Josh B, Brad, Dee T, Josh and Bek S, Bek T and the rest... may we keep on!

BIBLIOGRAPHY

30 Rock. Audition Day (2009) NBC TV Thursday 5 November.

Access All Areas (1997) 'Hunting For A Moment' ABC TV 16 March.

AirDisaster.com (1982) 'Cockpit Voice Recorders: Transcripts: Air Florida 90' n.d. [Online article] Available from http://www.airdisaster.com/cvr/af90tr.shtml (accessed 29/1/11).

Akiskal, H.S., & Akiskal, K. (1996) 'Re-assessing the prevalence of bipolar disorder: clinical significance and artistic creativity' in Schildkraut, J.J., & Otero, A. (ed) *Depression and the Spiritual in Modern Art: Homage to Miro*. John Wiley and Sons. Chichester, UK. pp 221–238.

Akiskal, H.S., & Akiskal, K. (1996) 'Abstract Expressionism as Psychobiology: The Life and Suicide of Arshile Gorky' in *Psychiatry Psychobiology*. 3: 29–36.

Albert Einstein quotes. [Online] Available at http://www.brainyquote.com/quotes/authors/a/albert_einstein_9.html (accessed 29/1/11).

Allthingswilliam.com *People* n.d. [Online] Available at http://www.allthingswilliam.com/people.html (accessed 29/1/11).

Ambrose, S. (2001) *Band Of Brothers: E Company, 506th Regiment, 101st Airborne from Normandy to Hitler's Eagle's Nest*. Simon and Schuster, New York, UK.

American Bar Association, Juvenile Justice Centre (2004) *Cruel and Unusual Punishment: The Juvenile Death Penalty. Adolescence, Brain Development and Legal Culpability*. Washington, D.C. American Bar Association, January 2004. Available online at http://www.americanbar.org/content/dam/aba/publishing/criminal_justice_section_newsletter/crimjust_juvjus_Adolescence.authcheckdam.pdf (accessed 11/5/11)

Anderson, C. et. al. (2011) *Life at Google*. [Online video] Available at http://www.youtube.com/lifeatgoogle (accessed 29/4/11).

Andreason, N.C. (1996) 'Creativity and Mental Illness' in Schildkraut, J.J., & Otero, A. (ed) *Depression and the Spiritual in Modern Art: Homage to Miro*. John Wiley and Sons. Chichester, UK.

Assayas, M. (2005) *Bono: In Conversation with Michka Assayas*. Penguin Books. London, UK.

At The Movies (2008) ABC TV. 4 May.

Averill, J. R. (1999) 'Individual differences in emotional creativity: Structure and correlates' in *Journal of Personality*, 67: 331–371.

Baumeister, R. F., De Wall, C. D. & Vohs, K. D. (2009) 'Social Rejection, Control, Numbness, and Emotion: How not to Be Fooled by Gerber and Wheeler'. *Perspectives in Psychological Science*. 1 September. V4n5 pp 489–493.

Baumeister, R. F., (2008) 'Interpersonal Rejection in the Laboratory' in *Interpersonal Acceptance*. [Online article] January. V2n1. Available at http://www.isipar.org/files/Newsletters/ISIPAR%20Newsletter%20vol%202%20number%201.pdf (accessed 29/1/11).

Bellis, M. A. et al. (2007) 'Elvis to Eminem: quantifying the price of fame through early mortality of European and North American rock and pop stars' *Journal of Epidemiology and Community Health* 61: 930–931.

Berger, J. (1972) *Ways of Seeing: Based on the BBC television series with JOHN BERGER*. British Broadcasting Corporation. London.

Bink, M.L. & Marsh, R.L. (2000) 'Cognitive Regularities in Creative Activity' in *Review of General Psychiatry*. v4n1: 59–78.

Bono, The Edge, Clayton, A., Mullens Jr. L. & McCormick, N. (2006) *U2 by U2*. It Books. New York, NY.

Bukowski, C. (2003) *Sifting through the Madness for the Word, the Line, the Way*. Ecco. New York, NY.

Cameron, J. (2002) *The Artist's Way: A Spiritual Path to Higher Creativity*. Jeremy P. Tarcher/Penguin. New York, NY.

Carsen, S.H, Peterson, J. B., Higgins, D.M. (2003) 'Decreased Latent Inhibition Is Associated with Increased Creative

Achievement in High-Functioning Individuals' in *Journal of Personality and Social Psychology.* V85n3 pp 499 – 450.

Catalyst 'Body Clock' (2008) ABC TV. 4 September.

CBS News (2010) *The Key To Sting and Trudie's Relationship* [Online Video] 13 May. Available at http://www.cbsnews.com/video/watch/?id=6481095n (accessed 24/6/11).

Chaplin, J. P. (1985) *Dictionary of Psychology* Dell. New York, NY.

Child, Lee [Online] available at http://www.leechild.com/runningblind_research.php (accessed 16/4/11).

Ciarrochi, J., Forgas, J. R. & Mayer, J. D. (Eds) (2006) *Emotional Intelligence in Everyday Life.* Psychology Press. New York, NY.

Clare, A. W. & Milligan, S. (1994) *Depression and How to Survive It.* Arrow Books. London, UK.

Clinton, "I did not have sexual relations with that woman..." [Online video] Available at http://www.youtube.com/watch?v=KilP_KDQmXs (accessed 29/1/11).

Corliss, R. & Schickel, R. (2005) 'All Time 100 Movies' in *TIME Magazine.* Feb 12. [Online article] Available at http://www.time.com/time/specials/packages/article/0,28804,1953094_1953142_1953314,00.html (accessed 29/1/11).

Cowan, G. (2007) *Back from the Brink,* Bird in Hand Media. Gordon, NSW.

Cowen, M. (dir) (2006) *We Stand Alone Together: The Men of Easy Company* [DVD] USA. Home Box Office.

Cozolino, L. (2006) *The Neuroscience of Human Relationships.* W.W. Norton. New York, NY.

Crabtree, J. R. (2008) *Placing Non-Congregational Music In A Congregational Setting.* A thesis presented for the degree of Master Of Arts With Honours. Sydney: Macquarie University.

Cross Fit Journal (2010) *Roundtable in Tahoe: The Psychological Component.* [Online video] 13 November. Available at http://journal.crossfit.com/2010/11/roundtabletahoe-psychological.tpl (accessed 29/1/11).

Csikszentmihalyi, M. (1990) *Flow: The Psychology of Optimal Experience.* Harper and Row. New York, NY.

Csikszentmihalyi, M. (1997) *Creativity: Flow and the Psychology of Discovery and Invention.* Harper Perennial. New York, NY.

Csikszentmihalyi, M. (1999) 'Implications of a Systems Perspective for the Study of Creativity' in Sternberg, R. J. (ed) (1999) *Handbook of Creativity* Cambridge University Press. New York, NY. pp 313–335.

CTV British Columbia (2011) *Shania Twain Lost Singing Voice From Stress Of Divorce.* [Online Video] 9 May. Available at http://www.ctvbc.ctv.ca/servlet/an/local/CTVNews/20110509/shania-twain-singing-voice-110509/20110509/?hub=BritishColumbiaHome accessed (14/5/11).

Dacey, J. S. & Lennon, K. H. (1998) *Understanding Creativity: The Interplay of Biological, Psychological, and Social Factors.* Jossey-Bass Inc. San Francisco, CA.

De Bono, E. (1999) *Six Thinking Hats.* Back Bay Books. Boston, MA.

De Bono, E. (1990) *Parallel Thinking.* Penguin Books. London, UK.

De Lauzirika, C. (dir) (2007) *Dangerous Days: Making Blade Runner.* [DVD] USA. Warner Home Video.

De Mille, A. (1991) *Martha: The Life and Work of Martha Graham.* Random House. New York, NY.

Doctor Bob and the Amazing Disciples of Groove (1995) *The Doctor Is In* [CD] Australia. Token Resistance Music.

Doctor Bob and the Amazing Disciples of Groove (2000) *Therapy* [CD] Australia. Token Resistance Music.

Eno, B. (1996) *A Year: With Swollen Appendices.* Faber and Faber. London, UK.

Eno, B. & Schmidt, P. (2001) *Oblique Strategies: Over one hundred worthwhile dilemmas.* 5th edn. Brian Eno/Peter Schmidt. London, UK.

Farnes, N. (2010) *Memories of Milligan.* Fourth Estate. London, UK.

Farrell, S P (prod) (2011) *The Last Word: Sidney Lumet* [Online Video] The New York Times, New York, NY. Available at http://video.nytimes.com/video/2011/04/09/obituaries/1194838961597/lwlumet.html?nl=todaysheadlines&emc=*thab1*

(accessed 15/4/11).

Fletcher, A. (2001) *The Art of Looking Sideways*. Phaidon Press. London, UK.

Florida, R. (2002) 'The Rise of the Creative Class' in *Washington Monthly*. May [Online article] Available from http://www.washingtonmonthly.com/features/2001/0205.florida.html (accessed 29/1/11).

Frankl, V. E. (1959) *Man's Search for Meaning*. Washington Square Press. Boston, MA.

Fry, S. (2010) *The Fry Chronicles: An Autobiography*. Michael Joseph. London, UK.

Gann, K. (2007) *Mysteries of the Composing Brain*. [Online article] 6 June. Available at www.artsjournal.com/postclassic/2007/06/mysteries_of_the_composing_bra/ (accessed 29/1/11)

Gardner, H. (2001) 'Creators: Multiple Intelligence' in Pfenniger and Shubik (eds.) *The Origins of Creativity* Oxford University Press. Oxford, UK.

Gerasimov, A. (1947) *V. Lenin on the Tribune*. The State Tretyakov Gallery. Moscow, Russian Federation.

Gierland, J. (2003) 'Go with the Flow: According to Mihaly Csikszentmihalyi, great websites are not about navigating content, but staging experience' in *Wired* [Online article] Available at http://www.wired.com/wired/archive/4.09/czik_pr.html (accessed 29/1/11).

Gladwell, M. (2000) *The Tipping Point: How Little Things Can Make a Big Difference*. Abacus. London, UK.

Gladwell, M. (2008) *Outliers: The Story of Success*. Penguin Books. London, UK.

Goleman, D., Boyatzis, R. & McKee, A. (2002) *Primal Leadership: Learning to Lead with Emotional Intelligence*. Harvard Business School Press. Boston, MA.

Gottman, J. M. (1994) *Why Marriages Succeed or Fail: And How You Can Make Yours Last*. Fireside. New York, NY.

Gottman, J.M. & Silver, N. (1999) *The Seven Principles for Making Marriage Work*. Three Rivers Press. New York, NY.

Graham, P. (2009) *Maker's Schedule, Manager's Schedule* [Online article] July. Available at www.paulgraham.com/makersschedule.html (accessed 29/1/11).

Grazebrook, K., Garland, A. & BACP (2005) *What are Cognitive and/or Behavioural Psychotherapies?* Paper prepared for a UKCP/BACP mapping psychotherapy exercise. [Online article] July. Available at http://www.babcp.com/silo/files/what-is-cbt.pdf (accessed 29/1/11).

Grossman, L. (2010) 'Person of the Year 2010 Mark Zuckerberg' in *TIME Magazine*. 15 Dec.

Guggenheim, D. (dir) (2009) *It Might Get Loud* [DVD] USA. Sony Pictures.

The Harry Potter Lexicon *Patronus* n.d. [Online] Available at http://www.hp-lexicon.org/magic/spells/spells_p.html#Patronus1 (accessed 29/1/11).

Hamilton, I. (1983) *Robert Lowell: A Biography*. Vintage Books. London, UK.

Heath, C. (2010) 'Ryan Reynolds Wants Out of the Box' in *GQ Magazine*. October.

The Holy Bible New King James Version. Thomas Nelson Publishing. Nashville, TN.

Hugh Laurie Interview Ellen Show. [Online video] Available from http://www.dailymotion.com/video/x1fp7n_hugh-laurie-interview-ellen-show_fun (accessed 28/1/11).

Internet Movie Data Base.http://www.imdb.com/name/nm0000059/bio (accessed 3/3/11)

Jamison, K. R. (1994) *Touched with Fire: Manic-Depressive Illness and the Artistic Temperament*. Free Press Paperbacks. New York, NY.

Jamison, K.R. *Manic-Depressive Illness and Creativity* [Online article] No longer available from http://www.geocities.com/SoHo/Workshop/4296/creativity.html. (accessed 25/12/07).

Janis, I. L. & Mann, L. (1977) *Decision making: A psychological analysis of conflict, choice, and commitment*. Free Press. New York, NY.

joabj@delphi.com (1992) 'An unpublished Brian Eno interview' *Enoweb* [Online] Available from http://music.hyperreal.

org/artists/brian_eno/ (accessed 28/1/11).

Leibenluft. E. (1996) 'Circadian Rhythms Factor in Rapid-Cycling Bipolar Disorder' in *Psychiatric Times* 13: 5.

Levitin, D. (2006) *This Is Your Brain on Music: The Science of Human Obsession*. Dutton/Penguin. New York, NY.

Joffe, M (dir) (1996) *Cosi* [DVD] Australia. Roadshow Home Video

Kilroy, C. (1982) 'Special Report: Air Florida Flight 90' *AirDisaster.com* n.d. [Online article] Available from http://www.airdisaster.com/special/special-af90.shtml (accessed 29/1/11)

Koehler, B. (2006) *Gordon Claridge: Psychosis and Creativity* [Online article] Available at http://isps-us.org/koehler/claridge.htm (accessed 29/1/11).

Lehrer, J. (2010) 'Are Distractible People More Creative?' *Wired* [Online article] Available at http://www.wired.com/wiredscience/2010/09/are-distractible-people-more-creative/ (accessed 29/1/11)

Lewin, K. & Weiss, G. (1948) *Resolving Social Conflicts*. Harper & Row. New York, NY.

Lewis, R. (1995) *The Life and Death of Peter Sellers*. Arrow Books. London, UK.

Lowe, R. (2011) *Stories I Only Tell My Friends, The Autobiography*. Transworld Publishers, London, UK.

Ludwig, A.M. (1992) 'Creative achievement and psychopathology: Comparisons among professions' in *American Journal of Psychotherapy* 46: 330–356.

Ma, Hsen-Hsing. (2009) 'The Effect Size of Variables Associated With Creativity: A Meta Analysis' in *Creativity Research Journal*. v21n1: 30–42.

Mackay, H. (2010) *What Makes Us Tick? : The Ten Desires that Drive Us*, Hachette. Sydney, NSW.

Maddox, G. (2008) 'There wasn't anything I wouldn't try or do. The Hot Seat: Robert Luketic talks to Garry Maddox.' *Sydney Morning Herald*. 3 May.

Marano, H. E. (1995) 'At last – a rejection detector!' in *Psychology Today* November. [Online article] Available at http://www.psychologytoday.com/articles/199511/last-rejection-detector (accessed 29/1/11).

Meusburger, Peter (2009). 'Milieus of Creativity: The Role of Places, Environments and Spatial Contexts' in Meusburger, P., Funke, J. and Wunder, E. *Milieus of Creativity: An Interdisciplinary Approach to Spatiality of Creativity*. Springer. New York, NY.

Miles, B. (1997) *Paul McCartney: Many Years from Now*. Owl Books. New York, NY.

Milligan, S. (1971) *Adolf Hitler: My Part in His Downfall*. Penguin Books. London, UK.

Moir, A. & Jessel, D. (1989) *Brain Sex: The Real Difference Between Men and Women*. Dell Publishing. New York, NY.

Morgan, J. & Maddox, G. (2010) 'Actors Search for the Light after Dark Roles.' *The Sydney Morning Herald* 2 Jan. [Online article] Available at http://www.smh.com.au/news/entertainment/film/actors-search-for-the-light-after-dark-roles/2010/01/01/1261982389763.html (accessed 03/01/10).

National Transportation Safety Board (1982) *Aircraft Accident Report Air Florida, Inc., Boeing 737-222, N62AF, Collision with 14th Street Bridge near Washington National Airport, Washington, DC*

January 13, 1982. [Online] Available from http://www.ntsb.gov/publictn/1982/AAR8208.htm (accessed 29/1/11).

Nauert, R. (2011) *Social Rejection Hurts Like Physical Pain* [Online] Available at http://psychcentral.com/news/2011/03/29/social-rejection-hurts-like-physical-pain/24790.html (accessed 18/4/11).

Nowakowska, C., Strong, C. M., Santosa, C. M., Wang, P. W. & Ketter, T. A. (2005) 'Temperamental commonalities and differences in euthymic mood disorder patients, creative controls, and healthy controls.' in *Journal of Affective Disorder* 85: 207–215.

Oscar Levant Quotes [Online] Available at http://thinkexist.com/quotes/oscar_levant/ (accessed 29/1/11).

Parkinson Episode S02E15 (1999) BBC 17 December.

Peterson, C. & Seligman, M. (2004) *Character Strengths and Virtues: A handbook and classification.* Oxford University Press. Oxford, UK.

Pink Floyd. (1975) *Wish You Were Here* [CD] UK. Harvest/EMI.

Pray, D. (dir) (2009) *Art & Copy: Inside Advertising's Creative Revolution.* [DVD] USA. PBS Distribution.

Prayerworks (1998) *Prayerworks* [CD] Australia. Seam of Gold.

Prayerworks (2003) *True* [CD] Australia. CCC Worships.

Pressfield, S. (2002) *The War of Art.* Grand Central Publishing. New York, NY.

Pressfield, S. (2009) *Episode 2:"The Citizen Vs. The Tribesman"* [Online video] Accessed 29/1/11. http://www.stevenpressfield.com/ep-2/

Reiner, R. (dir) (1984) *This is Spinal Tap.* [DVD] USA. MGM.

Right Music. (2009) *Michael Jackson Memorial Service Full Video* [Online video] 9 July. Available at http://music.rightcelebrity.com/?p=2700 (accessed 29/1/11).

Robin Williams on Inside the Actors Studio [Online video] Available at http://www.youtube.com/watch?v=IL2Iv-kbc68&feature=related (accessed 29/1/11).

Rorem, N. (2006) *Facing the Night: A Diary (1999-2005) and Musical Writings.* Shoemaker & Hoard. Emeryville, CA.

Rybakowski, J., Klonowska, P., Patrzata, A. & Jaracz, J. (2008) 'Psychopathology and Creativity' in *Archives of Psychiatry and Psychotherapy* 1: 37–47.

The RS 500 greatest songs of all time. *Rolling Stone Magazine,* November 2004. Available from http://web.archive.org/web/20080622145429/www.rollingstone.com/news/coverstory/500songs (accessed 28/1/11).

Schildkraut, J.J., Hirshfeld, A.K. & Murphy, J. (1996) 'Depressive Disorders, Spirituality and Early Deaths in the Abstract Expressionist Artists of the New York School' in Schildkraut, J.J., & Otero, A. (ed) *Depression and the Spiritual in Modern Art: Homage to Miro.* John Wiley and Sons. Chichester, UK. pp 196–220.

Schutz, W. C. (1966) *The Interpersonal Underworld.* Science & Behavior Books. Palo Alto, CA.

Schmajuk, Nestor, Aziz, Dyana R. & Bates, Margaret J.B. (2009) 'Attentional-Associative Interactions in Creativity' in *Creativity Research Journal.* V21n1:92–103.

Scott, R. (dir) (1982) *Blade Runner* [DVD] USA. Warner Brothers.

Sexton, L.G. and Ames, L (Eds.) (1977) *Anne Sexton: A Portrait in Letters.* Houghton Mifflin. Boston, MA.

Shakespeare, W. (1601) *Hamlet* Orbis Publishing, London, UK.

Smolensky, M. & Lamburg, L. (2000) *The Body Clock Guide to Better Health.* Henry Holt. New York, NY.

Stephenson, P. (2002) *Billy Connolly* HarperCollins Entertainment. New York, NY.

Sternberg, R. J. (ed) (1999) *Handbook of Creativity* Cambridge University Press. New York, NY.

Stone, I. (1961) *The Agony and the Ecstasy.* Doubleday. New York, NY.

Strauss, L. (2006) *10 Reasons Creative Folks Make Us Crazy* [Online] Available from http://www.successful-blog.com/1/10-reasons-creative-folks-make-us-crazy/ (accessed 28/1/11).

Talking Heads (1979) *Fear of Music* [CD] USA. Sire.

TED Conference 2006 *Ken Robinson says schools kill creativity.* [Online video] Available from http://www.ted.com/talks/lang/eng/ken_robinson_says_schools_kill_creativity.html (accessed 28/1/11).

TED Conference 2009 *Elizabeth Gilbert on nurturing creativity.* [Online video] Available from http://www.ted.com/talks/lang/eng/elizabeth_gilbert_on_genius.html (accessed 28/1/11).

TED Conference 2010 *Brene Brown: The power of vulnerability.* [Online video] Available from http://www.ted.com/talks/lang/eng/brene_brown_on_vulnerability.html (accessed 28/1/11).

TEDx Mid Atlantic Conference 2010 *Charles Limb: Your brain on improv.* [Online video] Available from http://www.ted.

com/talks/lang/eng/charles_limb_your_brain_on_improv.html (accessed 28/1/11).

TIME Magazine (1982) 'We're Going Down, Larry'. 15 February. [Online article] Available at http://www.time.com/time/magazine/article/0,9171,925270-1,00.html (accessed 29/1/11).

Tuckman, B. W. (1965) 'Developmental sequence in small groups' [Online article] Available from http://www.mph.ufl.edu/events/seminar/Tuckman1965DevelopmentalSequence.pdf (accessed 29/1/11).

U2.com (2009) *Eno's Moment of Surrender.* [Online Video] Available from http://www.u2.com/media/index/mediaplayer/mediaId/385/type/video/setId/17 (accessed 28/1/11).

Wachowski, L. & Wachowski, A. (2002) *The Matrix* [DVD] USA. Warner Brothers Motion Pictures.

Williams, R. & Stockmeyer J. *Wallis' model of the Creative Process* [Online] Available from http://members.optusnet.com.au/charles57/Creative/Brain/wallis.htm. (accessed 28/1/11).

Winchester, S. (2008) *Bomb, Book & Compass: Joseph Needham and the Great Secrets of China.* Viking. London, UK.

Werner, K. (1996) *Effortless Mastery – Liberating the Master Musician within* Jamie Aebersold Jazz. New Albany, IN.

Who Magazine, Issue 931–932: 4 Jan 2010, Pacific Magazines. Sydney, NSW.

Wolfe, T. (1979) *The Right Stuff.* Bantam Books. New York, NY.

Yancey, P. (2000) *Reaching for the Invisible God.* Zondervan. Grand Rapids, MI.

Young, W. P. (2007) *The Shack.* Windblown Media. Los Angeles, CA.

Zeidner, M., Matthews, G. & Roberts, R. 'Emotional Intelligence, Coping with Stress, and Adaptation' in Ciarrochi, J., Forgas, J. R. & Mayer, J. D. (Eds) (2006) *Emotional Intelligence in Everyday Life*. Psychology Press. New York, NY. pp 100-128.

Zollo, P. 1997 *Songwriters on Songwriting: Expanded Edition*. Da Capo Press. New York, NY.

Zuckerman, A. (2010) *Music* Hachette. Sydney, NSW.

Zuckerman, A. (2008) *Wisdom* Hachette. Sydney, NSW.